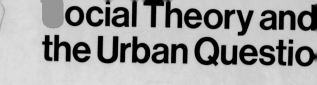

Social Theory and
the Urban Question

Peter Saunders

Social Theory and the Urban Question

Sociology Editor
Howard Newby
Reader in Sociology
University of Essex

by the same author

Urban Politics: A Sociological Interpretation

Social Theory and the Urban Question

Peter Saunders

Lecturer in Sociology, School of Cultural and Community Studies, University of Sussex

Hutchinson
London Melbourne Sydney Auckland Johannesburg

Hutchinson & Co. (Publishers) Ltd
An imprint of the Hutchinson Publishing Group
17–21 Conway Street, London W1P 6JD

Hutchinson Group (Australia) Pty Ltd
30–31 Cremorne Street, Richmond South, Victoria 3121
PO Box 151, Broadway, New South Wales 2007

Hutchinson Group (NZ) Ltd
32–34 View Road, PO Box 40–086, Glenfield, Auckland 10

Hutchinson Group (SA) (Pty) Ltd
PO Box 337, Bergvlei 2012, South Africa

First published 1981
Reprinted 1982

© Peter Saunders 1981

Set in Times Roman

Printed in Great Britain by The Anchor Press Ltd
and bound by Wm Brendon & Son Ltd
both of Tiptree, Essex

British Library Cataloguing in Publication Data

Saunders, Peter
  Social theory and the urban question.
  1. Sociology, Urban
  I. Title
  301.36   HT151

ISBN 0 09 143600 1 cased
      0 09 143601 X paper

Contents

Preface

As an undergraduate student some ten years ago, I chose to follow an optional course in urban sociology. The course was nothing if not varied, for over the next two terms I read about voluntary organizations in West African towns, the effects of residential propinquity on patterns of social relationships, the power elite in Atlanta, Georgia, the differences and similarities between life in Bethnal Green and life in the Surrey commuter belt, and a number of other aspects of economic, political and cultural relationships which had nothing in common other than the fact that they happened to occur in towns or cities. Even this common element was undermined somewhat, however, by a body of literature that indicated the difficulties in defining what an urban settlement actually was, for it was apparent that definitions in terms of size were purely arbitrary and had little sociological significance, while more specifically sociological formulations in terms of peculiarly 'urban' cultural characteristics exhibited an unfortunate propensity to collapse in the face of empirical evidence demonstrating the existence of 'urban' phenomena in 'rural' areas or of 'rural' phenomena in 'urban' areas.

Even more disturbing, perhaps, was the fact that so many of the themes and problems addressed by the urban sociology literature appeared to have been lifted from other areas of the discipline. In our seminars we discussed racial divisions in Birmingham, the extended family in Cairo and conflict over local political issues in New Haven, but had we not already confronted precisely these questions in other courses on race and stratification, the sociology of the family and political sociology? Gradually the suspicion began to grow that there was no such thing as urban sociology! Certainly in the context of advanced capitalist societies, it seemed that there was nothing specifically 'urban' about the problems we had been discussing for two terms.

Given this conclusion, it was perhaps somewhat perverse to have spent the next two years as a research student studying one aspect of what I still chose to call urban sociology; namely, the character of political power relationships in a borough in outer London. Following that, I spent three years as a member of a research team studying the character of political power relationships in a 'rural' area of East Anglia, but this only served to reinforce an uneasy feeling that very little had actually changed in this switch from urban to rural research. Indeed, we published a paper on 'rural community power' (Saunders *et al.* 1977) in which the theoretical problems addressed were identical to those that I had earlier considered in relation to a study of a concrete jungle with a population of a third of a million. The change of context from office blocks to thatched cottages was clearly not as dramatic as may originally have seemed, and it appeared that, whatever urban sociology was, rural sociology was not much different.

Finally, in 1979 I published a book under the title of *Urban Politics* which, in addition to reporting the case study of the London borough, attempted to review some of the key themes in the sociological literature on urban politics. Here too, however, the same nagging doubts resurfaced, for in the course of some 350 pages the book never actually confronted the basic question as to what was 'urban' about the political problems it was discussing. In retrospect, I believe that this question can be answered, and an attempt to do so can be found in the final chapter of the present work, but this is only possible once we explicitly recognize the problem and move beyond tacit and commonsense notions of what urban questions refer to.

This book is intended first and foremost as a text on major theoretical perspectives in urban sociology. Having taught courses in urban sociology for the last four years (and thus no doubt provoked in later generations of students the same bewilderment and scepticism regarding the viability of the subject as I experienced when I first encountered it), I have become acutely aware of the lack of such a text, and this book is an attempt to plug the gap. It does not, however, simply report on major theories; rather, an attempt is made to present and evaluate the different perspectives with reference to the different ways in which they conceptualize 'the urban'.

Four main approaches are discussed which may broadly be identified as ecological, cultural, Weberian and Marxist. In addition, the first chapter considers the way in which Weber, Durkheim and Marx and Engels came to address the urban question in their historical works and in their analyses of contemporary capitalism, while the penultimate chapter discusses a particular current of recent

Marxist work which confronts the question of urbanism from a rather different starting point than that which has generally characterized both Marxist and non-Marxist approaches within urban sociology.

The theme that runs throughout these chapters is that each of the different approaches to urban sociology has foundered on the attempt to fuse a theory of specific social processes with an analysis of spatial forms. The conclusion reached in Chapter 8 is that these two questions are, with one minor exception, distinct and mutually exclusive. There are, in other words, interesting things to be said about the economic, political and ideological significance of space in modern capitalist societies, just as there are important questions to be raised about certain social processes that occur within spatial contexts; but each of these two approaches constitutes a distinct area of analysis and they cannot be held together in a single theory of urbanism. To the extent that an urban sociology is a viable proposition, it must either devote its attention to the social significance of space (which, I suggest, is very limited), or focus on particular social processes which cannot be confined within particular spatial locations. In Chapter 8, I attempt to develop the second of these two possibilities, and the conception of urban sociology that results is therefore premised upon the abandonment of space as its peculiar theoretical concern. Seen in this way, urban sociology will clearly take account of space (and, indeed, of time) just as any other branch of the discipline must take the spatial and temporal dimensions of social relationships into consideration when addressing its particular theoretical problem, but it cannot any longer be defined in terms of a specific concern with spatial forms.

One further point should be noted concerning the limitations of this book, for it is concerned almost exclusively with theoretical approaches within urban sociology. Obviously such approaches are illustrated and examined in the context of empirical studies, but much of what has customarily passed as urban sociology (e.g. community studies) is not discussed in the pages that follow. In part this is due to the restrictions of length for a book such as this, and in part it is because such work has already been admirably reviewed and evaluated elsewhere (see, for example, Bell and Newby 1971). The main reason, however, is that my main criterion for including particular bodies of literature has been that they should represent a distinctive attempt to conceptualize the urban. Work such as the community study tradition has therefore been excluded on the grounds that it conspicuously fails to address this central theoretical question. There are many fascinating community studies, but it is by no means clear that these represent a contribution to urban, as opposed to any other, sociology.

Finally, I need to acknowledge the help and influence of a number of friends and colleagues who have contributed in one way or another to my work on this book. In particular I should mention John Lloyd, who was responsible for producing the first draft of Chapter 7, and Jenny Backwell, who provided précised translations of several books not currently available in English. Both also read and commented on various sections of the manuscript, as did Colin Bell, Alan Cawson, Ray Pahl and Andrew Sayer. I have also benefited enormously from discussions with colleagues and students in the urban studies and sociology subject groups at Sussex, and from the opportunity to present the arguments developed in Chapter 8 at seminars at Birmingham Polytechnic, Kingston Polytechnic, University College, and Reading and Liverpool universities. I am also most grateful to the University of Sussex for granting me a term's paid leave of absence to enable me to write the book, and for direct financial support towards research costs incurred in the process.

1 Social theory, capitalism and the urban question

Most areas of sociology today are characterized by a certain degree of theoretical and methodological pluralism, and urban sociology is no exception. Thus there are distinctive Marxist urban sociologies, Weberian urban sociologies and so on, each differing according to the questions they pose and the criteria of adequacy or validity they adopt. What seems to be peculiar to urban sociology, however, is that these various approaches have rarely paid much attention to what the so-called 'founding fathers' of the discipline actually wrote about the urban question. Contemporary Marxist urban theories, for example, make considerable references to Marx's discussions of the method of dialectical materialism, the theory of class struggle and the capitalist state and so on, but rarely pay much attention to his discussions of the town–country division or the role of the city in the development of capitalism. Similarly, Weberian urban sociology has tended simply to ignore Weber's essay on the city and to concentrate instead on his discussions of bureaucracy and social classes. Whereas other branches of the discipline have generally developed directly out of the substantive concerns of key nineteenth- and early twentieth-century European social theorists (for example the debates within industrial sociology over alienation and anomy, the concern with the question of bureaucracy in organizational sociology, the discussions of the state and political power in political sociology, the recurrent concern with secularization in the sociology of religion and with ideology in the sociology of knowledge), urban sociology has continually under-emphasized the work of these writers on the city, and has tended instead to take as its starting point the theory of human ecology developed at the University of Chicago in the years following the First World War.

The reason for this is not hard to find, for it is not that Marx, Weber, Durkheim and other significant social theorists had little to say about the city (far from it, for as Nisbet (1966) has suggested, this was in some ways a key theme in the work of all these writers), but rather that what they did say tends to suggest that a distinctive urban sociology cannot be developed in the context of advanced capitalist societies.

The central concern of all of these writers was with the social, economic and political implications of the development of capitalism in the West at the time when they were writing. The rapid growth of cities was among the most obvious and potentially disruptive of all social changes at that time. In England and Wales, for example, the 'urban population' (administratively defined) nearly trebled in the second half of the nineteenth century with the result that over 25 million people (77 per cent of the total population) lived in 'urban' areas at the turn of the century (see Hall *et al.* 1973, p. 61). This sheer increase in size was startling enough, but it also came to be associated in the minds of many politicians and commentators with the growth of 'urban' problems – the spread of slums and disease, the breakdown of law and order, the increase in infant mortality rates and a plethora of other phenomena – all of which attracted mounting comment and consternation on the part of the Victorian middle classes.

Of course, Marx, Weber and Durkheim were each fully aware of the scale and significance of these changes, yet it is clear from their work that none of them considered it useful or necessary to develop a specifically urban theory in order to explain them. In other words, all three seem to have shared the view that, in modern capitalist societies, the urban question must be subsumed under a broader analysis of factors operating in the society as a whole. While cities could provide a vivid illustration of fundamental processes such as the disintegration of moral cohesion (Durkheim), the growth of calculative rationality (Weber) or the destructive forces unleashed by the development of capitalist production (Marx), they could in no way explain them. For all three writers, what was required was not a theory of the city but a theory of the changing basis of social relations brought about through the development of capitalism, and it was to this latter task that they addressed themselves.

When they did discuss the city, they did so only in one of two ways. First, all three saw the city as an historically important object of analysis in the context of the transition from feudalism to capitalism in western Europe. In his essay on the city, for example, Weber showed how in the Middle Ages the towns played a highly significant role in breaking the political and economic relations of feudalism and establishing a new spirit of rationality which was later to prove crucial for the development of capitalist entrepreneurship and democratic rights of citizenship. Similarly, Durkheim showed how the medieval towns helped break the bonds of traditional morality and foster the growth of the division of labour in society, while Marx and Engels saw the division between town and country in the Middle Ages as the expression of the antithesis between the newly developing capitalist mode of production and the old feudal mode in this period. However, it is clear that all three writers agree that the city was significant only at a specific period in history, and that neither the ancient city nor the modern capitalist city can be analysed in these terms. The city in contemporary capitalism is no longer the basis for human association (Weber), the locus of the division of labour (Durkheim) or the expression of a specific mode of production (Marx), in which case it is neither fruitful nor appropriate to study it in its own right.

The second context in which the city appears in the work of these writers is as a secondary influence on the development of fundamental social processes generated within capitalist societies. The city, in other words, is analysed not as a cause, but as a significant condition, of certain developments. The clearest example here concerns the argument found in the work of Marx and Engels to the effect that, although the city does not itself create the modern proletariat, it is an important condition of the self-realization of the proletariat as a politically and economically organized class in opposition to the bourgeoisie. This is because the city concentrates the working class and renders more visible the stark and growing antithesis between it and capital. In rather different vein, Durkheim's concern with the effects of an advanced division of labour on the moral cohesion of modern societies similarly takes urbanization as an important precondition of the development of functional differentiation. In both cases, therefore, a developmental theory (the growth of class struggle, the growth of new forms of social solidarity) is made conditional upon the growth of towns.

We can now appreciate why urban sociology has tended to pay so little attention to what Marx, Weber and Durkheim had to say about the city, for it is apparent in their work that the city in contemporary capitalism does not itself constitute a theoretically significant area of study. It is hardly surprising, then, that subsequent attempts to establish an urban sociology have drawn upon other aspects of their work while generally bypassing their discussion of the urban question. We shall see in later chapters, for example, how Durkheim's work on the social effects of the division of labour came to be incorporated into ecological theories of city growth and differentiation in the 1920s, how Weber's writings on political domination and social stratification formed the basis for a conceptualization of the city as a system of resource allocation in the 1960s, and how in the 1970s Marx's analysis of social reproduction and class struggle was developed as the foundation for a new political economy of urbanism. The influence of these three writers over the development of urban sociology has been pervasive yet selective.

The aim of this chapter is to retrace the way in which Weber, Durkheim and Marx and Engels all came to the conclusion that the city in contemporary capitalism was not a theoretically specific object of analysis. The paths followed by their respective analyses are divergent, yet the end-point is the same. In other words, although these writers differed radically in their methods, their theories and their personal political commitments and persuasions, their application of their different perspectives and approaches nevertheless resulted in conclusions that are broadly compatible. In each case, therefore, we shall consider first the methodological principles that guided their work, and second the results of the application of these principles to an analysis of the urban question.

Marx and Engels: the town, the country and the capitalist mode of production

Marx's method arguably rests on two key principles. The first is that no single aspect of reality can be analysed independently of the totality of social relations and determinations of which it forms an integral part. His commitment to dialectical analysis – to the principle of the unity of opposites – led him to reject any mode of analysis that failed to relate the part to the whole, for although it was both possible and necessary to abstract elements from the whole, these had always to be reintegrated or synthesized in order to arrive at a scientific conception of the totality. As Swingewood argues, 'The dialectical approach in Hegel and Marx is pre-eminently a method for analyzing the interconnections of phenomena, of grasping facts not as isolated, rigid and external data but as part of an all-embracing process' (1975, p. 33). It is precisely because of this claim to be able to analyse the totality that Marxism has remained so intellectually attractive and powerful within the social sciences. It is also this that explains why it is that, in contemporary urban studies, geographers, sociologists, political scientists and economists who have adopted a Marxist method have tended to converge in their interests and concerns to the point where disciplinary affiliation has become virtually insignificant (see, for example, Chapter 7), for the application of a dialectical method must result in a mode of analysis that denies the very basis on which such academic boundaries are drawn. *good point* ✓

The second key principle is that the material world exists prior to our conceptions of it, and that the way in which this world appears to us may conceal or distort its essential character. Marx recognizes that our ideas about the world must bear some relation to what that world is actually like, but he denies that reality is directly reflected in consciousness. Indeed, he suggests that there would be no need for science if this were the case since there would be nothing for it to discover beyond immediate experience. Consciousness is thus not a reflection of material reality but the mediation of it, and it follows from this that the essential reality that science attempts to discover may be obscured by the phenomenal forms through which this reality is represented in our everyday experience: 'Unlike phenomenal forms, Marx holds, essential relations need not be transparent to direct experience. Phenomenal forms may be such as to mask or obscure the relations of which they are the forms of manifestation' (Derek Sayer 1979, p. 9).

For Marx, therefore, the task of science is to penetrate the realm of appearances in order to discover the essential relations that give rise to these appearances. Unlike ideology, which takes the phenomenal forms as given, science goes beyond the world of commonsense experience: 'The forms of appearance are reproduced directly and spontaneously, as current and usual modes of thought; the essential relation must first be discovered by science' (Marx 1976, p. 682). Any theory (such as bourgeois political economy) that remains at the level of appearances (for example formally equivalent exchange) and attempts to explain reality in terms of the categories of everyday experience (say, land, labour and capital as three factors of production) will inevitably fail to provide scientific explanations (for instance of the process of valorization of capital), but will simply formalize and legitimate existing ideological modes of thought.

All this, however, raises the obvious question of how Marx's dialectical method can discover essential relations when other methods cannot, given that the essence cannot be known through its phenomenal forms. There are basically two different interpretations of Marx on this key problem.

The first suggests that science involves two stages: first, an analysis of a general conceptualization of the world into its simplest elements, and second, a reconceptualization of the world in terms of a synthesis of these elements. McBride summarizes this method as 'A movement from broad generalizations to endless specifics to generalities qualified by facts' (1977, p. 56), and shows how this corresponds to the familiar dialectical schema of a development from thesis to antithesis and thence to synthesis. To cite an example given by Marx (1973) himself, science begins with a 'chaotic' concept such as population, analyses this down into its simplest elements (for example, the population is broken down into classes, which in turn necessitates a conceptualization of the relation between wage labour and capital, which itself rests on a concept of exchange and division of labour, and so on), and then reconstructs reality in terms of this conceptual system in order to render it intelligible. The outcome of this dialectical method is that the essence of reality comes to be known through the application of analytical abstractions to concrete cases: 'The method of rising from the abstract to the concrete is only the way in which thought appropriates the concrete, reproduces it as the concrete in the mind' (Marx 1973, p. 101). The further this procedure is carried, the closer scientific conceptions of reality come to 'mapping' the material reality itself: 'Progress in science is essentially progress towards an ever closer approximation to objective truth' (Collier 1978, p. 15).

Now there is some debate among Marxists as to whether this method of rising from the abstract to the concrete was intended by Marx as a statement of his mode of investigation or simply as his mode of exposition. Certainly the structure of *Capital* corresponds to this formula (Marx sets out his argument by starting with the simplest abstraction – the commodity – and then gradually builds up to the full complexity of actual capitalist societies), yet in the Postface to the second edition of that work he states explicitly that 'the method of presentation must differ in form from that of inquiry' (1976, p. 102). Furthermore, just two years after he wrote the 1857 Introduction in which this method is most fully elaborated, he rejected this formulation on the grounds that 'any anticipation of results still to be proved appears to me to be disturbing', and he argued instead that 'the reader who on the whole desires to follow me must be resolved to ascend from the particular to the general' (1969, p. 502). In other words, the prescription given in the 1857 Introduction is reversed, and the method of analysis is described in terms of a movement from particular 'concrete' cases (i.e. specific capitalist societies) to more general abstractions.

This leads us to the second interpretation of Marx's method as a mode of analysis based upon careful and rigorous empirical investigation. Derek Sayer, for example, argues that a mode of investigation that began with abstractions would have to be premised on the assumption that Marx had some magical and privileged insight into the essential reality of capitalism before he actually studied any existing capitalist societies, and there is clearly no justification for such a view:

Marx's historical categories . . . are generated neither from 'simple abstractions' in general, nor from transhistorical categories in particular. They are emphatically *a posteriori* constructs, arrived at precisely by abstraction from the 'real and concrete'. Marx has no mysteriously privileged starting point. [D. Sayer 1979, p. 102]

But if Marx begins with the 'concrete' and generates his abstractions through the study of existing societies, how does this method manage to penetrate phenomenal forms and reveal the essential relations which lie behind them? Sayer's answer is that Marx's method is, in a sense, conjectural. In other words, he posits the existence of certain relations which, if they did exist, would account for phenomenal appearances: 'The "logic" of Marx's analytic is essentially a logic of hypothesis formation, for what he basically does is to *posit* mechanisms and conditions which would, if they existed, respectively explain how and why the phenomena we observe come to assume the forms they do' (D. Sayer 1979, p. 114). This method is neither deductive (since there are no *a priori* covering laws or transhistorical generalizations from which essential relations can be deduced), nor inductive (since the discovery of regularities in the world of appearances cannot itself imply the necessity of certain underlying essences). It is, rather, a 'retroductive' method.

The logic of retroductive explanation involves the attempt to explain observable phenomena by developing hypotheses about underlying causes. It cannot support *any* conjecture, since the hypothesized causes must be able to explain evidence at the level of appearances, but it is equally a weak form of inference since the hypotheses can never be directly tested. In other words, it is never possible finally to demonstrate that a posited 'law' of capitalist development is actually true since such a law refers to processes which, even if they do exist, remain hidden. Furthermore, it is never possible to demonstrate that the essential relations posited by the theory are the correct ones since there is always the possibility that other essences could be put forward which could explain phenomenal forms equally as well.

Marx's method, understood as a method of retroduction, thus carries no guarantees of truth and no privileged insight into the inner workings of society. There is no warrant in this method for dismissing alternative theories that can also explain phenomenal appearances, nor for claiming a monopoly over the 'correct' scientific mode of analysis. Equally, of course, it makes no sense to attack this method on the grounds that its results cannot be directly tested against experience, since its very purpose is to theorize processes that by definition cannot be amenable to direct observation. The results of the application of such a method must be evaluated on its own terms (for example, does the posited essence explain phenomenal forms? are the predictions – as opposed to the prophecies – that arise out of this method borne out historically? how well does the theory explain comparative variations between societies? and so on). As Sayer concludes,

If we require all the propositions in a scientific explanation to be open to empirical refutation, we must conclude that Marx was no scientist. If, on the other hand, we demand merely that it must be possible to provide independent empirical evidence which bears on its truth or falsity, then we may reasonably regard *Capital* as a paradigm of scientific research. [D. Sayer 1979, p. 141]

In short, Marx's method can be used fruitfully to generate theories that are plausible to a greater or lesser extent but can never finally be demonstrated, and it follows that there is no necessary and compelling reason to accept such theories other than one's own political values and purposes. Marxism, in other words, is as much a guide to political practice as a method of scientific analysis.

For Marx and Engels, the historic division between town and country that characterizes all human societies from antiquity to the period of modern capitalism is both the expression and the basis of the division of labour. In *Capital*, for example, Marx writes: 'The foundation of every division of labour which has attained a certain degree of development, and has been brought about by the exchange of commodities, is the separation of town from country. One might well say that the whole economic history of society is summed up in the movement of this antithesis' (1976, p. 472). Similarly, in his essay on the housing question, Engels (1969b) argues that the separation of town and country can be overcome only through the abolition of the division of labour consequent upon the transition to socialism. It follows from this that any analysis of the town–country division must be grounded in an analysis of the mode of production that creates and sustains it.

According to Marx, the first real class society was that of the ancient city state (notably Rome). Roman society was based on a slave mode of production in which the wealth of the ruling class was founded on agricultural land ownership. Ownership of the means of production became increasingly concentrated into great estates – the *latifundiae* – as a result of the progressive collapse of the independent peasantry, but although the great landowners lived in the city itself, the mode of production remained rural: 'Ancient classical history is the history of cities, but cities based on landownership and agriculture' (Marx 1964, p. 77).

In antiquity, therefore, the city never became the locus of a new mode of production. The relation of Rome to its provinces was entirely political; the city was nothing more than an administrative centre superimposed upon a slave-agriculture mode of production. It followed from this that internal struggles could destroy this political bond but that there was no basis in this society for the development of a qualitatively new mode of production out of the ruins of the old: 'Rome, indeed, never became more than a city; its connection with the provinces was almost exclusively political and could, therefore, easily be broken again by political events' (Marx and Engels 1970, p. 90). Rome collapsed, it was not transcended, and this is because the tension between town and country, centre and periphery, was never more than political. Ancient society disappeared 'without producing a different mode of production, a different society. . . . Why? Because the town in antiquity consisted of a closed system. Internal struggle could only harm it from the inside without being able to open up another practical reality' (Lefebvre 1972, p. 40). With the collapse of Rome, the break-up of the *latifundiae* and the fall of a slave mode of production, all that happened was a return to individual peasant agriculture.

The history of human societies up to the Middle Ages is therefore a history of the countryside. In the feudal or Germanic period, however, this begins to change: 'The middle ages (Germanic period) starts with the countryside as the locus of history, whose further development then proceeds through the opposition of town and country; modern history is the urbanization of the countryside, not, as among the ancients, the ruralization of the city' (Marx 1964, pp. 77–8). In other words, in the feudal era, for the first time, the division between town and country comes to express an *essential contradiction* which eventually brings about the transcendence of feudalism itself.

According to Marx, the growth of a merchant class in the established towns during the Middle Ages had the important effect of extending trading links between different areas, thereby facilitating a division of labour between different towns and stimulating the growth of new industries: 'The towns enter into relations with one another, new tools are brought from one town into the other, and the separation between production and commerce soon calls forth a new division of production between the industrial towns, each of which is soon exploiting a predominant branch of industry' (Marx and Engels 1970, p. 72). However, the development of industrial capital was hindered by the existing relations of production in the established towns, for the guild system both restricted entry into manufacture and regulated the movement of labour. Capitalist manufacture, based originally on weaving, was thus propelled out of the corporate towns and was at the same time attracted into the countryside where there was water power to drive the new machinery and labour power to work it:

> The money capital formed by means of usury and commerce was prevented from turning into industrial capital by the feudal organization of the countryside and the guild organization of the towns. These fetters vanished with the dissolution of the feudal band of retainers, and the expropriation and partial eviction of the rural population. The new manufacturers were established at sea-ports, or at points in the countryside which were beyond the control of the old municipalities and their guilds. [Marx 1976, p. 915]

The new system of capitalist manufacture, facilitated by merchants' capital in the medieval towns, thus took root in the countryside, and the great cities of the Industrial Revolution grew up around it. Whereas the towns of antiquity had represented a closed system, these new industrial towns represented an opposition to the mode of production that had spawned them. The hierarchical obligations of feudalism and the corporate regulation of the medieval towns were here replaced by relations based entirely on the cash nexus. The new social relations of capitalism thus became established as the antithesis to the old social relations of feudalism, and the contradictions between them, expressed in the class antagonism between industrial bourgeoisie and feudal landowners, came to be represented directly and vividly in the conflict between town and country.

In the feudal period, therefore, the division between town and country not only reflected the growing division of labour between manufacture and agriculture, but was also the phenomenal expression of the antithesis between conflicting modes of production. Although the new industrial towns were not themselves the cause of the transcendence of feudalism, they were the form it took. In this sense, the town was at this time an historical subject:

> For Marx, the dissolution of the feudal mode of production and the transition to capitalism is attached to a *subject*, the town. The town breaks up the medieval system (feudalism) while transcending itself . . . the town is a 'subject' and a coherent force, a partial system which attacks the global system and which simultaneously shows the existence of this system and destroys it. [Lefebvre 1972, p. 71]

The stark contrast between town and country is, of course, in no way overcome by the establishment of a capitalist mode of production. Indeed, Engels suggests that this contrast is 'brought to its extreme point by present-day capitalist society' (1969b, p. 333). However, the significance of this division changes with the development of capitalism, for the essential contradiction within the capitalist mode of production (that between capital and labour) no longer corresponds to the phenomenal forms of town and country in the way in which that between capital and feudal landownership once did. Once capitalism has become established, it permeates throughout social production, and (in time) agriculture becomes characterized by capitalist social relations just as manufacturing industry does. The town and the country are thus no longer the real subjects of analysis or of political struggle, for although the separation between them becomes ever more vivid, it does not itself set the parameters within which the struggle for socialism is to be waged. Put another way, the struggle between proletariat and bourgeoisie extends across urban–rural boundaries as workers in town and countryside are increasingly drawn into the capital relation.

Having said that, it is nevertheless the case that Marx and Engels look to the *urban* proletariat to lead the struggle for socialism. As Williams (1973) has pointed out, there is something of an ambivalence in their analysis of the role of the city in capitalist societies, for they argue on the one hand that the city expresses most vividly the evils of capitalism, and on the other that it is within the city that the progressive forces of socialism are most fully developed. What this indicates is not so much an 'emotional confusion' (as Williams 1973, p. 37, suggests) as a dual focus in their work on capitalist urbanization. In other words, Marx and Engels study the capitalist city in two ways: first as an illustration or a microcosm of processes occurring at a different rate throughout capitalist society, and second as an important condition of the development of certain specific processes within that society.

When they discuss the city as a microcosm, their concern is not with the city *per se* but with capitalist processes that are most clearly revealed in an urban context: 'From this perspective, seen in this light, the town provides the backcloth; on that backcloth lots of events and notable facts come to pass which analysis detaches from their relatively unimportant decor' (Lefebvre 1972, p. 106). It is, in other words, not the city that is held responsible for the poverty and squalor of the urban proletariat, but the capitalist mode of production. Engels makes this abundantly clear both in his early work on the condition of the English working class, where he argues that 'the great cities really only secure a more rapid and certain development for evils already existing in the germ' (1969a, p. 150), and in his later essay on the housing question. In both works the city

is portrayed as the hothouse of capitalist contradictions, the exaggerated expression of essential tendencies within capitalism itself, and in both Engels leaves us in no doubt that urban poverty can be overcome only through a transformation of the society as a whole.

As his work developed, so his treatment of the urban question became ever more firmly grounded in a critique of capitalism. In his essay on the housing question (written some thirty years after his discussion of the condition of the English working class), he states explicitly that 'The housing shortage from which the workers and part of the petty bourgeoisie suffer in our modern big cities is one of the innumerable *smaller* secondary evils which result from the present day capitalist mode of production' (Engels 1969b, p. 305). And whereas in his earlier work, written before he met Marx, he had been tempted to suggest that the 'Big Whigs' of Manchester were perhaps in part responsible for perpetuating the pattern of urban deprivation in that city (see Engels 1969a, pp. 80–1), he is clear in his later essay that it is the capitalist system itself, and not the conscious and deliberate actions of individual capitalists, that explains the deplorable conditions under which large sections of the proletariat are obliged to live. Indeed, he argues that the bourgeoisie has sometimes attempted (out of self-interest) to alleviate these conditions, but that such attempts necessarily fail as the logic of capitalism constantly reasserts itself:

> Capitalist rule cannot allow itself the pleasure of generating epidemic diseases among the working class with impunity. . . . Nevertheless the capitalist order of society reproduces again and again the evils to be remedied, and does so with such inevitable necessity that even in England the remedying of them has hardly advanced a single step. [Engels 1969b, p. 324]

This notion of an 'inevitable necessity', an inexorable capitalist logic, recurs throughout this essay. There is, according to Engels, no possibility of resolving the housing question within capitalist society. Every attempt at what today would be termed 'urban renewal' results in the eradication of slums in one area and their simultaneous reappearance in another:

> The breeding places of disease, the infamous holes and cellars in which the capitalist mode of production confines our workers night after night, are not abolished; they are merely shifted elsewhere! The same economic necessity which produced them in the first place produces them in the next place also! As long as the capitalist mode of production continues to exist it is folly to hope for an isolated settlement of the housing question or of any other social question affecting the lot of the workers. The solution lies in the abolition of the capitalist mode of production. [Engels 1969b, pp. 352–3]

The city is not, however, only a reflection of the logic of capitalism, for Marx and Engels also see in the development of urbanization the necessary condition for the transition to socialism. This is not because the city is the locus of a new mode of production, as was the case in the medieval period, but because it is in the city that the revolutionary class created by capitalism, the proletariat, achieves its 'fullest classic perfection' (Engels 1969a, p. 75). Precisely because the tendencies within capitalism are most fully developed in the great cities, it is there that the conditions for effective struggle against capital reach their maturity:

> Since commerce and manufacture attain their most complete development in these great towns, their influence upon the proletariat is also most clearly observable here. Here the centralization of property has reached the highest point . . . there exist here only a rich and a poor class, for the lower middle class vanishes more completely with every passing day. [Engels 1969a, p. 56]

dualism

The tendencies for capital to become concentrated and for the classes to polarize develop in the cities, and it is therefore in the cities that the concentration and common deprivation of the proletariat is most likely to result in the growth of class consciousness and revolutionary organization:

> If the centralization of population stimulates and develops the property-holding class, it forces the development of the workers yet more rapidly. The workers begin to feel as a class, as a whole. . . . The great cities are the birth-places of labour movements; in them the workers first began to reflect upon their own condition and to struggle against it; in them the opposition between proletariat and bourgeoisie first made itself manifest. . . . Without the great cities and their forcing influence upon the popular intelligence, the working class would be far less advanced than it is. [Engels 1969a, p. 152]

Here, then, is the source of the ambivalence noted by Williams, for although the city represents a concentration of the evils of capitalism, it also constitutes the necessary conditions for the development of the workers' movement that will overthrow it. The conditions of life in the countryside cannot sustain a coherent class challenge to the bourgeoisie because 'the isolated dwellings, the stability of the surroundings and occupations, and consequently of the thoughts, are decidedly unfavourable to all development' (Engels 1969a, p. 291). This is why Marx and Engels develop the well-known argument in the *Communist Manifesto* to the effect that the bourgeoisie has rendered a service to the workers' movement by creating large cities which have 'rescued a considerable part of the population from the idiocy of rural life' (1969, p. 112).

It is important to recognize, however, that it is not urbanization itself that forges a revolutionary working class any more than it is urbanization that gives rise to poverty, squalor and disease. The development of potentially revolutionary conditions is a tendency inherent within the development of capitalism, and the growth of cities is a contingent condition influencing whether and how such conditions come to be acted upon by the working class. The city is only of secondary significance in Marx's analysis of capitalism and the transition to socialism.

What this means, of course, is that there is no basis in the work of Marx and Engels for the development of a specific theory of urbanism in capitalist societies. The city may illustrate the manifestations of essential tendencies within capitalism, and it may even influence the way in which these manifestations come to be articulated in political struggles, but it is not the essential cause of such developments, nor is it the phenomenal form of an underlying contradiction as was the case in feudal society. A Marxist analysis that seeks to go beyond the level of appearances and to posit the existence of essential relations will not take the city as an object of analysis, but will rather consider the phenomena that become manifest in cities in terms of the underlying relations and determinations of which they are but one manifestation. From a Marxist perspective, it seems that urbanism may constitute a valid concept in the analysis of feudalism (where the city is, for the first and last time, an historical subject), and it may perhaps refer to a real and essential contradiction in some contemporary 'Third World' societies (as Lipton 1977 suggests); but in the context of modern capitalism it would seem to constitute an 'ideological' concept by means of which we make sense of everyday experience ('urban' problems, 'urban' decay, etc.) rather than a 'scientific' one by means of which we analyse and explain it.

Max Weber: the city and the growth of rationality

Weber's approach to sociological explanation represents almost a total reversal of Marx's method. While Marx emphasizes totality, the need to relate everything to everything else, Weber argues that only partial and one-sided accounts are ever possible. Where Marx seeks to identify essential causes behind phenomena, Weber's concepts represent logical purifications of phenomenal forms. Marx's notion of praxis, the inherent fusion of scientific analysis and political struggle, is directly opposed to Weber's insistence on the separation of science and politics, facts and values. And while Marx is interested in individuals only in so far as they are personifications of objective relations, Weber sees individual actions and individual consciousness as the very basis of sociological analysis.

The basic concept in Weber's sociology is that of the human subject endowed with free will who, in interaction with others, attempts to realize certain values or objectives. He recognizes that not all human actions are rational since individuals may be unaware of certain possibilities for realizing their aims, and their actions may in any case be contaminated by habit or emotion. Sociology in his view can therefore perform a technical service by clarifying what people want to achieve (e.g. by pointing to inconsistencies between different sets of values to which they are committed), and by indicating which strategies are most likely to result in the required effects.

At the heart of Weber's sociological enterprise, therefore, is the attempt to relate subjective motives to particular courses of action. It follows from this that the explanation of social action will be premised upon an understanding of the subjective meaning that that action has for the individual concerned. Hence Weber's well-known definition of sociology as 'A science concerning itself with the interpretative understanding of social action and thereby with a causal explanation of its course and consequences' (1968, p. 4). By social action, Weber means human action which is subjectively meaningful and which takes account of the actions of others.

Implied in this definition is a rejection of any attempt to explain social phenomena as the result of anything other than subjectively meaningful human actions:

> Action in this sense of subjectively understandable orientation of behaviour exists only as the behaviour of one or more *individual* human beings. . . . collectivities must be treated as *solely* the resultants and modes of organization of the particular acts of individual persons, since these alone can be treated as agents in the course of subjectively understandable action. [Weber 1968, p. 13]

Thus, when using collective concepts such as 'social class' or 'state', the sociologist should always remember that it is not a class or a state that acts, but rather the individuals who comprise it.

The explanation of social action involves two stages. First, the sociologist must attempt to provide a plausible account of the actors' motives. This is possible because certain types of subjective meanings are generally attached to certain types of actions in certain types of situations (e.g. chopping wood on a cold day may be indicative of a desire to light a fire). There is, of course, no guarantee that the posited motive is the actual motive (the more rational the action, the greater is the likelihood that we will understand it correctly), and having adduced a possible motive, the sociologist must then go on to show that this individual tends to act in similar ways in other similar situations. In other words, an adequate sociological explanation must attempt both to understand the meaning of a given action for those involved, and to demonstrate the probability of its occurrence in particular types of situations. As Weber puts it,

> If adequacy with respect to meaning is lacking, then no matter how high the degree of uniformity and how precisely its probability can be numerically determined, it is still an incomprehensible statistical probability, whether we deal with overt or subjective processes. On the other hand, even the most

perfect adequacy on the level of meaning has causal significance from a sociological point of view only insofar as there is some kind of proof for the existence of a probability that action in fact normally takes the course which has been held to be meaningful. [Weber 1968, p. 12]

Correlations and generalizations explain nothing if we fail to understand what lies behind them, just as understanding of subjective meanings is useless if we cannot predict typical patterns of action.

Two points in particular should be noted about this argument. The first is that Weber only ever talks of *adequate* explanations; even when the attribution of meaning is successfully combined with an analysis of probability, we can never be certain that the explanations we put forward are correct. Furthermore, the element of free will in social life means that there must always be an element of uncertainty in the explanation of social action, for if individual actions are not determined then the most that sociology can achieve is statements of probability regarding the likely occurrence of certain types of actions in certain types of situations. It follows from this that laws of social life (including Marxist laws) are impossible, since each action is a unique (though often predictable) event. The so-called 'laws' of the social sciences (for example, the law of supply and demand) are in fact statements of typical probability regarding the likelihood of certain types of action occurring in certain types of situations.

The second point is that, although all social events are historically unique, there is clearly a need for some means whereby social phenomena can be classified in general terms, for only in this way is it possible to understand typical motives and to recognize typical patterns of action. It is, in other words, necessary to generalize in order to explain unique events. In Weber's sociology, this function of generalization is fulfilled through the construction of *ideal types*. These are mental constructs which serve to specify the theoretically most significant aspects of different classes of social phenomena. They may be either 'individual' types (Calvinism, capitalism, bureaucracy, etc.) or generic types (such as the four different types of social action). As Burger has pointed out, individual types clearly refer to numerous empirical cases (for example, there are many different capitalist societies): 'This type of ideal type is not called "individual" because it refers to one individual phenomenon, but because the occurrence of the constellation of elements described in it characterizes, from the point of view adopted by the historian, a class of phenomena occurring in a distinct unique, i.e. individual, historical epoch' (1976, pp. 131–2). Generic types, on the other hand, are ahistorical and serve to specify the elements from which individual types are constructed. One of the defining features of Weber's ideal type of the spirit of capitalism, for example, is goal-oriented rational action (one of four generic types of social action). As Torrance suggests, 'On the whole, Weber's position appears to be that types are constructed out of general conceptual elements, but may be additionally defined by a specific historical reference to times, places or persons' (1974, p. 136).

Weber insists that ideal types are indispensable in sociological explanation and that we constantly construct and use them whether or not we realize it. Whenever we refer to 'capitalist societies', for example, we are employing an ideal type construct, for there are many variations between, say, France and the United States which we choose to ignore for the purposes of classification while emphasizing those aspects that they have in common and that appear most relevant for our theoretical purposes. Social reality is infinite, and we can never know all there is to know about a given phenomenon. When we come to study some aspect of social life, therefore, we are immediately confronted with a chaotic complexity of sense impressions, and the only way to impose order on this chaos in order to distinguish that which is relevant to our concerns from that which is not is through the application of conceptually pure types. Ideal types are the yardsticks by means of which empirical reality can be rendered accessible to analysis. In the absence of such constructs we would be left only with an infinite range of different unique cases, each with its own history and characteristics, and we would lack any criteria for determining which of these characteristics are significant for our theoretical purposes.

Although they are mental constructs, ideal types are not simply conjured up out of nothing in the mind of the researcher, but are developed on the basis of existing empirical knowledge of actual phenomena. They involve the logical extension of certain aspects of reality into a pure, artificial yet logically possible type against which existing phenomena can be measured and compared. While their basis lies in empirical reality, ideal types do not express that reality but rather exaggerate certain aspects of it while thinking away others. The only test of an ideal type consists in the assessment of its logical coherence. Since its purpose is to clarify reality in order to facilitate the development of hypotheses, it clearly makes no sense to criticize an ideal type on the grounds that it fails to reproduce the real world in all its bewildering complexity. Ideal types are not intended as descriptions. Indeed, it is quite possible to construct any number of different ideal types of the 'same' phenomenon according to which aspects of it are deemed most significant for any given purpose. While these different types may vary in their fruitfulness for research, they cannot be evaluated against each other in terms of their empirical validity since they will each involve extensions of different aspects of the phenomenon in question. Ideal types, in other words, are always partial: 'There is no absolutely "objective" scientific analysis of culture or . . . of "social phenomena" independent of special and "one-sided" viewpoints according to which – expressly or tacitly, consciously or unconsciously – they are selected, analysed and organized for expository purposes' (Weber 1949, p. 72).

Now it has often been suggested that this emphasis on the one-sidedness of sociological constructs leads Weber into a hopeless relativism in which any one account is as good as any other. Hindess (1977), for example, finds in Weber's approach a 'systematic epistemological relativism' and concludes in relation to the ideal type method that 'There is no reason why the social scientist should not let his imagination run wild. He has nothing to lose but the chains of reason' (p. 38). Such arguments, however, ignore the fact that for Weber ideal types are simply the means of analysis, not its end product. It does not follow that a partial account cannot be objective, for although ideal types are subjective constructs and cannot be tested, the hypotheses developed on the basis of them can and must be: 'Essentially, all that Weber meant by objectivity was that, within the limits of the inescapably one-sided viewpoint, it is both possible and necessary to validate one's substantive propositions' (Dawe 1971, p. 50). All explanations are partial, but not all are valid (or to be more precise, adequate). Any sociological account must be demonstrated through historical and comparative evidence.

Where Weber does endorse relativism is not in the realm of facts but in the realm of values. Thus, although he argued that scientific explanations had to be evaluated in terms of their empirical adequacy, he denied that ethical judgements could ever be evaluated in the same way. For him, the moral realm necessarily consists of fundamental dilemmas which individuals must resolve for themselves. 'The ultimately possible attitudes toward life are irreconcilable, and hence their struggle can never be brought to a final conclusion' (Weber 1948a, p. 152). Science, therefore, can never legislate on moral questions, and the basic reason for this is that, as we have seen, science is itself partial in that the ideal types that it employs are constructed according to the relevance of particular aspects of reality for the scientist's own moral and practical concerns: 'The problems of the social sciences are selected by the value-relevance of the phenomena treated . . . cultural (i.e. evaluative) interests give purely empirical scientific work its direction' (Weber 1949, pp.21–2). Sociology is therefore grounded in ethical concerns from the very outset: 'An attitude of moral indifference has no connection with scientific "objectivity" ' (1949, p. 60).

It follows from this, as Dawe suggests, that, 'Weber is arguing for the centrality of value to social science, not merely as a "principle of selection of subject matter", but as the *sine qua non of all meaningful knowledge of social reality.* Without the attribution of value, knowledge of social phenomena is inconceivable' (Dawe 1971, p. 42). This being the case, sociology clearly cannot be used to justify a particular value position, since, 'If sociology is shaped by value, it cannot become the justification for that value; the argument would be entirely circular' (pp.55–6). Weber's concern is not to create a dry and morally indifferent social science, but rather to ensure that the inherently one-sided accounts of social science are not used to provide a spurious resolution to fundamental moral questions which individuals must confront for themselves: 'Weber is more concerned with defending the value sphere against the unfounded claims of science than with protecting the scientific process from valuational distortions' (Bruun 1972, p.54).

Hindess suggests that Weber's method gives rise to 'plausible generalizations and plausible stories, nothing more' (1977, p.48). This is true in the sense that, for Weber, there can be no final guarantee of truth (his criterion of science is one of adequacy, not truth), and there are many different sides to any one question. But as we saw in the previous section, Marx's logic of retroduction is similarly unable to offer guarantees of truth, and despite its emphasis on dialectical totality, it too may be seen as partial and one-sided (for example in the emphasis it places on economic factors). The significance of Weber's method is precisely that it recognizes the partiality of sociological explanations and thus takes account of the theoretical pluralism that has always characterized the social sciences. For Weber, no one approach ever enjoys a monopoly over 'correct' scientific knowledge of social reality. As we shall see in Chapter 5, attempts by Marxists to argue otherwise appear entirely unconvincing.

Weber's ideal type method is clearly evident in his study of the city; indeed, one commentator has suggested that this study contains 'the most fully worked out typology' in his economic sociology (see Freund 1968, p.168). The study begins by rejecting size as an adequate basis for conceptualizing the city (see page 90), and goes on to distinguish two aspects of the city that appear crucial from Weber's perspective, namely economic and political organization. As regards the former, he suggests that cities are defined by the existence of an established market system: 'Economically defined, the city is a settlement the inhabitants of which live primarily off trade and commerce rather than agriculture . . . the city is a market place' (Weber 1958, pp.66–7). He then distinguishes between consumer, producer and commercial cities on the basis of this economic criterion, adding that 'It hardly needs to be mentioned that actual cities nearly always represent mixed types' (p.70) and that these are therefore ideal constructions that enable classification.

As regards the political dimension, he suggests that partial political autonomy is a key criterion: 'The city must . . . be considered to be a partially autonomous association, a "community" with special political and administrative arrangements' (p.74). On this basis, he distinguishes the 'patrician city', run by an assembly of notables, and the 'plebeian city', run by an elected assembly of citizens. He further suggests that, in its pure form, political autonomy entails some independent basis of military power in the form of a fortress or garrison, although he recognizes at various points in the study that, in the Middle Ages, the political autonomy of the cities in northern Europe was achieved on the basis of economic rather than military power.

Taking these two dimensions together, Weber then constructs his ideal type city:

> To constitute a full urban community a settlement must display a relative predominance of trade-commercial relations with the settlement as a whole displaying the following features: 1. a fortification; 2. a market; 3. a court of its own and at least partially autonomous law; 4. a related form of association; and 5. at least partial autonomy and autocephaly, thus also an administration by authorities in the election of whom the burghers participated. [Weber 1958, pp. 80–1]

Clearly this is an ideal type which is useful only in the analysis of the city at particular historical periods. This reflects Weber's concerns in this study which are basically to trace the significance of the medieval European city in the development of Western capitalism, and to show why cities in ancient times and those in other parts of the world in the Middle Ages failed to create these conditions. As Bendix (1966) recognizes, this study is therefore an essential complement to Weber's earlier work on the Protestant ethic, and it reflects the same historical interest in the question of the peculiar origins of Western capitalism. It would therefore be ridiculous to look to this study for guidance in respect of research on the modern capitalist city, just as it would be ridiculous to attempt to employ Weber's ideal type of sixteenth-century Calvinism in an analysis of modern-day religious communes. The ideal type city that Weber puts forward is an individual type and cannot therefore be taken as a definition of the city at all times and in all places. Martindale, in his introduction to Weber's essay, therefore misses the point when he suggests that the conspicuous lack of fortresses in modern cities, together with their political subordination to the nation-state, means that, 'The age of the city seems to be at an end' (Weber 1958, p.62), for this is an altogether meaningless statement. The age of the medieval city is at an end – by definition – but if we wish to analyse the modern city, then we must turn to Weber's methodological writings, and not to his specific historical analysis, for guidance on how to proceed. In other words, we must determine which aspects of the modern city are most relevant for our current theoretical concerns and construct our own ideal type accordingly (see Chapter 8). The implication of this, of course, is that, just as Weber studied the ancient and medieval city because it appeared significant in respect of his theoretical concerns with the origins of capitalism, so too should any attempt to study the modern city be guided by a particular theoretical problem. If we learn any lesson from Weber's essay on the city, therefore, it is that the city is not itself a problem to be studied in its own right, and that there appears little point in trying to develop a theory of the city *per se*. Like Marx and Engels, Weber analysed the city only in the context of a broader theoretical concern with the question of capitalism.

Having developed this ideal type, Weber notes that general approximations to it are found only in the Occident. Thus, although there are many similarities between East and West, both in antiquity and in the Middle Ages, it was only in the West in the medieval period that the city came to be the basis of human association. In other places and in previous times, urban residents formed associations on the basis of kinship and estate, but in the western city in the Middle Ages, they came together for the first time as *individuals*:

Here, in new civic creations burghers joined the citizenry as single persons. The oath of citizenship was taken by the individual. Personal membership, not that of kin groups or tribe, in the local association of the city supplied the guarantee of the individual's personal legal position as a burgher. [Weber 1958, p. 102]

This contrasts with both the ancient city, where 'the individual could be a citizen . . . but only as a member of his clan' (p. 101), and with the Oriental and Asiatic city, where 'when the urban community appears at all it is only in the form of a kin association which also extends beyond the city' (p. 104).

Weber argues that a major factor explaining this difference was ✸ Christianity, for it helped dissolve clan associations while other religions such as Islam reinforced clan and tribe structures: 'By its very nature the Christian community was a confessional association of believing individuals rather than a ritualistic association of clans' (p. 103). It was also significant that there was no centralized hierarchical bureaucracy in the West as there was, for example, in China, for this meant that there were no religious or political barriers to the development of the city as an association of individuals.

The main form of association that emerged in the Western medieval cities was the guild (and, later, the corporation). As time went on, the guilds became less and less associated with particular crafts and businesses, and more and more associated with the *de facto* political control of the city. Citizenship rights became dependent upon guild membership, and non-urban, non-industrial classes such as the large nobles and bishops had therefore to join the guilds in order to achieve access to political power: 'The English guild often bestowed the civic rights. . . . Nearly everywhere the guild was actually, though not legally, the governing association of the city' (Weber 1958, p.134). Like Marx, therefore, Weber sees the city in the Middle Ages as highly significant in the break with feudalism and the foundation of the conditions for the development of capitalism: 'Neither modern capitalism nor the modern state grew up on the basis of the ancient cities while medieval urban development, though not alone decisive, was carrier of both phenomena and an important factor in their origin' (p.181).

This significance was both economic and political. Economically, the guilds laid the basis for the development of economic rationality: 'Under the domination of the guild the medieval city was pressed in the direction of industry on a rational economic model in a manner alien to the city of antiquity' (p. 223). This is not to suggest that capitalist industry developed within the guild system, for Weber agrees with Marx that 'the new capitalistic undertakings settled in new locations' (p. 189) away from the traditional forms of enterprise and the constricting organization of labour represented by the city guilds and corporations. The economic importance of the Western medieval city was not, therefore, that it spawned capitalist industry, but that it created the ideological and institutional legacy that 'formed the urban population of medieval Europe into a "ready-made" audience for the doctrines of the great Reformers' (Bendix 1966, p. 79). In other words, the development of the spirit of capitalism from the sixteenth century onwards, which Weber traces to the influence of puritanism, can be seen as the germination of a seed sown some 400 years earlier in the medieval city.

The city was equally significant politically. First, under the rule of the nobility Weber shows how constant feuding and rivalry within the patrician class led to the emergence of 'a noble professional officialdom' (Weber 1958, p. 130) – the Italian *podesta* – which attained its greatest perfection in the first half of the thirteenth century. This entailed the formation of a class of officials and of legally trained assistants, and this in turn led to the rational codification of law and to the possibility of an inter-local system of legal administration. Second, it was within the cities that the political power of the nobility came to be challenged and undermined (in Italy by the development of the *popolo*), and that the basis for modern democratic forms of government came to be established. While these developments took different forms in northern Europe than in the Mediterranean area, the result was broadly similar in that the locus of political power shifted from the militarily based power of the nobility to the economically based power of the entrepreneurial class in the towns: 'In the Middle Ages resident citizen entrepreneurs and small capitalistic craftsmen played the politically central role. Such strata had no significant role within the ancient citizenry' (p. 204). The medieval city in Europe was thus crucial in breaking from feudalism, both economically and politically.

Weber makes it clear that the city became the basis of human association only at a specific period in history. In antiquity the basis for such association, even within the cities, was kinship; in the modern period it is the nation-state. It was only in the Middle Ages, therefore, that the city was significant as the basis for social relationships, and there is a clear parallel here with Marx's argument that it is only in the feudal period that the city expresses essential social relations. Both Marx and Weber, therefore, analyse the city historically in terms of its role in the development of modern capitalism, and their analyses are in fact remarkably similar. Neither of them sees the city today as an important area of study; Marx, because the essential basis of the town–country division is eroded by the establishment of capitalist relations throughout the society, Weber because the city is no longer economically or politically autonomous and does not constitute the basis of human association. Both therefore cast a long shadow of doubt over the possibility or fruitfulness of a theory of urbanism in capitalist societies. If urban sociology is to have any rationale, therefore, it would seem necessary to argue that cities still perform some theoretically significant role within contemporary capitalism. (*Saunders*)

Émile Durkheim: the city, the division of labour and the moral basis of community

Durkheim's method provides a direct contrast to the approaches of both Marx and Weber. Like Marx, he accepts that the essence of social reality may be hidden and distorted by everyday common-sense ideas about it, but unlike Marx he suggests that the appearance of phenomena can nevertheless be taken as the expression of their essence if such phenomenal appearances are directly observed without conceptual encumbrances. In other words, Durkheim rejects the Marxist method of theorizing essences, and argues instead that essences can be directly ascertained through pure observation of appearances. Like Weber, therefore, Durkheim assumes that reality is given in observation, but unlike Weber he denies the necessity for any conceptual abstraction of partial aspects of that reality and he asserts the ability of sociology to penetrate to the essence of social phenomena. Put simply, it is Durkheim's commitment to empiricism that most sharply separates his approach from that of the other two writers discussed in this chapter, for what is specific to his method is the assertion of observation as the basis of knowledge and the consequent denial of any *a priori* theorization or conceptualization as a condition of knowledge.

Durkheim's firm commitment to empiricism has often led commentators to suggest that his is a positivist sociology. To some extent this is correct, for his endorsement of a purely experiential basis for knowledge, his equation of the logic of explanation between the natural and social sciences and his rejection of actors' ideas about the world as an important aspect of sociological explanation are all commonly associated with sociological positivism (see Giddens 1974). Against this, however, Durkheim rejects the positivist prescription of value-freedom and ethical neutrality of science, arguing that if science cannot prescribe ends then it loses all point, and that valuations of good and bad can be derived from observation of normal and pathological forms of phenomena. He also rejects individualistic explanations in favour of those that seek the causes of phenomena in collective forces which are not themselves directly observable. As Keat and Urry argue, it is therefore too simple to summarize his method as positivist since 'there are in Durkheim elements of both positivist and realist conceptions of science' (1975, p. 81). As we shall see, it is precisely the strain between these two conceptions that results in the final internal incoherence of his approach.

Basic to Durkheim's method is his argument that reality cannot be known through ideas about it. Science must address itself to the facts themselves if it is to avoid the ideological contamination of common-sense ideas, and this entails the eradication of all preconceptions: 'We must, therefore, consider social phenomena in themselves as distinct from the consciously formed representations of them in the mind; we must study them objectively as external things' (Durkheim 1938, p. 28). Science thus begins with 'a complete freedom of mind' (1933, p. 36) in which the objectivity of social facts can impress itself upon the senses. Only then is it possible to develop definitions of social facts which can identify their essential and inherent qualities: 'In order to be objective, the definition must obviously deal with phenomena not as ideas but in terms of their inherent properties. It must characterize them by elements essential to their nature' (1938, p. 35).

Sociological definitions are thus built up inductively, for it is only by observing a range of cases that the common elements essential to them all can be ascertained. Theory, in other words, plays no part in the definition, identification and classification of phenomena, but rather is developed on the basis of prior empirical observation. The classic problem of induction, of course, is that we can never be sure that we have identified an element common to all cases since the next empirical observation may prove to be an exception. Durkheim, however, denies that this is a problem for his method, and argues explicitly that there is no need even to aim for completeness of observation:

A satisfactory method must, above all, aim at facilitating scientific work by substituting a limited number of types for the indefinite multiplicity of individuals. . . . But for this purpose it must be made not from a complete inventory of all the individual characteristics but from a small number of them, carefully chosen. [Durkheim 1938, p. 80]

The reason why exhaustiveness is not required (and, incidentally, why this method is far removed from the conceptual partiality of Weber's ideal types) is that, for Durkheim, observable cases provide the means for identifying the common essence that lies behind them. The inductive analysis of a small number of cases is therefore sufficient to establish the common essential element of which each case is an expression.

Durkheim is careful to argue that the initial definition of social facts does not itself penetrate to their essence. All that is possible at this first stage is the identification of the surface features of phenomena: 'Since the definition in question is placed at the beginnings of the science, it cannot possibly aim at a statement concerning the essence of quality; that must be attained subsequently. The sole function of the definition is to establish contact with things' (1938, p. 42). Social facts, in other words, leave visible traces which provide indications of their essence; different types of social solidarity, for example, give rise to and are therefore indicated by different types of law, so that it becomes possible to distinguish the moral basis of different societies by means of an initial definition of legal forms (see below). Sociology therefore relies on observable phenomena as indicators of the essence of social facts, just as, say, the physicist relies on observation of movement of mercury in a thermometer to indicate temperature.

This argument, of course, assumes that there is a direct causal link between indicator and essence – that what we can observe is the direct expression of social facts that remain hidden. In order to establish such a link, Durkheim advances two principles of causality. The first is that social phenomena have social causes: 'The determining cause of a social fact should be sought among the social facts preceding it and not among the states of the individual consciousness' (1938, p. 110). The explanation of social facts cannot therefore be reduced to an analysis of individual actions any more than the explanation of biological facts can be found in the analysis of the chemical composition of living organisms. Social facts, the collective phenomena of social life, have an existence external to individuals, and individual actions are constrained by them in various ways (for

instance by the moral authority of laws, by the determinacy of socialization, by the 'currents' generated in collective life, and so on). It
follows that there exists a distinct social reality which sociology alone
can study, and that the causes of social phenomena cannot be sought
through psychology or any other science: 'Products of group life, it is
the nature of the group which alone can explain them' (1933, p. 350).

The second principle of causality is that any social fact has only one
social cause: 'A given effect can maintain this relationship with only
one cause, for it can express only one single nature' (1938, p. 127). If
there appear to be several causes, then this can only mean that there
are, in fact, several different phenomena to be explained. For
example, if, as Durkheim (1952) suggests, there are three principal
causes of suicide, then there must be three types of suicide corresponding to them. The morphological classification of social facts can
therefore be followed by analysis of the causes of each of the facts
identified.

Taken together, the argument that social phenomena are *sui
generis*, and that single facts have single causes, enables Durkheim to
assert the inherent connection between visible indicators and the
essences of which they are a function. To return to our previous
example, if there are two types of law then there must be two distinct
types of social phenomena that have given rise to them. The question
then is how are these social causes to be discovered?

Durkheim's answer is that the discovery of causes proceeds
through the method of 'concomitant variation': 'We have only one
way to demonstrate that a given phenomenon is the cause of another,
viz., to compare the cases in which they are simultaneously present or
absent, to see if the variations they present in these different combinations of circumstances indicate that one depends on the other'
(1938, p. 125). If a consistent correlation is found in a number of
different cases, then a real relationship is to be assumed between
them: 'As soon as one has proved that, in a certain number of cases,
two phenomena vary with one another, one is certain of being in the
presence of a law' (p. 133). Observable correlations therefore point to
the existence of an essential causal relation.

It is only at this point that theory plays a part in the analysis, for
having demonstrated concomitant variation, the sociologist must
attempt to explain it:

When two phenomena vary directly with each other, this relationship must
be accepted. . . . The results to which this method leads need, therefore, to be

interpreted. . . . We shall first investigate, by the aid of deduction, how one of the two terms has produced the other; then we shall try to verify the result of this deduction with the aid of experiments, i.e., new comparisons. If the deduction is possible and if the verification succeeds, we can regard the proof as completed. [Durkheim 1938, p. 132]

The example given by Durkheim concerns the statistical relationship between levels of education and suicide rates. Since education cannot itself explain an increase in the tendency to suicide, we must attempt to identify some common factor that can account for both. Such a factor is the break-down of traditional religion, which increases both the desire for knowledge and the tendency towards suicide, and the task is then to show that wherever such religions have been eroded, both education and suicide increase accordingly. If this is demonstrated, then a sociological proof has been established.

The major question that must be posed to Durkheim's method, however, is whether theory really is limited to the secondary role that he attributes to it, and thus whether he has in fact developed an objective empirical science freed from contaminating preconceptions. The first point to be noted is that the initial process of classification and identification of visible phenomena is itself dependent upon theoretically derived criteria. The identification of 'facts' is theoretically derived:

'Facts', supposedly, can be identified and classified on the basis of 'experience' and 'observation' alone, without prior theory or interpretation. Classification is, however, a theory-dependent exercise. It requires observation and comparison, of course, but it also requires a knowledge of its field of operation, criteria of identity, difference and relevance for characteristics of the 'objects' classified. [Benton 1977, p. 89]

Durkheim's phenomenalism thus reveals the classic weakness of positivist approaches which rest on the assumption of a purely experiential basis of knowledge.

There is, however, also a second problem which derives from his attempt to assert this postulate of phenomenalism while at the same time drawing the distinction between observable phenomena and their hidden essences. The point, quite simply, is that, far from discovering essences through the method of concomitant variation and theoretical deduction, Durkheim's method assumes their existence from the outset. The existence of essences, and their relation to observable phenomena, is therefore pre-established in the assumptions on which the method is premised. Thus Durkheim's starting point, that observable phenomena are significant as expressions and embodiments of an essential reality to which they are causally linked, depends upon a prior theory of essences and their relation to appearances which is, according to his own prescriptions for eradicating preconceptions, illegitimate. As Hirst shows, he can only assert the phenomenal as the basis of knowledge by positing an essence theoretically: 'Durkheim's sociology . . . is a theoretical mechanism for the reproduction of the "given". It is a device for "saving" the phenomena of immediate experience: at one and the same time it promotes these phenomena to primacy ("the given") and it installs an essence behind their groundless existence' (Hirst 1975, p. 103). The result of the application of such a method is, as Hirst suggests, self-confirming, since Durkheim's sociology begins by identifying 'social facts' on the basis of unacknowledged theoretical criteria, and then asserts the necessity of these facts by 'discovering' essential causes which are similarly the product of prior theoretical assumptions: 'The essence to which we refer tells us nothing but what we already know' (p. 101).

This problem of the prior role of theory in positing the existence of an underlying essence as the basis for phenomenal forms is, in fact, explicitly recognized by Durkheim in his study of suicide (1952). There he argues that the method of morphological classification cannot be followed since it is not possible to identify different types of suicide on the basis of the empirical study of individual cases (i.e. the official records do not distinguish different types of suicide). He therefore proposes to reverse the order of study and to proceed from a *theoretical* identification of the different causes of suicide (anomy, egoism and altruism) to an empirical classification of the different types (see pp. 145–7). In other words, he assumes that his theory, which argues for three causes of suicide, is correct in order to identify different types of cases on the basis of which the theory can be tested. While he apparently sees this problem as specific to this particular analysis (in that available data are inadequate for the purposes of classification), it is clear that his procedure in this study is in fact entailed in his very method, the difference being that the theory-dependency of classification and of the identification of the essential causes of phenomena is here made explicit.

To summarize, then, Durkheim's method is inherently contradictory. If he wishes to assert the theoretical neutrality of observation of social facts as the basis for subsequent sociological explanation, then there is no ground in his method for the identification of essences causally linked to such facts. If, on the other hand, he wishes to assert the existence of an essential social reality to account for phenomenal appearances, then there is no basis in his method for rejecting the role of theory in constituting knowledge. This dilemma between phenomenalism and realism is irresolvable within the terms of Durkheim's method, and as we shall see in Chapter 2, it is a dilemma that recurs in the work of the Chicago school of human ecology whose exponents, like Durkheim, attempted to hold to a positivist approach to the source of knowledge while at the same time explaining observed phenomena as the result of unobservable hidden forces in human society.

Durkheim's method was set out most explicitly in *The Rules of Sociological Method* (1938), but as Giddens notes, this work 'explicates the methodological suppositions already applied in *The Division of Labour*' (Giddens 1971, p. 82). This latter text, Durkheim's first major work, is the most significant of his writings as regards our present concern with the role of the city in Durkheim's sociology.

The theme of the book concerns the moral basis of social solidarity, that is the social origins and foundation of the social cohesion of collective life. In it, Durkheim is concerned to show that social solidarity may be a function of either homogeneity or heterogeneity, of similarity between the 'parts' comprising the social whole or of the complementary differences between them. The problem, however, is that the moral basis of social life is not itself directly observable. The resolution to this problem, in line with his methodological prescriptions, is to identify an observable indicator that reveals it:

Social solidarity is a completely moral phenomenon which, taken by itself, does not lend itself to exact observation nor indeed to measurement. To proceed to this classification and this comparison, we must substitute for this internal fact which escapes us an external index which symbolizes it and study the former in the light of the latter. This visible symbol is law. [Durkheim 1933, p. 64]

His argument, therefore, is that different types of law, which can (he suggests) be classified directly through observation, are the effects of different types of solidarity: 'Since law reproduces the principal forms of social solidarity, we have only to classify the different types of law to find therefrom the different types of social solidarity which correspond to it' (p. 68).

The two types of law he identifies are 'repressive' (the imposition of punishment through suffering or loss) and 'restitutive' (the restoration of normality to counterbalance an infraction). Both are social in origin but their forms are different (indicating that they arise from different social conditions).

Repressive law is indicative of the existence of strong, generalized collective sentiments in society – a strong 'collective conscience' – to which all normal members of the society subscribe. An offence against this collective morality is thus not merely an offence against an individual, but is a transgression of something that is felt to be sacred and above any individual. Repressive law is thus the means by which the collectivity avenges itself: 'Since these sentiments are collective it is not us they represent in us, but society. Thus, in avenging them, it is surely society and not ourselves that we avenge, and moreover, it is something superior to the individual' (p. 101). Clearly, such a law based on a generalized collective morality can derive only from a society based on 'essential social likenesses' (p. 105), for it is only in such a society that a high degree of moral conformity and collective sentiment can be sustained. Repressive law, in other words, is both product of and indicative of what Durkheim terms social bonds of 'mechanical solidarity'. Such a society is maintained and perpetuated on the basis of the similarity between its members, and challenges to this solidarity meet with a strong collective response through the use of repressive sanctions.

Restitutive law, by contrast, does not reflect a strong collective conscience (although its origin remains social) in that an offence against such law does not provoke a generalized moral outrage but merely an attempt to rectify the wrong that has been done. The only collective sentiment expressed in restitutive law relates to the ethic of individualism: 'The only collective sentiments that have become more intense are those which have for their object, not social affairs, but the individual' (p. 167). This type of law, therefore, is indicative of a society that derives its solidarity from the complementary differences between individuals and in which mechanical bonds of similarity have been replaced by 'organic' relations of interdependence. In such a society, the force of collective sentiments has given way to a positive union of co-operation brought about by the social division of labour: 'It is the division of labour which, more and more, fills the role that was formerly filled by the common conscience. It is the principal bond of social aggregates of higher types' (p. 173). The bonds of interdependence forged by the growth of the division of labour are infinitely stronger than the mechanical bonds of similarity, and the development of advanced societies is the history of the transition from the latter to the former.

Having classified the two types of social solidarity, Durkheim then considers the causes of the growth of division of labour which brings about the transition from one to the other. It is at this point that the analysis of the city becomes important.

His argument is that two factors give rise to an increased division of labour in society: 'material density' (by which he means density of population in a given area) and 'moral density' (which refers to the increased density of interaction and social relationships within a population). In *The Division of Labour* (1933) he argues that the two are in practice inseparable and that 'it is useless to try to find out which has determined the other' (p. 257), although he later revised this view, arguing that social concentration cannot simply be deduced from physical concentration (since this would be to admit to the origins of a social fact in a physical rather than a social cause), and that the key cause of the division of labour was therefore an increase in moral density (see 1938, p. 115).

The increase in moral density of a society is expressed through urbanization: 'Cities always result from the need of individuals to put themselves in very intimate contact with others. There are so many points where the social mass is contracted more strongly than elsewhere' (1933, p. 258). In simple segmental societies characterized by only the most rudimentary division of labour and by mechanical bonds of solidarity, cities do not exist. The history of the advanced societies, on the other hand, reveals a continuous expansion of urban life which, 'Far from constituting a sort of pathological phenomenon . . . comes from the very nature of higher social species' (p. 259). Urbanization, together with the associated development of new means of transportation and communication, is the cause of the division of labour. The reason is simple; a concentrated human population can survive only through differentiation of functions: 'In the same city, different occupations can co-exist without being obliged mutually to destroy one another, for they pursue different objects . . . all condensation of the social mass, especially if it is accompanied by an increase in population, necessarily determines advances in the division of labour' (pp. 267–8). As we shall see in the next chapter, this explicit application of Darwinian principles to the analysis of functional differentiation in human societies is one of the principal themes that later urban sociologists abstracted from Durkheim's work.

There is, however, no guarantee that an increase in moral density will result in increased division of labour, since it may simply lead to, say, the collapse of the society or to the elimination of weaker competitors within it. Moral density is, in other words, a necessary but not a sufficient condition. What is necessary in addition is that the moral weight of the collective conscience be weakened, since 'the progress of the division of labour will be as much more difficult and slow as the common conscience is vital and precise' (p. 284). Here too, however, the development of the city performs an important role. This is because cities grow principally through immigration rather than through natural increase and thus attract new residents from surrounding areas whose attachment to traditional beliefs and values is thereby weakened: 'Nowhere have the traditions less sway over minds. Indeed, great cities are the uncontested homes of progress. . . . When society changes, it is generally after them and in imitation . . . no ground is more favourable to evolutions of all sorts. This is because the collective life cannot have continuity there' (p. 296).

Durkheim's characterization of the city as a force for change presents what has since become a very familiar analysis of the nature of urban life. His argument that the city undermines traditional controls, that the collectivity cannot possibly impose a single code of moral conduct over the diverse spheres of action in which the urbanite becomes involved, that the individual enjoys freedom as a result of the necessary anonymity of the city, that small moral communities may develop in different parts of the city but that their sphere of influence over the individual is circumscribed, that the city extends its influence over the surrounding countryside and thus 'urbanizes' the society as a whole – all of this is reflected in the work of the Chicago school of urban ecology (Chapter 2), in Wirth's essay on urbanism as a way of life (Chapter 3) and in countless community study monographs up to the present day. And what these subsequent developments have also taken over from Durkheim is the recognition that, while the city is undoubtedly a force for progress and individual freedom, it may also become associated in the most vivid way with the pathological aspects of modern society.

It is Durkheim's concern to show that, while the development of the division of labour contains within it the possibility for a new and stronger basis of social solidarity, it may nevertheless come to be expressed through 'abnormal' forms. In other words, the erosion of collective morality that it entails may, in certain circumstances, result not in a new organic solidarity of interdependence, but in a state of moral deregulation or anomy. Where this occurs (i.e. where the division of labour has not become sufficiently institutionalized as the moral basis of social life), the moral cohesion of society itself is threatened, and according to Durkheim this was the explanation of the malaise of the advanced societies at the time when he was writing. Given the role of the city as the primary force for change, it is naturally in the cities themselves that the anomic character of modern societies becomes most evident: 'The average number of suicides, of crimes of all sorts, can effectively serve to mark the intensity of immorality in a given society. . . . Far from serving moral progress, it is in the great industrial centres that crimes and suicides are most numerous' (pp. 50–1). This is why (as we noted at the start of this chapter) the cities tend to be associated with social 'problems', for they are the most developed expression of the pathology generated as a result of moral deregulation in the society as a whole.

Given his commitment to a science of ethics, Durkheim attempts in *The Division of Labour* to diagnose the causes of this social malaise and to prescribe a remedy. The latter he finds in the establishment of a modern form of occupational guild system, nationally organized. His argument here is particularly relevant to our present concern with the urban question, for he suggests that the medieval guilds and corporations were at that time the 'normal mould' for the organization of economic interests (p. 20) and that the town was thus the cornerstone of medieval society. However, as large-scale capitalist industry developed, so the urban corporation of merchants and traders became less and less suited to its organizational needs:

While, as originally, merchants and workers had only the inhabitants of the city or its immediate environs for customers, which means as long as the market was principally local, the bodies of trades, with their municipal organization, answered all needs. But it was no longer the same once great industry was born. As it had nothing especially urban about it, it could not adapt itself to a system which had not been made for it. . . . An institution so entirely wrapped up in the commune as was the old corporation could not then be used to encompass and regulate a form of collective activity which was so completely foreign to the communal life. [Durkheim 1933, p. 22]

The erosion of the corporation of the Middle Ages (which in France was finally completed in the Revolution of 1789) has, however, left a vacuum precisely at the time in history when economic life has become central to collective existence. This vacuum cannot be filled by the state, for it is too remote from individuals and is ill-equipped to regulate the complexity of modern economic relations. Nor can it be filled by a resurrection of the medieval guild system, since this is totally inappropriate to a society in which the advanced division of labour has become extended far beyond the locality:

> There are not many organs which may be completely comprised within the limits of a determined district, no matter how far it extends. It almost always runs beyond them. . . . The manner of human grouping which results from the division of labour is thus very different from that which expresses the partition of the population in space. The occupational environment does not coincide with the territorial environment any more than it does with the familial environment. [Durkheim 1933, pp. 189–90]

It can, therefore, be filled only by nationally organized occupational corporations which alone can regulate the moral basis of economic life and thereby overcome the anomic condition of modern industrial societies.

It is clear from this argument that, like Marx and Weber, Durkheim does not consider the modern city relevant to the key concerns of social theory in advanced capitalist societies. Like them, he argues that it is only in the Middle Ages that the city was significant in itself since it was only during that period that it provided the organizational expression for functional economic interests. Just as Marx and Weber see the city in antiquity as theoretically unimportant, so too does Durkheim, arguing that 'Rome was essentially an agricultural and military society' (p. 19), and that the basis of association was familial rather than urban. And just as Marx and Weber deny the theoretical significance of the modern city (since for Marx it no longer expresses essential class relations, and for Weber it is no longer the basis for human association), so too Durkheim argues that the distinction between the city and the society as a whole in the modern period is no longer meaningful, that the society itself can now be likened to one great city (p. 300), and that localism has been undermined by the extension of the occupational and social division of labour. As he puts it,

> As advances are made in history, the organization which has territorial groups as its base (village or city, district, province, etc.) steadily becomes effaced. . . . These geographical divisions are, for the most part, artificial and no longer awaken in us profound sentiments. . . . Our activity is extended quite beyond these groups which are too narrow for it, and, moreover, a good deal of what happens there leaves us indifferent.[Durkheim 1933, pp. 27–8]

Like the other two theorists discussed in this chapter, Durkheim therefore addresses the urban question in two ways. First, he sees the city as an historically significant condition for the development of particular social forces (that is to say, it creates a social concentration which stimulates the division of labour, while at the same time it facilitates this development by breaking down the bonds of traditional morality); second, he sees in the modern city the expression of the current (abnormal) development of these forces (pathological disorganization reflecting the anomic state of modern society). What appears as the most striking (and, given the divergences in their methods, astonishing) feature of any comparative reading of the works of Marx, Weber and Durkheim in relation to the urban question is thus their unanimity in their approach to the city, for all three see the medieval city as historically significant while addressing the modern city simply as the most visible expression of developments in the society as a whole. The lesson from all three seems all too clear; the development of an urban history appears a valid and fruitful project, but the development of an urban sociology does not. As we shall see in the following chapters, the subsequent development of urban sociology and the fate of the various attempts to conceptualize the urban in the conditions of advanced capitalist societies would appear to bear this out.

2 The urban as an ecological community

In his review of various attempts by sociologists to develop a specifically urban theory, Leonard Reissman suggests that the ecological perspective advanced between the wars by Robert Park and his colleagues at the University of Chicago remains 'the closest we have come to a systematic theory of the city' (1964, p. 93). Certainly human ecology was the first comprehensive urban social theory, and in the United States it has some claim to have been the first comprehensive sociological theory, for it developed at a time when American sociology was gaining institutional recognition as a discipline but lacked an indigenous body of theory. As Hawley observes, 'The reformist phase of sociology was drawing to a close and the subject was gaining acceptance as a respected discipline in the curricula of American universities. . . . Ecology opportunely provided the necessary theory' (1968, p. 329).

From its very inception, therefore, human ecology exhibited a certain tension as regards the scope of its applicability. On the one hand, it was represented as a theory of the city and thus as an attempt to develop an explanation of patterns of city growth and urban culture. In this sense, human ecology could be seen as a sub-discipline within sociology with its own object of study; while some sociologists studied education and others studied the family, those interested in human ecology studied the city. On the other hand, however, it claimed to be a discipline in its own right with its own distinctive body of theory. Indeed, the human ecologists argued that the ecological perspective addressed a problem that could not be subsumed under any other discipline, including sociology. Human biology studied the individual organism, human psychology the individual psyche, human geography the organization of space, and the various social sciences the different aspects, economic, political or cultural, of social organization. In contrast with all of these, human ecology was concerned with the specific theoretical problem of how human populations adapted to their environment. As we shall see, it then followed from this formulation that human ecology was the basic social science that established the framework within which economic, political and moral phenomena could be investigated. As one of Park's students was later to suggest, 'Human ecology, as Park conceived it, was not a branch of sociology but rather a perspective, a method, and a body of knowledge essential for the scientific study of social life and hence, like social psychology, a general discipline basic to all the social sciences' (Wirth 1945, p. 484).

This tension between human ecology as an approach within urban sociology, and human ecology as a distinct and basic discipline within the social sciences, runs throughout the work of the Chicago school. It is basically a tension between defining the perspective in terms of a concrete, physical, visible object of study – the community – and defining it in terms of a theoretically specific problem – the adaptation of human populations to their environment. Whenever Park addressed himself to such methodological questions (which was not very often), he adopted, as Wirth suggests, the latter position, arguing that a science was defined by the theoretical problem it posed rather than the concrete object it studied. Yet throughout his writings, Park nevertheless emphasized the ecological concern with the community as a visible and real entity. This confusion, which lies at the heart of the problems associated with human ecology, is reflected in, and was exacerbated by, the ambiguity inherent in Park's concept of 'community', for this term is employed to refer both to the physical community and to the ecological process. In the former case it refers to an empirical object of analysis, in the latter to a theoretical one.

Community and society

Many different intellectual influences can be discerned through an examination of Park's writings, among them those of Simmel, Comte, Spencer and W. I. Thomas. However, it does appear that two writers were especially significant. At risk of some oversimplification, it may be suggested that it was from Émile Durkheim that Park derived his methodological framework, and from Charles Darwin that he derived his theory.

Durkheim's influence can be found first in Park's ontological assumptions regarding 'human nature' and the relationship between the individual and society. In his first important statement of the ecological perspective in 1916, for example, Park wrote, 'The fact seems to be that men are brought into the world with all the passions, instincts and appetites uncontrolled and undisciplined. Civilization, in the interests of the common welfare, demands the suppression sometimes, and the control always, of these wild, natural disposi- tions' (1952, p. 49). Just as Durkheim sought the conditions for social stability and cohesion in the subordination of the individual to the moral authority of society, so Park takes as his starting point the tension between individual freedom and social control. Like Durkheim, Park explains personal and social disorganization in terms of the erosion of moral constraints, for *Homo ecologicus* is an inherently egoistical and unsocial creature who needs to be kept in check by society for the good of himself and of others.

Of course, Park recognized that the social control of human nature was not, and never could be, total. Indeed, in the same way that Durkheim noted that social disorganization (within limits) was the necessary price to be paid for human progress, and that too much moral constraint was as bad as too little since it resulted in individual fatalism and social stagnation, so Park found in the break-down of traditional moral controls a cause for both concern and celebration. On the one hand, he saw that the growth of the cities had undermined the social cohesion once maintained by the family, the church and the village, and he pointed to the threat of the mob 'swept by every new wind of doctrine, subject to constant alarms' (1952, p. 31). Yet on the other, he saw the potential for individual freedom and self-expression that the city represented, and he noted how disorganization could be seen as a prelude to reorganization at a new level of human organization involving new modes of social control.

Human nature and moral constraint thus constantly confronted each other, and it followed that any form of human organization was necessarily an expression of both. This was certainly true of the city, for despite the regular geometrical form of many American cities, which suggested artificial rather than natural causes, Park maintained that 'The structure of the city . . . has its basis in human nature, of which it is an expression', and that, because of this, 'There is a limit to the arbitrary modifications which it is possible to make (1) in its physical structure and (2) in its moral order' (1952, p. 16). In other words, the city is as much a manifestation of natural and invariant forces as it is of political and conscious choices, and it is no more possible to abolish the ghettos and the dens of iniquity than it is to programme men's passions or eliminate their instincts.

For Park, then, human society involves a double aspect. On the one hand, it is an expression of human nature, and this is revealed in the competition for survival in which relationships with others are entirely utilitarian (a view that Park finds in the work of Herbert Spencer). On the other, it is an expression of consensus and common purpose (a view that he traces to Comte). On one level individual freedom is supreme; on the other individual will is subordinated to the 'collective mind' of society as a superorganism (to what Durkheim termed the *conscience collective*). The first level Park terms 'community', and the second 'society'; 'The word community more accurately describes the social organism as Spencer conceived it. Comte's conception, on the other hand, comes nearer to describing what we ordinarily mean by society' (1952, p. 181).

As we shall see later, this distinction between community as the biotic level of social life and society as its cultural level proved highly problematic. In particular, Park's writings on the subject exhibit some inconsistency as regards the methodological status of the dichotomy, for on some occasions he refers to community and society as analytical categories, while on others he treats them as empirical realities. The distinction is, however, basic to his ecological approach, for it enables Park to identify the peculiar concerns of human ecology in relation to the other social science disciplines. 'Ecology', he writes, 'is concerned with communities rather than societies, though it is not easy to distinguish between them' (1952, p. 251). The ecological approach to social relations, therefore, was characterized by an emphasis on the biotic as opposed to the cultural aspect of human interaction, the Spencerian rather than the Comtean view of social relations. This did not mean that human ecology denied the relevance of consensus and culture in the study of social life; only that it concentrated on the unconscious and asocial aspects as its specific area of interest.

By thus delimiting the field of ecological inquiry, Park was able to draw upon the work of Darwin in order to show how the forces that shape plant and animal communities also play a significant role in the evolution of human communities. Central to Darwin's thesis was the notion of a 'web of life' through which all organisms were related to all others in ties of interdependence or 'symbiosis'. This balance of nature was a product of the tooth and claw struggle for survival which served to regulate the population size of different species and to distribute them among different habitats according to their relative suitability. Competition for the basic resources of life thus resulted in the adaptation of different species to each other and to their environment and hence to the evolution of a relatively balanced ecological system based upon competitive co-operation among differentiated and specialized organisms. Needless to say, this was an entirely natural and spontaneous process.

It was Park's contention that the same process operated in the human community: 'Competition operates in the human (as it does in the plant and animal) community to bring about and restore the communal equilibrium when, either by the advent of some intrusive factor from without or in the normal course of its life history, that equilibrium is disturbed' (1952, p. 150). Competition between individuals, he argued, gave rise to relations of competitive co-operation through differentiation of functions (division of labour) and the orderly spatial distribution of these functions to the areas for which they are best suited. His analysis, in other words, is both functional and spatial: 'The main point is that the community so conceived is at once a territorial and a functional unit' (1952, p. 241).

His discussion of the development of functional differentiation and interdependence in the human community draws heavily on Durkheim's analysis of the origins of the division of labour. Just as Durkheim argues that the transition from a relatively homogeneous to a relatively differentiated society is effected by an increase in material and moral density, so too Park suggests that an increase in population size within a given area, together with an extension of transport and communication networks, results in greater specialization of functions (and thus stronger ties of interdependence). Park then goes on to argue, however, that this functional differentiation is also expressed spatially, for competition not only stimulates a division of labour, but also distributes the different economic groups to different niches in the urban environment. The pattern of land use in the city therefore reveals the pattern of economic interdependence.

The ecological concept that explains the congruence between spatial and economic differentiation is that of dominance. Again with reference to Darwin, Park suggests that 'In every life community there is always one or more dominant species' (1952, p. 151). The beech tree, for example, has achieved dominance over its natural habitat in the sense that only those plants, such as bluebells, that flower at a time when the tree has no leaves can flourish under its branches. In the human community, analogously, industry and commerce are dominant, for they can outbid other competitors for strategic central locations in the city. The pressure for space at the centre therefore creates an area of high land values, and this determines the pattern of land values in every other area of the city, and thus the pattern of land use by different functional groups. As Park puts it, 'The struggle of industries and commercial institutions for a strategic location determines in the long run the main outlines of the urban community . . . the principle of dominance . . . tends to determine the general ecological pattern of the city and the functional relation of each of the different areas of the city to all others' (1952, pp. 151–2). Differences in land values are thus the mechanism by which different functional groups are distributed in space in an orderly, efficient yet unplanned manner.

It follows from all this that the natural state of the ecological community, be it human or otherwise, is one of equilibrium. Change, which may result either from internal expansion or from external disruption, is represented as basically a cyclical and evolutionary process involving, first, a destabilization of the existing equilibrium; second, a renewed outburst of competition; and, finally, the development of a new (and 'higher') stage of adaptation. Basic to this conception are two assumptions. The first is that, having reached a 'climax' stage (an optimal point at which population size and differentiation is most closely adapted to environmental conditions), a community will remain in a state of balance unless some new element emerges to disturb the *status quo*. The second is that the process of community change involves an evolution from the simple to the complex through the adaptive process of differentiation of functions. This theory of community change was most explicitly set out by one of Park's colleagues at the University of Chicago, Roderick McKenzie.

McKenzie (1967) argued that the size of any human community is limited by what it can produce and by the efficiency of its mode of distribution. Thus a primary service community (such as one based on agriculture) cannot grow beyond a population of around 5000, whereas an industrial town can grow to many times that size provided its industries are serviced by an efficient system of market distribution. It was McKenzie's contention that any particular type of community tended to increase in size until it reached its climax point at which the size of population was most perfectly adjusted to the capacity of the economic base to support it. The community would then remain in this state of equilibrium until some new element (e.g. a new mode of communication or a technological innovation) disturbed the balance, at which point a new cycle of biotic adjustment would begin involving movement of population, differentiation of functions, or both of these processes. Competition, in other words, would again sift and sort the population functionally and spatially until a new climax stage was reached.

Drawing again on Darwin's work, the human ecologists referred to this process of structural community change as succession – 'that orderly sequence of changes through which a biotic community passes in the course of its development from a primary and relatively unstable to a relatively permanent or climax stage' (Park 1952, p. 152). Just as in nature one species succeeds another as the dominant life form in a particular area, so too in the human community the pattern of land use changes as areas are invaded by new competitors which are better adapted to the changed environmental conditions than the existing users. Such a process of invasion and succession is reflected in the human community in changes in land values with the result that competition for desirable sites forces out the economically weaker existing users (e.g. residents) who make way for economically stronger competitors (e.g. business). Following a successful invasion, a new equilibrium is then established and the successional sequence comes to an end.

It is these related processes of competition, dominance, succession and invasion that provide the basis for the well-known model of community expansion proposed by Burgess (1967). He suggested that the city could be conceptualized ideally as consisting of five zones arranged in a pattern of concentric circles. The expansion of the city occurred as a result of the invasion by each zone of the next outer zone, so that the central business district tended to expand into the surrounding inner-city zone of transition, which in turn tended to expand into the zone of working-class housing around it, and so on. This physical process of succession therefore results in the segregation of different social groups in different parts of the city according to their suitability: 'In the expansion of the city, a process of distribution takes place which sifts and sorts and relocates individuals and groups by residence and occupation. . . . Segregation offers the group, and thereby the individuals who compose the group, a place and a role in the total organisation of city life' (pp. 54 and 56).

This constant process of change and adjustment, invasion and succession, disorganization and reorganization, is especially marked in the inner-city zone of transition. The outward pressure of the central business district accelerates the deterioration of the area around it by increasing the value of surrounding land while threatening the existing housing stock, and existing inhabitants progressively move out while their place is taken by new migrants into the city who find their niche in the decaying properties. In time, these migrants themselves move out and are replaced by later arrivals, and so the process of physical expansion and social turnover goes on. Burgess recognizes that mobility is therefore most pronounced in the inner-city areas that are in an almost constant state of flux, and he sees this as the explanation for the social disorganization (crime, vice, poverty etc.) that tends to characterize these areas. Mobility, in other words, is a source of change and of personal and social disorganization, and where mobility is greatest, so too is the lack of social cohesion and the demoralization of the human spirit.

All of these processes that we have described so far involve the natural and spontaneous response of human populations to changes in the environment in which they live. However, we noted earlier that Park and his colleagues recognized that human populations had certain characteristics that were not shared by plant and animal communities. In particular, human beings enjoyed scope for mobility which plants did not possess, and they had a capacity for consciously changing their environment which had no parallel in the plant and animal worlds. As McKenzie observed, 'The human community differs from the plant community in the two dominant characteristics of mobility and purpose, that is, in the power to select a habitat and in the ability to control or modify the conditions of the habitat' (1967, pp. 64–5). Human beings, in other words, shared a culture.

According to the Chicago ecologists, the cultural aspect of human organization, which they associated with the concept of society as opposed to community, developed at the point where the biotic struggle for existence had established a natural equilibrium. Competition led naturally to one form of human organization by forcing increased functional and spatial differentiation and thereby creating utilitarian ties of mutual interdependence (symbiosis). Once distributed functionally and territorially, however, the members of a human population were then in a position to develop new and qualitatively different bonds of cohesion based not on the necessities of the division of labour but on common goals, sentiments and values. From its origins in unconscious competition, human organization thus developed a new basis in consensus and conscious co-operation, for while competition resulted in specialization and individuation, consensus involved communication and the subordination of the individual's primordial instincts to the collective consciousness. As Park writes,

It is when, and to the extent that, competition declines that the kind of order which we call society may be said to exist. In short, society, from the ecological point of view, and in so far as it is a territorial unit, is just the area within which biotic competition has declined and the struggle for existence has assumed higher and more sublimated forms. [Park 1952, pp. 150–1]

There are therefore two types of human association: the symbiotic, brought about by competition, and the social, brought about by consensus:

The distinction is that in the community, as in the case of the plant and animal community, the nexus which unites individuals of which the community is composed is some kind of symbiosis or some form of division of labour. A society, on the other hand, is constituted by a more intimate form of association based on communication, consensus and custom. [Park 1952, p. 259]

This does not mean, however, that at the level of society there is no competition or conflict, for although he never defines the term it is clear that for Park consensus refers to shared orientations rather than shared objectives, to a common frame of reference for action rather than universal agreement over what that action should be (see Weber 1968, appendix I, for a similar formulation of the concept). Thus Park suggests that, on the social level, competition takes the form of conflict (1952, p. 153), by which he means that competition becomes conscious and collectively organized (for example through political parties) and thereby patterned by cultural norms: 'In human as contrasted with animal societies, competition and the freedom of the individual is limited on every level above the biotic by custom and consensus' (1952, p. 156). Competition is therefore mediated by culture, but the cultural form does not fundamentally alter the underlying biotic process.

This distinction between the biotic and the cultural, community and society, is fundamental to the classical perspective of human ecology, for as we have seen it is on the basis of this dichotomy that Park identifies the specific area of concern that is peculiar to this approach. The methodological basis of this crucial distinction is, however, never clearly established.

On some occasions, Park refers to communities and societies as empirical categories and thus as real entities which can be distinguished (albeit with some difficulty) in empirical research. Following Durkheim, he designates communities and societies as 'things' which can be directly studied and which exist independently of our ideas and conceptualizations of them. Communities are in this sense identified as locally based functional systems which are irreducible to the elements (that is, to human individuals) from which they are composed. Communities are therefore visible objects which can be studied in their own right: 'The community is a visible object. One can point it out, define its territorial limits, and plot its constituent elements, its population and its institutions on maps' (1952, p. 182). Empirical research can therefore begin with the study of communities because community is the framework within which society develops, and because it is more immediately visible than society and thus more amenable to statistical analysis. From such a starting point, it should be possible to discover empirical regularities between different communities, and thereby inductively to develop plausible hypotheses and scientific generalizations.

Elsewhere, however, Park treats the community–society dichotomy as an analytical construct. This follows from his argument that a science is distinguished not by a specific object of study but by the theoretical problem it poses in relation to some aspect of that object: 'What things are for any special science or for common sense, for that matter, is determined largely by the point of view from which they are looked at' (1952, p. 179). This suggests that human ecology is defined, not by its empirical concern with communities, but by its mode of conceptualizing 'community'. In this sense, community refers to a specific aspect of human organization which is identified theoretically as the unorganized and unconscious process whereby human populations adjust to their environment through unrestricted competition. Community here is not a thing but a process, not a separate and visible area of human existence but a distinct perspective on human existence. Seen in this way, the concept of community is merely a shorthand term for the biotic forces operating in human society, in which case it is clearly not possible to distinguish it from society in any empirical research setting.

Of these two approaches, the latter appears to achieve more prominence in Park's writings. Like Durkheim, he is concerned to analyse the complexity of society by first tracing the simplest and most basic unit of human organization, and this he finds in the concept of community. Only through exhaustive analysis of the impact of biotic forces on human society is it possible to begin to identify the significance of cultural factors. As Wirth (1945) explained it, the basic physical and natural forces at work in human society establish the framework and the context within which men act, and human ecology is therefore basic and complementary to the analysis of social organization and social psychology: 'Human ecology is not a substitute for, but a supplement to, the other frames of reference and methods of social investigation' (p. 438).

Having first established the scope of the biotic in human affairs, Park then attempts to reconstruct the complexity of social reality by taking into account the additional significance of human technology and cultural values. While conceptually distinct, he therefore recognizes that the biotic and the cultural are empirically interrelated:

Human ecology has, however, to reckon with the fact that in human society competition is limited by custom and culture. The cultural superstructure imposes itself as an instrument of direction and control upon the biotic substructure. Reduced to its elements the human community, so conceived, may be said to consist of a population and a culture, including in the term culture (1) a body of customs and beliefs and (2) a corresponding body of artifacts and technological devices. To these three elements or factors – (1) population, (2) artifact (technological culture), (3) custom and beliefs (non-material culture) – into which the social complex resolves itself, one should, perhaps, add a fourth, namely, the natural resources of the habitat. It is the interaction of these four factors that maintain at once the biotic balance and the social equilibrium when and where they exist. [Park 1952, p. 158]

Having torn asunder the biotic and the cultural at the conceptual level, Park therefore reunites them at the level of empirical reality, for his four elements of the 'social complex' include ecological and cultural factors as inherently interrelated aspects.

Clearly, then, Park recognizes the mutual interdependence of the biotic and the cultural in the 'real' social world. Indeed, he takes the analysis further by suggesting that it is possible to conceptualize a hierarchy of constraints on the individual in terms of the operation of the ecological, economic, political and moral orders, such that the freedom of the individual is progressively restricted beyond the biotic level: 'The individual is more free upon the economic level than upon the political, more free on the political than the moral' (1952, p. 157). Such a formulation can be understood only analytically, and such an interpretation is reinforced in one of the last essays Park published where he developed a model of human society 'as a kind of cone or triangle, of which the basis is the ecological organisation of human beings' (1952, p. 260). Furthermore, in this essay he added that on this basic ecological level 'the struggle for existence may go on, will go on, *unobserved* and relatively unrestricted' (p. 260; my emphasis), thereby demonstrating beyond doubt that the ecological community is not a thing but a theoretically defined aspect of social organization.

How, then, can a view of community as an empirical category – an observable and measurable object – be reconciled with the parallel view of community as an analytical construct? That both views are present in Park's writings cannot be doubted. That he never explicitly recognized their incompatibility is also apparent. His essays on human ecology span twenty-three years, yet in all that time he seemingly never felt obliged to address what appears as an obvious and fundamental confusion surrounding the dichotomy on which his entire approach was based.

The source of the confusion lies in the methodology that Park derived from Durkheim. As we saw in Chapter 1, this is basically an empiricist methodology, in that Durkheim (and Park) argues that knowledge is derived directly from the sense experiences and that phenomena must therefore be defined solely in terms of their external characteristics. It is for this reason that Park emphasizes community as an empirical and visible object. However, both Durkheim and Park are also committed to an holistic view of social collectivities in the sense that they wish to avoid reducing such collectivities to their individual components. Community (for Park) and society (for Durkheim) are therefore objects of study *sui generis*. There is an evident tension between these two postulates of phenomenalism and holism, for when we actually observe human communities and societies all we ever actually see are individuals. In other words, the very apprehension of a social collectivity as a thing is necessarily conceptual rather than phenomenal. The commitment to holism thus necessarily undermines the empiricist methodology by postulating a reality beyond direct experience. As Keat and Urry observe, 'When positivists seek to put into operation their methodology they often find themselves employing realist arguments or positing realist-type entities, albeit in an unsystematic and confused way' (1975, p. 82).

Such was the case with Durkheim in his study of the suicidogenic current which he saw as the underlying yet unobservable cause of the social suicide rate. Such is also the case with Park in his study of biotic forces as the underlying yet unobservable cause of functional and spatial organization. The way in which Durkheim side-stepped this problem was by reversing his own prescriptions as regards causal analysis. Because he was unable to observe the variations in the suicidogenic current, Durkheim inferred them from their supposed consequences in the suicide statistics (in other words, rather than tracing the effect of the current on the suicide rate, he deduced these effects from variations in the suicide rate, thereby developing an entirely tautological analysis). The way in which Park attempted to resolve what was essentially the same problem as regards the biotic forces behind human organization was by eliding an empirical category – community – which he argued could be observed, with an analytical one – the biotic level – which could not. In this way, he tried to fuse a phenomenal form with a realist concept. The way in which he did this was through the development of perhaps the most important concept of all in the ecological dictionary – that of 'natural area'.

We have seen that both Park and McKenzie argued that the biotic forces of competition always tend to produce a natural equilibrium at the point where the population is optimally adjusted to its environment. At this climax stage, the community is functionally and spatially differentiated such that different functional groups are located in different areas according to their relative suitability. As this unstable biotic equilibrium develops, so too do distinctive cultural forms corresponding to the different areas: 'The general effect of the continuous processes of invasions and accommodations is to give to the developed community well-defined areas, each having its own peculiar selective and cultural characteristics' (McKenzie 1967, p. 77). These different areas within the city, fashioned by competition and characterized by both functional and cultural differentiation, are termed 'natural areas'.

The significance of the concept of natural area for the Chicago school's human ecology is twofold. First, it overcomes the empirical problem associated with the biotic–cultural division by specifying an observable object – the ghetto, the red light district, the suburb or whatever – in which these two aspects of human organization have become fused. A natural area, that is, is also a cultural area. It is on the one hand an area characterized by division of labour and competitive co-operation, while on the other it is a moral area characterized by consensus and communication. It therefore represents an object, a 'thing', which can be studied both ecologically and sociologically, as a natural unit or as a social unit. Human ecology is therefore provided with an object of analysis in the sense that visible natural areas constitute a laboratory in which biotic processes of population change and adaptation can be studied.

The second point is related to this, for the natural area not only provides a concrete object of study, but also represents the conceptual framework within which such studies can be developed. Because natural areas are seen as the manifestations of natural forces operating in any and every human settlement, it follows that the different regions of one city should be directly comparable with those of another. Categories such as the ghetto or the suburb are treated generically, so that, for example, the cultural form of one ghetto should be similar to that of all others. Park writes,

The natural areas of the city ... serve an important methodological function. They constitute, taken together, what Hobson has described as 'a frame of reference', a conceptual order within which statistical facts gain a new and more general significance. They not only tell us what the facts are in regard to conditions in any given region, but in so far as they characterise an area that is natural and typical, they establish a working hypothesis in regard to other areas of the same kind. .... Most facts that can be stated statistically, once they have been plotted in this conceptual scheme – this ecological frame of reference – can be made the basis of general statements which may be eventually reduced to abstract formulae and scientific generalizations. [Park 1952, p. 198]

Empirical research is thus situated within a framework that enables the development of inductive generalizations (i.e. what Park sees as the transition from concrete fact to conceptual knowledge). Because biotic forces are assumed to be at work, the hidden causes of visible phenomena in natural areas, it is possible to develop scientific knowledge about them by studying their effects in different comparable locations: 'The result of every new specific enquiry should reaffirm or redefine, qualify or extend, the hypotheses upon which the original enquiry was based. The results should not merely increase our fund of information, but enable us to reduce our observations to general formulae and quantitative statements true for all cases of the same kind' (1952, p. 198).

Faced with the same methodological problems as Durkheim (how to develop knowledge of an underlying force in human society when the only valid knowledge is that grounded in experience of 'concrete facts'), Park therefore resorts to much the same solution (assume the existence of the force and search empirically for phenomena that are deemed to be manifestations of that force). Implicitly, however, Park seems to recognize that such an approach is hardly consistent with his positivist methodology, and it is for this reason that he also suggests that the natural area is itself an object of study in which the biotic as well as the cultural may be directly analysed.

This, then, is the source of the confusion referred to earlier between community as an empirical category and as an analytical construct. For Park it has to be both a thing that can be observed directly, and a force in human organization which can be theorized on the basis of such observation. The natural area concept is pressed into service to perform this dual function as both an observable object and a manifestation of an unobservable force. Once we recognize this uneasy tension in Park's methodology between positivism and realism, the analysis of communities and the theorization of the biotic forces that are at work within them, we can understand how it is that human ecology itself exhibits a dual identity, as on the one hand a sociological method for studying the city, and on the other a distinct discipline within the human sciences. Park's human ecology was from the very beginning set upon two stools. It was only a matter of time before the critics kicked them apart.

Human ecology is dead. . .

'By 1950, the ecological approach as developed by Park, his colleagues and students at the University of Chicago was virtually dead ' (Berry and Kasarda 1977, p. 3). The demise was gradual and cumulative, brought about by a combination of essentially misguided criticisms (which nevertheless served to call the approach into question) and fundamental critiques.

What I term the 'misguided criticisms' fell into three categories. The first, stated most forcibly by Davie (1937), accepted the basic assumptions of human ecology – that city growth was the product of 'automatic forces' involving competition and selection – but took issue with Burgess's application of these ideas through the hypothesis of a concentric zone pattern. In a study of New Haven, Davie showed that patterns of residential location were largely a function of patterns of industrial location, and that industry located near lines of communication which exhibited no uniform pattern. Recognizing that Burgess's model was conceived as an ideal type, Davie nevertheless concluded that 'There is no universal pattern, not even of an "ideal type" ' (p. 161). His study then stimulated a series of other projects on other cities in which various authors engaged in increasingly elaborate mapping exercises, but this whole line of research and criticism inevitably led up a cul-de-sac since it was addressed only to the descriptive question of urban form. The theoretical problems of the ecological analysis of such forms remained unexamined. In retrospect it does seem that Burgess's famous paper has received disproportionate attention over the years, and this has resulted in widespread concern with the question of spatial distribution to the neglect of the more basic question of functional differentiation (a tendency which, as we shall see, was later 'corrected' by Hawley).

The second misconceived (yet in a different context very significant) criticism concerned the mode of statistical analysis in ecological research. Robinson (1950) drew a distinction between ecological correlations (correlations between aggregate phenomena such as that between the proportion of blacks in a population and the rate of illiteracy) and individual correlations (correlations between indivisible units). He then pointed to the fallacy of using an ecological correlation as evidence for an individual one, for the fact that there may be a strong correlation between the illiteracy rate and the proportion of blacks in a given population does not necessarily justify the deduction that it is the blacks who are illiterate. Indeed, Robinson showed that ecological correlations invariably over-emphasized (and occasionally even reversed) individual ones.

Robinson's paper represents an important criticism of research which does aim to deduce individual statistical relationships from correlations based on aggregate data (one famous example being Durkheim's *Suicide*). This was not, however, the intention of the Chicago ecologists, for as Menzel (1950) pointed out, ecological correlations in their research were used to demonstrate 'a common underlying cause inherent not in the individuals as such but in inter-individual differences and relationships – properties of areas as such' (p. 674). Indeed, we saw in the previous section that Park was concerned to emphasize the irreducibility of the ecological community to its individual components. Thus a correlation between, say, divorce rates and crime rates would not be used to imply that divorcees are criminals, but as evidence of how the characteristics of a particular area (and in particular a high level of mobility) generate high levels of social disorganization which are reflected in the divorce rate, the crime rate and so on. Ecological correlation thus performed the same function as Durkheim's concomitant variation (see page 38).

The third criticism that is basically misguided is one developed by Alihan (1938), among others, to the effect that there is a disjuncture between the theoretical and the empirical products of the Chicago school. Reviewing the research monographs of those like Anderson (on the hobo) and Zorbaugh (on the slum), Alihan suggests that they invariably fail to distinguish biotic and cultural forces, and that they are no more than sociological studies in which territorial distribution is taken into account on a descriptive level: 'If we take a territorially demarcated unit as a basis of study, we do not discriminate between certain activities carried on within the area as those of "society" and others which are those of "community" ' (p. 82). Alihan's argument here is true but irrelevant, for while it certainly is the case that the various Chicago monographs do not draw this distinction, it is equally the case that it was never intended that they should. As we saw in the last section, such studies were premised on the assumption that the areas under investigation had been created by biotic forces, and their objective was to study the cultural forms that had developed as a result with a view to developing theoretical generalizations. The biotic–cultural division, in other words, provided the initial framework for such studies rather than their object of analysis. Thus Alihan's comment that Park and his colleagues 'waver between the complete scission of the two concepts on the one hand, and their fusion on the other' (pp. 69–70) cannot in itself be deemed a criticism, since it was precisely Park's intention to separate the two analytically and to fuse them empirically.

This line of attack was, nevertheless, pursued with much enthusiasm by critics of the Chicago school, and most notably by Firey (1945). He suggested that human ecology explained locational activity purely in terms of economic maximization, and argued against this that space may have a symbolic as well as economic value, and that locational activity may therefore reflect sentiment as much as economic rationality. Reporting his study of land use in Boston, he then showed how upper-class residents had remained in Beacon Hill for 150 years because of their sentimental attachment to the area and despite the economic advantages of selling up and moving out; how 'sacred sites' such as the common and civil war burial grounds had been preserved from development even though they occupied the most valuable ground in the city and caused economically wasteful traffic congestion; and how, even in an Italian slum, the first generation immigrants were loath to leave the area owing to their commitment to the values of family and *paesani* which were upheld in the slum but were threatened outside it. It followed from all this that cultural values and intersubjective meanings were clearly crucial variables in the explanation of patterns of land use, and that the ecological concern with biotic forces had therefore to be modified.

Park, however, never denied the empirical significance of cultural factors. Indeed, as we have seen, he included both technology and 'non-material' cultural factors as two of the four elements of the 'social complex'. In terms of empirical research, he and his colleagues never intended that community could be analysed separately from society (as Alihan's critique suggested), nor that distributional patterns should be explained solely in terms of ecological forces (as Firey claims). The most that can be said about the difference between Park and Firey is that they are primarily interested in different questions: for Firey, the interesting question is why and how Beacon Hill has resisted invasion from business uses for a century and a half; for Park, it would be why and how Beacon Hill came to be associated with the upper class in the first place.

Where the work of writers such as Alihan and Firey *does* pose an important challenge to human ecology is not in their attacks on the biotic–cultural dichotomy, but in the implications that their arguments have for the fundamental methodological division (which underpins this dichotomy) between the community as a visible object and the community as an analytical construct. These implications are in fact brought out by Alihan, who suggests in relation to the Chicago ecologists that

One of their main difficulties lies in the confusion between abstraction and reality. Some of this confusion might have been avoided if the school had been familiar with the 'ideal type' method of investigation. The concept 'community' is approached in a way that denies its social attributes. In its very definition it is an abstraction of the asocial aspect of human behaviour. Yet the ecologists find themselves compelled in many ways to take account of the social factors which in reality are intrinsically related to and bound up with the asocial community. Had ecologists persisted in dealing with the concept of the 'natural order' as an abstraction, or as an 'ideal type', for the purposes of study these social factors could be treated apart from 'community', as conditioning, concomitant and intrusive phenomena of the 'natural order'. We would then have only the problem of the validity and scientific utility of a particular classification and of the particularistic philosophical ideology underlying the delimitation of the category 'community'. But ecologists do not pursue this course consistently; what is to them an abstraction at one time becomes a reality at another. [Alihan 1938, pp. 48–9]

Alihan here summarizes the main point at issue. If Park had consistently approached the concept of 'community' solely as an abstraction, an heuristic device for analysis, then his approach would have been methodologically (though not necessarily theoretically) valid. We may still have wished to argue that it was not useful to approach human society from such a naturalistic perspective, and that to do so was to resort to unwarranted biological determinism (see Gettys 1940), but there would be no methodological grounds for disputing the biotic–cultural distinction. The fact that Park did not, and could not, limit the concept in this way was due to his commitment to the positivist postulate of phenomenalism. In other words, for him any abstraction had to have a direct empirical reference. He could no more accept the idealism implicit in Alihan's reference to ideal types than he could the realism inherent in the alternative view of abstractions as referring to a level of reality beyond the senses. Following Durkheim, the ecologists were concerned above all with things: 'Their universe of discourse became limited to externalities and the interpretation of social life hinged upon its most concrete aspects. Reducing social behaviour to a common denominator of the tangible and the measurable . . . human ecologists became the expounders of the socially "given" '(Alihan 1938, p. 6).

In the light of this critique, human ecology was confronted with two options. Either it could retain its foundation in a positivist methodology while rejecting attempts to theorize the underlying forces determining the mode of human organization, or it could attempt to develop and justify the concept of the ecological community as an abstraction while rejecting the search for an observable and physical reference point. Human ecology could no longer have its cake and eat it, and the two questions of spatial form and functional process, which Park had attempted to unite, had at last to be severed.

Different analysts, faced with this dilemma, chose different options. Those who chose the first continued to undertake research on the observable and external characteristics of human communities, but this was now divorced from any rigorous theoretical framework, and what Mills (1959) refers to as 'abstracted empiricism' ran rampant as a result. Basically these studies fell into two categories: those concerned with statistical analyses of urban populations (tracing patterns of migration, mapping social phenomena, etc.) and those concerned with descriptive accounts of cultural forms (for example the tradition of community studies). Neither of these categories has provided coherent and cumulative data, for while the former merely amasses figures and trends, the latter provides a long series of non-comparable case studies on individual localities. Neither, in fact, can any longer be termed 'ecological', for while the first has disintegrated into the most descriptive demography, the second appears little different from cultural anthropology. In both, the theoretical specificity of the urban has disappeared.

Those analysts who chose the second option have fared somewhat better. This approach was first spelt out by Hawley (1944), who asserted (against the contemporary line of argument at that time) that human ecology was a viable theoretical perspective, but that it had been distorted by the Chicago School's emphasis on spatial distributions of social phenomena. Hawley sought to relocate human ecology in the mainstream of ecological thought, and in doing so he argued that space, far from being central, was incidental to the ecological problem. The traditional concern of the Chicago ecologists with the physical distribution of social phenomena (which, as we have seen, was the product of their commitment to the principle of phenomenalism) was, for Hawley, indicative not of a genuinely ecological framework but of a geographical one. Space, he suggested, was merely a factor that had to be taken into account by human ecology, just as it had to be taken into account by any other science. What was specific to human ecology was not, therefore, its concern with the physical human community, but rather its interest in a particular process; that of the adaptation of human populations by means of functional differentiation.

Six years after this article appeared, Hawley published a book which set out an ecological framework that has guided research in human ecology ever since. In the words of Berry and Kasarda, 'Hawley reformulated the ecological approach and initiated its present revival within the field of sociology' (1977, p. 3). So it was that human ecology re-emerged during the 1950s as a more modest, but methodologically more secure, approach than that first outlined by Park thirty-four years before.

. . . Long live human ecology!

Like Park, Hawley began from the position that a science should be distinguished according to its perspective rather than its object of study: 'A science is delimited by what it does rather than by any *a priori* definition of its field . . . it must bring into focus a set of problems not included within the scope of other disciplines to which scientific techniques can be, and are in fact being, applied' (1950, p. 10). The perspective that was specific to ecology was that which sought to explain how populations adapted collectively and unconsciously to their environment. This struggle to adapt was seen as a central problem for all species, including human beings, for although human beings had developed cultural artefacts which enabled them to adapt more efficiently and effectively than other species, the difference between them was quantitative rather than qualitative: 'The difference between men and other organisms in adaptive capacity, though great, seems to be a matter of degree rather than kind' (1950, p. 32). There was therefore no reason why the principles of ecological theory as a whole should not be applied to the analysis of adaptation by human communities in particular, and this is what Hawley set out to do.

It is important to recognize that Hawley does not suggest that an ecological approach to the human community is in any way exhaustive, for he argues that such communities are comprised of psychological and moral as well as functional relations, and that human ecology is concerned only with the latter. Nor does he suggest that these different aspects of social relationships can be empirically distinguished, for 'Sustenance activities and relationships are inextricably interwoven with sentiments, value systems and other ideational constructs' (1950, p. 73). Hawley never seeks to deny that values and individual motivations may play an important part in the development of human communities, but rather seeks to assert that this is irrelevant to the ecological problem. The theoretical objective of human ecology, he states, 'is to develop a description of the morphology or form of collective life under varying external conditions. With its problem stated in that manner, the irrelevance of the psychological properties of individuals is self-evident' (1950, p. 179). It is because human ecology is concerned with how human populations adapt collectively to their environment that questions of individual values and motivations have no place within it.

Hawley's analysis of adaptation is developed around the four ecological principles of interdependence, key function, differentiation and dominance. These principles are themselves derived and justified from certain 'cardinal assumptions' concerning the invariant conditions in which human populations are situated (see Hawley 1968). For example, every human population must afford some means whereby its members can achieve access to the environment in order to live; every human population develops some form of interdependence between its members; and so on. From such simple and seemingly non-contentious assertions, Hawley develops a complex and highly contentious theory. (It is worth noting here that Hawley's 'cardinal assumptions' are not dissimilar from those identified by Marx, for both writers emphasize the primacy of material production in society, and both stress the necessity for a system of social relations through which this can be accomplished. What is interesting about this is that, while both writers start from similar *a priori* assumptions regarding the conditions for social existence, they go on to develop very different theories, and this would tend to suggest that neither ecological nor Marxist theory can be justified simply in terms of logical deduction from general principles. As we saw in the discussion of Marx's methodology in Chapter 1, such abstract transhistorical generalizations are in fact very limited, and it follows from this that Hawley's claim to have 'deduced' the principles of ecological organization from such generalizations should be approached with some caution.)

The first of Hawley's ecological principles is interdependence, and he suggests that a major difference between his approach and that of earlier human ecologists concerns the relative emphasis on interdependence as opposed to competition. In any human population, the process of adaptation to the environment involves the development of interdependence among its members. This may take the form either of symbiotic relations (i.e. complementary relations between functionally dissimilar groups) or commensalistic relations (i.e. aggregation of functionally similar groups). In both cases, the combination of individual units increases their collective capacity for action beyond what would have been possible had they remained isolated. Thus a symbiotic union enhances the creative powers of human groups (for it enables specialization), while a commensalistic union enhances their defensive powers (for it increases numerical strength). Symbiotic unions are therefore productive while commensalistic unions are protective. Hawley terms the former 'corporate groups' and the latter 'categoric groups'. The main corporate groups in modern society are familial, associational and territorial, while the main categoric groups are those based on common occupation (for instance the trade unions).

The pattern of ecological organization of a given population within a given territory is therefore determined by the two axes of symbiosis and commensalism. The pattern will be far from simple, however, for Hawley recognizes that corporate groups (based on symbiotic interdependence) may sometimes function as categoric units (for example when responding to some external threat), while categoric groups (based on commensalistic aggregation) may sometimes develop corporate characteristics (for example by developing a specialized leadership stratum). Furthermore, the relations between various units may take either a symbiotic or commensalistic form, so that, for example, corporate units may establish categoric combinations while categoric units may develop symbiotic ties between them as a result of differentiation between their functions. Any human population therefore exhibits a complex pattern of interdependence between different units, but this complexity can nevertheless be analysed by means of the simple formal dichotomy between symbiosis and commensalism. For Hawley, in other words, the ecological community, which constitutes the object of analysis for human ecology, is the system of symbiotic and commensalistic relationships which enables a human population to carry on its daily life. As a system of interdependent relations, the ecological community is therefore irreducible to the units that comprise it: 'It is, in fact, the least reducible universe within which ecological phenomena may be adequately observed. . . . The community, then, is the basic unit of ecological investigation' (1950, p. 180).

Having thus identified the ecological community in terms of a system of functional and interdependent relationships, Hawley is then in a position to develop three further ecological principles. The first of these is the principle of the 'key function', by which he means that certain units within the system will tend to perform a more significant function in adapting the population to its environment than others: 'In every system of relationships among diverse functions, the connection of the system to its environment is mediated primarily by one or a relatively small number of functions' (1968, p. 332). Because the fundamental problem faced by human populations is that of adapting to the external environment, it follows that those units most centrally involved in this process must be the key functional units in the system. Although Hawley does not spell out the implications of this argument, it is clear from his work that the key function is therefore performed in a capitalist society by private enterprise firms which mediate both between the population and its natural environment (through material production) and between the population and its surrounding social environment (through trade).

The performance of the key function is crucial to the two remaining ecological principles identified by Hawley. The first of these is functional differentiation, the extent of which depends upon the productivity of the key function. Thus, while the low productivity of hunting and gathering societies inhibits the development of functional differentiation and specialization, the high productivity of societies organized around the key function of industry means that there is in principle no upper limit on the extent to which differentiation may proceed. This is significant because differentiation, involving an increasingly complex mode of social organization, is the principal way in which human populations adapt to their environment. In other words, given adequate productivity of the key function, differentiation restores the balance between population and environment where this is disturbed by competition (in the way Park suggested) or by improvements in transport and communications (in the way Durkheim suggested in his discussion of moral density).

The final ecological principle – that of dominance – is similarly dependent upon the key function, for the dominant positions within the ecological system are assumed by those units that contribute most to the key function: 'Dominance attaches to the unit that controls the conditions necessary to the functioning of other units. Ordinarily that means controlling the flow of sustenance into the community' (1950, p. 221). Interestingly, Hawley recognizes that one implication of this view is that the dominant units in a human population are likely to be economic rather than political:

It is commonly assumed that government assumes the dominant position. . . . Yet its dominance is not without qualification . . . government, especially in the United States, plays a passive part in the sustenance flow to the community. In effect, government shares and is in competition for the dominant position with associational units whose functions enable them to exert a decisive influence on the community's sustenance supply [Hawley 1950, p. 229]

The functional dominance of business within the ecological system is therefore expressed politically through business influence over community decision-making; a conclusion that Hawley later reaffirmed (1963) in a study of concentrated business power in relation to urban renewal programmes.

The functional dominance of business is expressed not only politically, but also spatially and temporally. It is expressed spatially through centrality, for the centre of human settlements is the point at which functional interdependence is integrated and administered.

Dominant units performing the key function therefore occupy central sites, while other units performing lesser functions are distributed according to their relative contributions: 'In general, units performing key functions have the highest priority of claim on location. Other units tend to distribute themselves about the key function units, their distances away corresponding to the number of degrees of removal separating their functions from direct relation with the key function' (Hawley 1968, p. 333). The functional hierarchy is thus expressed in the form of a spatial gradient, and although Hawley notes that the spatial distribution of different functional units may be affected by factors such as topography and transport routes, his analysis nevertheless results in a very familiar conclusion: 'A noticeable tendency appears for each class of land use to become segregated in a zone situated at an appropriate distance from the centre. The resulting series of more or less symmetrical concentric zones represents in general outline a universal community pattern' (1950, p. 264). Burgess's famous description of the pattern of land use is therefore reaffirmed by Hawley, but his analysis is not, for Hawley explains this pattern as the result of *functional* dominance rather than central dominance *per se*. Where business performs the key function in the system, it will be found at the centre of human settlements, but where other units (e.g. household units in pre-industrial societies) perform the key function, they will occupy the central locations. Thus, while evidence relating to the spatial pattern of pre-industrial cities appears to refute Burgess's model, it is entirely consistent with Hawley's.

The temporal dimension of dominance is revealed in the way in which the rhythm of the principal sustenance unit in the community becomes imposed upon other activities. Just as business dominance is expressed spatially in the pattern of land use, so it is expressed temporally in the rhythm of community activities, the most obvious example of this being the rush-hour.

The significance of these four principles of interdependence, key function, differentiation and dominance is that together they explain how it is that human populations exhibit a constant tendency towards functional equilibrium in their relationship with their environment. Thus Hawley suggests that these four factors tend to bring about a situation where 'development has terminated in a more or less complete system that is capable of sustaining a given relationship to environment indefinitely' (1968, p. 334). In such a closed system, differentiation of functions has been maximized (relative to the productivity of the key function) and organized in terms of corporate and categoric units; the performance of the key function itself has been concentrated in just one unit (or a categoric grouping of units) in order to maximize efficient control of other units of the system; all functions are mutually complementary and are organized at maximum efficiency so that the number of individuals involved in performing each function is just enough to maintain it adequately; and the different functional units have been arranged in space and time so that accessibility is directly proportional to the frequency of exchanges between them.

The tendency towards such an optimally adjusted and maximally efficient system is, however, only a tendency. The fact that such systems are never actually realized is due first to 'immanent change' (that is, change in the environment, such as a decline in non-replaceable natural resources, which necessitates constant readjustment of the ecological system), and second to 'cumulative change' (expansion of the system itself consequent upon the growing productivity of the key function). Because the ecological system is never static it never attains a state of closure, but the underlying tendency within the ecological community is nevertheless always towards the re-establishment of equilibrium. System change is thus fundamentally an evolutionary process involving expansion and readjustment of the ecological system.

This emphasis on evolutionary change lies at the heart of contemporary ecological theory. It is found, for example, in the work of Otis Dudley Duncan, one of the leading exponents of Hawley's approach to human ecology, who writes, 'The most fundamental postulates of human ecology still are best elucidated in an evolutionary framework' (1964, p. 45). Like Hawley, Duncan conceptualizes the ecological community as 'equilibrium-seeking' (Duncan 1959). He suggests that the ecological system may be understood as a functionally interdependent 'ecological complex' consisting of population, environment, human technology and human organization. All four of these variables interact upon each other, although in general population and organization tend to be dependent while environment and technology are independent. In other words, just as Hawley traces the source of system change to external environmental conditions or to internal expansion of productivity, so too Duncan emphasizes the significance of environmental and technological changes in the evolution of the ecological complex as a whole. Changes in these two factors, together with associated changes in population size and organizational capacity, bring about the expansion of the system as a whole: 'Ecological expansion . . . may be characterized by a formula, the four terms in which have been called the "ecological complex": technological accumulation at an accelerated rate; intensified exploitation of environment; demographic transition (now popularly known as "population explosion"); and organizational revolution' (Duncan 1964, p. 75).

Contemporary human ecology is thus characterized above all by its emphasis on the tendency to equilibrium (homeostasis) and the evolutionary nature of system change. In both respects, it has come very close to the functionalist paradigm in sociology. Indeed, there are other parallels between ecological and functionalist perspectives, for not only do they both address themselves to the same problems of the maintenance of equilibrium and the evolutionary development of social systems, but both are oriented towards the analysis of system features rather than individual values and motivations (see Beshers 1962, ch. 2), and both attach considerable significance to patterns of functional interdependence between different units in social systems and to the process of cybernetic feedback within systems (for example through the mutual interaction of the four elements in Duncan's ecological complex). Duncan himself has recognized this close affinity between the two approaches, and has even argued that the ecological perspective may help to clarify some of the areas of confusion within functionalist sociology as a whole (see Duncan and Schnore 1959).

Given this affinity between ecological and functionalist approaches, it is not surprising that many of the familiar criticisms made against functionalist theory have also been made against postwar human ecology. Two in particular deserve mention. The first concerns the problem of teleology and tends to involve the argument that analysis of social systems cannot be accomplished without reference to the subjectively meaningful purposive actions of individual members. The second concerns the question of ideology and tends to involve the assertion that theories that are addressed to the problem of system maintenance are grounded in inherently conservative postulates.

The problem of teleology is that collectivities do not act purposefully, which renders problematic any explanation of a given phenomenon couched in terms of the social purpose, or function, it serves. According to Hawley, however, human ecology does not encounter the problem of teleology found in structural functionalism because it theorizes the control and regulation mechanisms within ecological systems: 'As an organization attains completeness it acquires the capacity for controlling change and for retaining its form through time' (1968, p. 331). In other words, as the ecological community develops towards a closed system, so there evolves a centralized and concentrated key function which effectively controls the development of other units within the system.

What remains unclear in this analysis, however, is how this control and integration on the part of the key functional unit is achieved. Thus according to Robson (1969), any such analysis of the functional role of institutions must implicitly resort to an analysis of the purposive actions of the individuals within them: 'A viewpoint which emphasizes the functional role of social institutions, as does Hawley's, makes assumptions as to motivations, attitudes, sentiments and values which must at least be recognized and considered' (p. 23). Hawley, however, seeks to develop a theoretical perspective which can put to one side questions of individual motives and values, yet according to Robson he conspicuously fails to demarcate the line between the cultural aspects which he does not wish to study and the ecological aspects which he does. Robson's argument is precisely that this line cannot be drawn and that any ecological analysis must take account of the subjective values and purposes of individual actors.

This sort of criticism is at one and the same time both profound and irrelevant. It is profound because it points to a basic problem in urban sociology in particular (see Chapter 4 on urban managerialism and Chapter 6 on the state and the urban system) and in sociology in general; namely, the division between the 'two sociologies' of system and action discussed by Dawe (1970).

Yet it is also irrelevant for the same reason, for it fails to articulate theoretically with the ecological perspective. As Castells (1977a, ch. 8) has suggested, criticisms of the ecological perspective that are grounded in a commitment to an action frame of reference represent less of a critique and more of an inversion. Human ecology is criticized not for what it is, but for what it is not. The debate between voluntaristic action theorists and deterministic systems theorists is as old as sociology itself, and it does not therefore appear particularly useful to criticize human ecology on these grounds.

The argument that human ecology is ideological is one that has more often been made in relation to the prewar than the postwar literature. Alihan (1938), for example, suggested that the Chicago school's emphasis on competition as 'the process basic to all other processes' (p. 91) was little more than an ideological judgement reflecting the core competitive ethic of American capitalism at the time when Park and his colleagues were writing. Similarly Gettys (1940) pointed to the biologistic and naturalistic claims of the Chicago school as fundamentally misrepresenting and mystifying what were essentially social processes – a criticism that has subsequently been developed more fully by Castells (1977a), who has suggested that the apparently 'natural' forces identified by Park must rather be explained as forces specific to the capitalist mode of production (see Chapter 5).

With the work of Hawley and Duncan, however, the emphasis on competition as a basic process in human organization has been replaced by an emphasis on interdependence, while assertions about the natural basis of ecological processes have become blurred as a result of the attempt to dispense with the biotic–cultural dichotomy. Nevertheless, postwar human ecology is still open to the charge of ideology for much the same reason as the work of the Chicago school was, for fundamental to the claims of contemporary ecological theory is the view that certain processes are constant and invariant. Human ecology, in other words, is still concerned to identify transhistorical generalities – forces and processes that invariably operate in all human societies.

We noted earlier that the range of transhistorical generalizations that can safely be made concerning necessary features of all societies appears very limited, and that Hawley's set of cardinal assumptions (that individuals must have access to the environment; that this access must involve some degree of interdependence; that individuals are time-bound; and so on) do not take us very far. The problem is that Hawley believes that other principles can logically be deduced from these initial assumptions (for example principles of dominance and the key function) and that these principles are also invariant. It is in this respect that his work can be attacked as ideological, for there appear no necessary logical grounds for arguing that, for example, certain groups must exercise a dominant function and must therefore attain political, spatial and temporal dominance in society, or that dominant groups must always occupy central locations from which they can control the whole system. Although Hawley avoids discussion of natural biotic forces, the whole thrust of his analysis is nevertheless towards the conclusion that centralized power and extreme division of labour are natural and necessary. Indeed, his conceptualization of the closed ecological system, towards which all systems are said to exhibit a constant tendency, appears as much a political as a theoretical 'ideal', and it is one that, with its implications of extensive corporate power and all-embracing political control, many people are concerned to work and fight against.

Like structural functionalism, therefore, human ecology has tended to develop theoretical explanations (and hence, implicitly, justifications) for a particular mode of political and economic organization. It is a theory of the *status quo* that supports arrangements by explaining them as the outcome of invariant principles. Its concerns are the concerns of the dominant groups in society – it talks of maximizing efficiency but has nothing to say about optimizing social justice; it talks of maintaining equilibrium through gradual change and readjustment and rules out even the possibility of fundamental restructuring. In one sense, the ecological perspective can be enlightening in that it points to the processes that need to be overcome if fundamental changes are to be worked for. But in another sense it is totally restricting and inhibiting in that it denies the possibility of acting on these processes. At best it is mildly reformist; at worst it is crushingly reactionary.

Whether all this is sufficient to dismiss human ecology as ideological depends on how ideology is conceptualized, and this in turn depends on whether it is possible to distinguish science and ideology. This is a question that is taken up in Chapter 5. For the moment, the least that can be said is that this body of theory presents a picture of the social world that is likely to prove particularly unattractive to those who are committed to working for change.

As regards its contribution to the development of a specifically 'urban' social theory, however, we are in a position to draw more definite conclusions regarding the claims and achievements of human ecology. It is clear from Duncan's work that the application of the ecological perspective to the urban question is now problematic. For a start, Duncan (1959) argues convincingly against Hawley's claim that the community represents a microcosm which can be studied in its own right as the smallest indivisible ecological unit, for he points out that the scope of the interdependency between the four elements of the ecological complex now extends far beyond the community to the 'supra-local'. Indeed, it may be suggested that, given the interdependency of localities, regions and states in the world today, the only viable ecological unit is the world system! Clearly urban sociology loses its specificity entirely when the theoretical processes in which it is interested, and the objects of study that it is concerned to analyse, can only be represented quite literally as the world and its entire contents.

Second, it is also clear from Duncan's work that ecology has become a theoretical perspective which has no necessary connection with urban analysis. In a defence of the ecological perspective, for example, Duncan and Schnore (1959) suggest that it can fruitfully be applied to the study of any aggregate phenomenon, and they cite as examples the analysis of bureaucracy and stratification as well as urbanization. The distinctiveness of the ecological approach, in other words, lies solely in its emphasis on the problem of how human aggregates adapt to changing conditions, and there is nothing specifically 'urban' about that.

Appreciation of this point enables us to situate human ecology more precisely in terms of its relationship to structural functionalism, for it is apparent that ecology has become merely one specialized area of study *within* the functionalist paradigm. The problem that it poses is one of the four key functional problems identified by Parsons in his famous 'AGIL' scheme, the other three being goal definition (which on a societal level refers to the political system), integration (which refers to institutions performing social control functions) and latency or pattern maintenance (which refers to the process of socialization) (see Parsons, Bales and Shils 1953). For Parsons, adaptation, the fourth cell in the typology, is achieved by the economic system, for this mediates between the social system as a whole and its external non-social environment.

It is interesting in the light of this to note that, in his attempt to distinguish the theoretical concerns of human ecology from those of other social science disciplines, Hawley (1950, ch. 4) encounters the greatest difficulty in distinguishing it from economics, and he re-solves his problem only by claiming that ecology is broader than economics in that it focuses on interdependencies beyond those grounded in mere exchange values. It may be, therefore, that the ecological system should replace the economic system in Parsons's AGIL typology, for what is clear is that Parsons's theoretical identi-fication of the problem of adaptation coincides exactly with the theoretical concerns of the postwar human ecology.

Once human ecology is located as a sub-discipline within struc-tural–functionalism, its significance for urban analysis can more readily be evaluated. We have seen in this chapter that, as originally developed by the Chicago school, human ecology represented an attempt to generate both a distinct theoretical approach to human society and a specific theory of the city, and that the irreconcilable tension between these two resulted eventually in its collapse. Hawley was able to resurrect human ecology only by jettisoning its specific relevance to the city, and his development of the ecological approach as a sociological perspective rather than as an urban theory was then taken further by Duncan with the result that the relation between ecological theory and urban theory became purely contingent. Now that ecology has found its niche within the functionalist paradigm, we may debate its validity and its usefulness in that context, but irrespective of the conclusions we draw from such a debate, it is clear that human ecology is no longer essentially an urban theory and that it cannot provide a conceptual framework within which a specifically urban social theory can be developed.

3 The urban as a cultural form

There is in Anglo-Saxon culture a deep and enduring tension between the image of the town and that of the countryside. The imagery is that of opposites, for the virtues of rural life – family, traditional morality, community – are mirrored in the vices of the city – egoism, materialism, anonymity – while the advantages of urban living are similarly reflected in the disadvantages of rural existence. As Raymond Williams observes,

On the country has gathered the idea of a natural way of life: of peace, innocence and simple virtue. On the city has gathered the idea of an achieved centre: of learning, communication, light. Powerful hostile associations have also developed: on the city as a place of noise, worldliness and ambition; on the country as a place of backwardness, ignorance, limitation. A contrast between country and city, as fundamental ways of life, reaches back into classical times. [Williams 1973, p. 1]

While the prevailing image of the city, which can be traced in literature and, more recently, in film, includes both positive and negative aspects – progress as well as pollution, liberty as well as loneliness – it does appear that evaluation is more often hostile than favourable: 'Life in the countryside is viewed as one of harmony and virtue. The town is disorganized; the countryside is settled. The town is bad; the countryside is good' (Newby 1977, p. 12). In part this may be the legacy of the fear of the town by the dominant classes in the nineteenth century, for as Glass (1968) has argued, the expanding Victorian cities represented a concentration of the industrial pro-letariat which the guardians of the *status quo* viewed with some appre-hension. Then as now, industrialists, philanthropists and visionary planners sought to re-establish the moral bonds of the small community by developing company towns and new model com-munities which would reintegrate the individual into society and demobilize the mob (see Dennis 1968, Heraud 1975). Yet this is far from a complete explanation for the durability and pervasiveness of anti-urban sentiment in Western cultures, for as Williams demonstrates, the tendency to compare the urban present with an idyllic version of a rural past has been in evidence for centuries. We shall consider Williams's own explanation for this later in this chapter.

Not surprisingly, the tension between the urban and the rural and between the values that each represents has found expression not only in cultural forms, but also in social theory and philosophy, where it is revealed most clearly in the concept of community. Nisbet (1966) has suggested that community constitutes 'the most fundamental and far-reaching of sociology's unit-ideas' (p. 47), and this is the case because it is indicative of what appear to be some of the most basic dilemmas in social relationships. If, as Nisbet suggests, community encompasses relationships of personal intimacy, depth, commitment and continuity, then, either implicitly or explicitly, it represents a vivid contrast with other types of relationships which are characterized by indifference, superficiality, segmentalism and brevity. It is the contrast between emotion and intellect, altruism and egoism, affection and instrumentalism, and so on.

What needs to be emphasized at the outset, however, is that such dualisms which are evoked by and entailed in the concept of community refer not specifically to different types of human settlement – the country as opposed to the city – but rather to different patterns of human relationships. The classic dichotomy drawn by Tonnies (1963) between *gemeinschaft* and *gesellschaft*, for example, is not in itself a typology of forms of settlement, although Tonnies did argue that ways of life in the village were generally characteristic of the former while those in the city tended to characterize the latter. As concepts, however, *gemeinschaft* and *gesellschaft* referred to types of social relationships, and more specifically to the contrast between the emotional and the rational, the personal and the contractual, the communal and the individual aspects of human interaction. As such, these two concepts were employed to designate the direction of change in society as a whole rather than differences between geographical areas within society at any one time. Indeed, as Bell and Newby (1976) point out, Tonnies recognized that the relationship between community as a pattern of social interaction and community as a physical location was a contingent one: 'For him, *gemeinschaftlich* relationships were linked to the "community of place" only insofar as those who affirmed a "community of blood" (kinship) and a "community of mind" (friendship) wished to live in reasonable proximity' (p. 196). The mere fact of being neighbours does not necessarily create neighbourliness, any more than the fact of being brothers creates fraternalism. While *gemeinschaft* and *gesellschaft* may come to be expressed in the country and the city respectively, they cannot be reduced to physical terms.

What Tonnies has in fact provided is not a dichotomy of rural and urban but a theory of social change. In his view, western European societies were in a process of transition from unions of *gemeinschaft* (e.g. social organization based on the family) to associations of *gemeinschaft* (e.g. the guild system) to associations of *gesellschaft* (e.g. the capitalist firm) and finally to unions of *gesellschaft* (e.g. corporate capitalism). As Mellor (1977) suggests, his is therefore a theory of the changes in social relations wrought by the development of capitalism, and despite his protestations to the contrary, his characterization of *gesellschaft* in terms of impersonality and self-interest is less a theory of urban life *per se* than of urban life in the context of a developed competitive capitalist exchange economy.

Much the same argument also applies to the various writers discussed in Chapter 1, for as we saw there, distinctions such as that between mechanical and organic bonds of social solidarity, or between traditional and rational action, are applied by Durkheim and Weber respectively to the analysis of different types of social relationships in different types of societies rather than to the dichotomy between the rural and the urban. This line of analysis was, however, developed most fully by Parsons (1951), who suggested that simple dichotomies such as that of Tonnies blurred several analytically distinct dimensions. Parsons suggested that the social actor confronted a series of dilemmas which he termed the pattern variables. Thus an actor may relate to an object according to universal or particular criteria; he may evaluate it according to its quality or its performance; he may act towards it affectively or with affective neutrality; and his relationship with it may be specific to one situation or diffused among many. In this way, Parsons differentiates the various dimensions of action implied in Tonnies's single dichotomy, thereby enabling both greater precision and greater flexibility in their application. *Gemeinschaftlich* relationships can therefore be identified in terms of their particularism, quality, affectivity and diffuseness, while those characterized by *gesellschaft* involve universalism, performance, affective neutrality and specificity. It then becomes possible to analyse empirical cases in a more refined way since it is possible that certain types of relationships may involve a mixture of the different pattern variables (e.g. they may be particularistic yet affectively neutral) which could only be violated by the imposition of a single blanket dichotomy.

What Tonnies, Durkheim, Weber and Parsons all share in common, therefore, is their attempt to distinguish different types of social relationships through the development of analytical dichotomies. In all four cases, the contrasts that are drawn refer to different patterns of social interaction, not to different types of human settlements. While the contrast between ways of life in the country and the city may be used (particularly in the case of Tonnies) to illustrate or exemplify these various distinctions, it is not essential to them. Thus in the work of all four writers, we look in vain for any specific theory of urban or rural ways of life.

During the twentieth century, however, there has developed another line of sociological thought which has attempted to relate distinct types of social relationships to distinct patterns of human settlement. Of particular significance here is the work of Georg Simmel, and notably his essay on the metropolis and mental life which was written in 1903 (in Wolff 1950). In his concerns with individuality, rationality and the division of labour, Simmel was located in the mainstream of nineteenth-century sociological thought, and this led him to draw similar contrasts to those identified by Tonnies, Durkheim and others. Yet Simmel also had certain distinctive concerns, the most significant of which was his interest in developing a sociology of number (i.e. an analysis of the significance of group size for social relationships). His famous essay on the metropolis can usefully be seen as the product of a fusion between these two lines of interest, for in it Simmel brought together (and to some extent confused) an analysis of the cultural forms of modern industrial capitalism and an analysis of the effects of size on group life. In Simmel's work, therefore, the metropolis became not only the illustration of certain types of social relationships, but also their source, and as a result, sociological analysis came to mirror literary imagery in its focus on the city as a specific social and cultural form.

The metropolis and mental life

It has often been suggested that Simmel's sociology is highly personal, wilfully eclectic and internally incoherent. However, the wide diversity of his writings does reveal a certain methodological unity and a degree of substantive continuity. The methodological unity is a function of his commitment to formalistic analysis and to the principle of the dialectic (the unity of opposites), while the substantive continuity is revealed in his recurring concern with the questions of individuality and freedom, modernity and the division of labour, and intellectual rationality and the money economy. All of these concerns are expressed in his essay on the metropolis and mental life.

Simmel's methodology was fundamentally neo-Kantian. Like Weber, he believed that knowledge of the world could be achieved only through the active mediation of a knowing subject – that is, through a prior mental process of selection of relevant aspects of concrete reality and of classification of these aspects through analytical constructs. The sociologist, in other words, imposed a conceptual order upon the world in order to understand it.

For Simmel, this order was achieved through the analytical separation of form and content. While the content of specific human actions could be explained only psychologically (the question of why certain individuals choose to embark upon certain courses of action was for Simmel a psychological question), the social form through which they were expressed was a sociological phenomenon. For example, in his analysis of the triad (the forms taken by three-person interaction), he identified three different forms that interaction between the parties could take. One party could adopt the role of referee or mediator between the other two, or he could attempt to profit from conflict between the other two while refusing to align himself, or he could adopt a strategy of divide and rule. These forms are given in the fact of triadic interaction, and may be applied to an infinite range of specific cases (e.g. interaction within a family, within a political system, or even between nations). Thus, although the sociologist cannot explain why one party should choose to adopt one strategy rather than another in any particular case, he can nevertheless analyse the form of strategy that is adopted. In this way, sociology is equipped to develop generalizations concerning underlying uniformities in a wide variety of historically unique events.

Sociology, therefore, is the science of the forms of human association as abstracted from real-world interaction. Just as grammar studies the forms of language rather than what is actually said, and epistemology studies the forms of knowledge rather than what is actually theorized, so sociology studies the forms of inter-action rather than what is actually done (see Levine 1971, introduction). Sociology is the geometry of social forms, for its relationship to the content of social action is 'like that of geometry with regard to physico-chemical sciences of matter: it considers form, thanks to which matter generally takes an empirical shape – consequently a form that exists in itself only as an abstraction' (Simmel, quoted in Freund 1978, p. 160).

Simmel's commitment to dialectical analysis emerges out of his methodological formalism, for he suggests that social forms are at one and the same time the means whereby individual actions come to be expressed and the source of constraint upon them. Not only is the individual in society, but society is in the individual. Society (in the sense of the forms of human association) is both the source and the negation of individuality:

Social man is not partially social and partially individual; rather his existence is shaped by a fundamental unity which cannot be accounted for in any other way than through the synthesis or coincidence of two logically contradictory determinations: man is both social link and being for himself, both product of society and life from an autonomous centre. [Simmel; quoted in Coser 1965, p. 11]

Social life is thus founded in an irresolvable paradox, for the expansion of society is both the condition of and the challenge to the growth of individuality.

This analysis becomes clearer in Simmel's discussion of the sociological significance of number. As we have seen, the difference between a group of two and a group of three is, according to Simmel, qualitative as well as quantitative. In the dyad, each partner can rely on only one other, and this results in intense commitment to the relationship and to the knowledge that no superpersonal level of constraint is operating. In the triad, however, it becomes possible for the first time for the group to prevail over the individual, for the individual can be outnumbered. 'Simmel put his finger on a fundamental sociological phenomenon: series really begin only with the number three' (Freund 1978, p. 163); for the transition from two to three is qualitative, whereas transitions thereafter are quantitative.

There is, however, another qualitative shift at the indeterminate point at which a small group becomes a large group. In the large aggregate, new phenomena are needed that are not necessary in smaller groupings:

It will immediately be conceded on the basis of everyday experiences that a group upon realising a certain size must develop forms and organs which serve its maintenance and promotion but which a small group does not need. On the other hand, it will also be admitted that smaller groups have qualities, including types of interaction among their members, which inevitably disappear when the groups grow larger. [Simmel; in Wolff 1950, p. 87]

The unity of the group is no longer preserved by direct interaction among its members, and the personal and emotional commitments of members of small groups are replaced by formal means of control such as agencies of the law. If custom is characteristic of small groups, law is characteristic of large ones. In the large group, therefore, the individual is more restricted by the operation of superpersonal agencies that confront him and are seemingly beyond his control. However, the individual's commitment to the large group is correspondingly less, for as groups expand, so different social circles begin to intersect and the individual spreads his commitments across each. The result is that the increasing constraint within large groups is offset by the growing area of individual freedom across them: 'The increased restriction is more bearable for the individual because, outside of it, he has a sphere of freedom which is all the greater' (in Wolff 1950, p. 102).

An increase in the size of a social group has implications not only for the scope of individual freedom, however, but also for the degree of individual distinctiveness. As a group expands, so it threatens to immerse the individual within the mass: 'It pulls the individual down to a level with all and sundry' (in Wolff 1950, p. 31). The intellect of the individual is eroded by the emotion of the masses, and social interaction is debased as social life becomes grounded in the lowest common denominator. The larger the group, the more impersonal group interaction becomes, and the less concerned members become with the unique personal qualities of others. Faced with this assault on his individuality, the member of a large human aggregate comes to emphasize his own subjectivity, both to others (e.g. by distancing himself from the crowd by emphasizing some distinctive attribute) and to himself: 'When the individual's relations begin to exceed a certain extensiveness, he becomes all the more thrown back upon himself' (in Levine 1971, p. 290). In the large group, the individual increasingly stands alone.

Simmel's work on the social effects of size thus leads to the conclusion that, in a large group (such as the modern city), custom is replaced by formal social control mechanisms, the individual's commitments become extended across a number of different social circles, the scope of individual freedom is increased, the character of social relations is highly impersonal, and the individual's consciousness of self is heightened. Exploration of the significance of number for social life is, however, only one theme in Simmel's sociology, and it is complemented by a second major concern which relates to the analysis of the social effects of modernity. Of particular significance here is the development of an advanced division of labour in society, together with the establishment of a money economy.

The growth of the division of labour in modern societies has three main effects for the forms of human association. First, it fragments and segmentalizes social life. In small-scale relatively homogeneous societies, the individual's group memberships form a concentric pattern; the individual belongs to a guild, which belongs to a confederation, etc. The individual is therefore vertically integrated into his society, and the pattern of association assumes a totality, engulfing all aspects of his life. With an advanced division of labour, however, the social circles in which the individual moves become tangential to each other, and his involvement in any one of them is partial and specific. As Simmel puts it, 'The point at which the individual momentarily touches the totality or the structure of the whole no longer pulls parts of his personality into the relationship that do not belong there' (in Levine 1971, p. 293).

Second, the division of labour reinforces the self-consciousness engendered by an increase in size. This is because, in a highly differentiated society, the individual is constantly exposed to an infinite variety of changing situations and sensations in which his own unique personality is the only constant factor:

The more uniformly and unwaveringly life progresses, and the less the extremes of sensate experience depart from an average level, the less strongly does the sensation of personality arise; but the farther apart they stretch, and the more energetically they erupt, the more intensely does a human being sense himself as a personality. [in Levine 1971, p. 291]

The division of labour therefore encourages egoism and individualism.

Third, the development of the division of labour in society brings about an alienation of the individual from the entire cultural world that he and others have created. For Simmel, alienation is the unavoidable effect of modernity (see Mellor 1977, p. 185), for the division of labour separates the creator from his creation, and therefore results in the reification of all human creations. The world of things that individuals have created thus confronts them as an objective spirit, while the essential creativity of individuals is increasingly impoverished. Increasingly, the objective spirit comes to dominate the subjective spirit: 'The price of the objective perfection of the world will be the atrophy of the human soul' (Coser 1965, p. 23).

These characteristics of modernity are expressed in, and reinforced by, the development of a money economy. Money is totally depersonalized, for its exchange leaves no trace of the personality of its previous owner. It is a leveller, for it reduces all qualitative values to a common quantitative base. It is a source of individual freedom and independence, for the development of a cash economy enables social expansion upon a world level on the one hand, yet individual freedom of choice on the other. It confronts the individual as an objective power. It is, in short, the finest expression of the rationality of the modern world.

We find in Simmel's work, therefore, a recurrent concern with three core themes: size, division of labour and money/rationality. At the risk of some oversimplification, it may be suggested that these three constitute the 'independent variables' of his analysis of the forms of human association in the modern world. It is for this reason that the metropolis assumes a central significance for Simmel, for it is here that the effects of size, differentiation and the money economy on social relationships are most immediately visible and most intensely felt. As Nisbet observes, 'The direction of history is toward metropolis, which for Simmel is the structure of modernism, performing for his thought the role that democracy does for Tocqueville, capitalism for Marx, and bureaucracy for Weber' (1966, p. 308). The metropolis is the crystallization of the objective spirit.

These three variables are prominent in his essay on the metropolis and mental life. According to Simmel, the sheer *size* of the metropolis is significant because it gives rise to 'one of the few tendencies for which an approximately universal formula can be discovered' (in Wolff 1950, p. 416). As we have seen, this formula is that larger social circles increase the scope of individual freedom while reducing the quality of relationships with others:

The reciprocal reserve and indifference and the intellectual life conditions of large circles are never felt more strongly by the individual in their impact upon his independence than in the thickest crowd of the big city. This is because the bodily proximity and narrowness of space makes the mental distance only the more visible. It is obviously only the obverse of this freedom if, under certain circumstances, one nowhere feels as lonely and lost as in the metropolitan crowd. For here as elsewhere it is by no means necessary that the freedom of man be reflected in his emotional life as comfort. [Wolff 1950, p. 418]

Similarly, the effects of *differentiation* are most pronounced in the metropolis, for 'cities are, first of all, seats of the highest economic division of labour' (Wolff 1950, p. 420). This extreme differentiation is itself a function of size, for Simmel argues (consistently with Spencer and Durkheim) that only large human aggregates give rise to and can support a wide variation of services. Because of this close association between the city and the economic division of labour, the effects of division of labour in terms of individuality and alienation are most clearly revealed there. The individual is driven constantly to exaggerate his own uniqueness and to 'adopt the most tendentious peculiarities, that is, the specifically metropolitan extravagances of mannerism, caprice and preciousness' (p. 421) in order to gain attention and assert his personality. The change and flux that characterize city life intensify nervous stimulation and lead to greater consciousness of self: 'The city sets up a deep contrast with small town and rural life with reference to the sensory foundations of psychic life. The metropolis extracts from man as a discriminating creature a different amount of consciousness than does rural life' (p. 410). Yet precisely because new sensations become the norm in the metropolis, the individual develops a blasé attitude towards them. His nerves are blunted by continual stimulation, and he becomes incapable of reacting to new sensations with the appropriate enthusiasm and energy. Put another way, he becomes 'sophisticated', and devalues the objective world around him.

This devaluation of the world 'in the end drags one's own personality down into a feeling of the same worthlessness' (p. 415) as the individual becomes alienated from the world in which he lives. Art, technology, science and other aspects of human culture all become devalued and grow increasingly distant from the individual whose creation they are: 'The individual has become a mere cog in an enormous organization of things and powers which tear from his hands all progress, spirituality and value in order to transform them from their subjective form into the form of a purely objective life' (p. 422). Other individuals, too, are devalued, and the urbanite develops an aversion and antipathy towards others as a shield against their indifference towards him. Metropolitan life thus becomes impersonal and calculative, and again Simmel points to the contrast with small-town life.

This impersonality is reinforced by the third defining feature of the metropolis, the *money economy*. 'The metropolis', argues Simmel, 'has always been the seat of the money economy' (in Wolff 1950, p. 411). Money is both the source and the expression of metropolitan rationality and intellectualism, for both money and intellect share a matter-of-fact attitude towards people and things and are indifferent to genuine individuality. Metropolitan man is guided by his head, not his heart, by calculation and intellect, not affection and emotion. 'Throughout the whole course of English history, London has never acted as England's heart, but often as England's intellect and always as her moneybag!' (p. 412). Money also contributes to the urbanite's devaluation of the things and people around him, for it is the 'most frightful leveller' in its capacity to express all variations in terms of a single measure of equivalence: 'Money expresses all qualitative differences of things in terms of "how much?" Money, with all its colourlessness and indifference, becomes the common denominator of all values' (p. 414).

In the metropolis, therefore, are found the basic dilemmas of social life. It is here that the struggle is waged by the individual 'to preserve the autonomy and individuality of his existence in the face of over-whelming social forces' (p. 409). It is here that the tension is most clearly revealed between the eighteenth-century ideal of the freedom of the individual from traditional bonds, and the nineteenth-century ideal of individuality in the face of the mass. The metropolis is for Simmel the crucible of modern life.

Many aspects of Simmel's work have attracted considerable criticism over the years. He has been attacked for his formalism, for his exclusive concern with the minutiae of social life, for his empiricism and for his assumption of the inevitability of the patterns of social relationships that he identifies (see, for example, Mellor 1977, ch. 5). His claims regarding the invariant relation between size and the quality of social relationships (his so-called 'universal formula') have been challenged, not least by Weber, who argued in the opening paragraph of his essay on the city that 'various cultural factors determine the size at which "impersonality" tends to appear' (1958, p. 65). From our present perspective, however, the basic question to which we must address ourselves is how far Simmel's work constitutes a specific theory of the city as opposed to a theory of social relations in modern industrial capitalist societies. Leaving aside questions of its empirical validity, its theoretical consistency and its methodological adequacy, therefore, we need to consider the extent to which Simmel's approach to the analysis of the metropolis provides the framework for a distinctive urban sociological theory.

Clearly it is a different approach from that developed by Tonnies or by the writers discussed in Chapter 1, for the contrasts drawn by these theorists relate to different types of social relationships found in different types of historical societies as a result of the development of capitalism, the division of labour, the spirit of rationality or whatever. This is not the case with Simmel, for although the distinction between cause and effect is far from clear in his analyses, it does seem that he sees in the metropolis itself the source of at least some of the features of modern life. He does not refer to the city merely as an illustration of the rationality, impersonality and the like that characterize social relationships in the modern era, but rather sees it as a causal factor in its own right in the explanation of such social forms. What is crucial here, and what separates Simmel from the other writers discussed, is his unique emphasis on the sociology of number. The metropolis is above all a large human agglomeration, and according to Simmel's writings on the sociological significance of size, this fact alone should be expected to create different patterns of human association from those found in small settlements such as rural villages. With regard to his emphasis on size, therefore, Simmel's essay does represent an attempt to theorize the city *per se*.

Equally clearly, however, Simmel draws on other factors apart from size (namely, the division of labour and the money economy) to explain the depersonalized and utilitarian character of social relationships in the city, and although these additional factors are, according to his argument, historically associated with the metropolis, they are not peculiar to it or explained by it. They are, in other words, features of the mode of organization of society as a whole. It is because his theory of metropolis includes factors that are 'social' rather than specifically 'metropolitan' that Simmel is obliged to define the city in other than merely geographical or numerical terms: 'A city consists of its total effects which extend beyond its immediate confines' (in Wolff 1950, p. 419). But applying this definition, we soon end up with an equation between the concepts of metropolis and society, in which case the arguments about the effect of size become irrelevant (since society includes both small and large settlements) and the use of the term 'metropolis' becomes redundant. With regard to his emphasis on the effects of division of labour and the money economy, therefore, Simmel's essay cannot be represented as a specifically urban theory.

This latter interpretation of Simmel's essay lies behind Becker's assertion that

> Simmel never thought of urbanization as an explanatory formula. . . . On the contrary, the cities that he had in view were exclusively of the kind manifesting an elaborate division of labour, a money economy, a wage system, marked industrialization and other characteristics peculiar to the western world from the fifteenth century until very recent times. [Becker 1959, pp. 230–1]

But Becker's argument that Simmel was 'really' writing about a particular type of society rather than a particular type of settlement pattern ignores the central significance accorded to the fact of size in his work. When we consider Simmel's essay on the metropolis, therefore, we are confronted with a classic (though unintended) Simmelian dualism, for it is on the one hand an analysis of the city, and on the other an analysis of modern Western society.

These two dimensions must be treated separately, yet in Simmel's work they are inextricably confused. As it stands, Simmel's essay on the metropolis appears highly plausible as a description, yet hopelessly muddled as an analysis. Any attempt to develop a theory of the city must be able to include the common essential features of all cities, irrespective of the mode of production in which they are located. As Louis Wirth observed, 'It is particularly important to call attention to the danger of confusing urbanism with industrialism and modern capitalism' (1938, p. 7). It was precisely such a confusion that characterized Simmel's approach, and it was just this confusion that Wirth, thirty-five years later, set out to correct.

Urbanism and ruralism as ways of life

Wirth's paper, 'Urbanism as a way of life' (1938) is arguably the most famous article ever to have been published in a sociology journal. Its intellectual pedigree is explicit, for it reflects on the one hand the influence of Simmel and on the other that of Park. Having said that, it should be noted that it is therefore the product of rather intense inbreeding, for Park was himself a student of Simmel's at Berlin, and his sociology was strongly (though by no means entirely) influenced by Simmel's work (see the introduction to Levine 1971 for a discussion of the connections and disjunctions between Park and

Simmel). As is often the case with the products of inbreeding, the essay reflects the weaknesses of its parentage.

In many ways, Wirth's essay can be seen as an extension, modification and development of Simmel's paper on the metropolis (a paper that Wirth described as 'the most important single article on the city from the sociological standpoint' – 1967, p. 219). From Simmel he derives a concern with the forms of human association in the city, with the dualism between town and country, and with the subjective experience of urban life. Like Simmel, he identifies size as a key explanatory variable, although Simmel's analysis of the division of labour is replaced in Wirth's paper by an analysis of heterogeneity, while the effects of a money economy are dropped from the analysis altogether.

As a student of Park's, on the other hand, Wirth also drew upon some of the insights developed by the Chicago human ecologists as regards the effects cf density on human organization and the dominance achieved by the city over its hinterland. He saw human ecology as one of three significant perspectives on the city (the other two being organizational and social–psychological, concerned respectively with forms of social relationships and personality characteristics), and argued that all three should complement each other: 'Human ecology is not a substitute for, but a supplement to, the other frames of reference and methods of social investigation' (Wirth 1945, p. 488). It was his intention, therefore, to develop a theory of the city that could account for the ecological, organizational and social–psychological characteristics of urbanism. Put another way, he set out to synthesize Park's human ecology and Simmel's analyses of the forms of association and the development of urban personality.

Wirth believed that such a systematic theory of the city was possible but had yet to be achieved (Weber and Park had, in his view, come closest to fulfilling this objective, but neither of their essays on the city provided an ordered or coherent framework for analysis). He was highly critical of contemporary work, which proceeded on the basis of arbitrary classifications of urban settlements – usually that employed by the American census, which defined an urban area as one of a certain population size – for he argued that such classifications were mechanical and unsophisticated and in no way correspond with actual entities. 'What we look forward to', he wrote in a paper shortly before he died, 'is not the piling up of a vast body of reliable, continuous information if this labour is to be largely wasted on a basic system of classification such as we have used up to now. The factor-by-factor analysis of any problem in terms of which rural and urban settlements have shown significant differences . . . leads to sterile results' (Wirth 1964, p. 224). The size of settlement was not in itself of any sociological interest unless it could be shown to affect forms of association: 'As long as we identify urbanism with the physical entity of the city, viewing it merely as rigidly delimited in space, and proceed as if urban attitudes abruptly ceased to be manifested beyond an arbitrary boundary line, we are not likely to arrive at any adequate conception of urbanism as a mode of life' (1938, p. 4).

For Wirth, therefore, the urban–rural dichotomy referred to two ideal types of human community, two basic patterns of human association that characterized the modern age. Different types of settlements were thus more or less urban or more or less rural: 'We should not expect to find abrupt and discontinuous variation between urban and rural types of personality. The city and the country may be regarded as two poles in reference to one or the other of which all human settlements tend to arrange themselves' (1938, p. 3). There is, in other words, a continuum between the urban and the rural, and the differences between any two existing settlements are differences in degree along this continuum (Wirth 1964, p. 224). The important point to note about this is that differences between different settlements have therefore to be determined empirically. The role of Wirth's ideal types is to provide a framework for such analysis which (unlike government census classifications) is relevant to sociological concerns and which can provide the basis for hypothesis formation: 'To set up ideal–typical polar concepts such as I have done, and many others before me have done, does not prove that city and country are fundamentally and necessarily different. . . . Rather it suggests certain hypotheses to be tested' (1964, p. 223).

The hypothesis that Wirth advances is that variations in patterns of human association may be explained as the effects of three factors – size, density and heterogeneity. These three constitute the parameters of his conceptualization of the urban: 'For sociological purposes a city may be defined as a relatively large, dense and permanent settlement of socially heterogeneous individuals' (1938, p. 8). The task for urban sociology is then to analyse the extent to which each of these three variables gives rise to definite forms of social relationships: 'We may expect the outstanding features of the urban social scene to vary in accordance with size, density and differences in the functional type of cities' (p. 7).

It is important to recognize, however, that Wirth emphasizes that 'folk' ways of life may still be found in cities, for previously dominant patterns of human association are not completely obliterated by urban growth, and also to recognize that 'urban' ways of life are likely to spread beyond the boundaries of the city, given the ecological dominance of the city over its hinterland. Furthermore, he notes that technological developments in transport and communications have led to the spillover of the city into the countryside and to a new accessibility of the city to rural dwellers, and that the pace of such changes has 'made such notions as we have about rural and urban likenesses and differences obsolete' (1964, p. 221). All this merely reinforces his argument that the designation of different localities as more urban or more rural is a conceptual exercise, and that while we should expect larger, denser and more heterogeneous settlements to exhibit more urban characteristics than smaller, more scattered and more homogeneous ones, this remains an empirical question which should not be 'resolved' by the *a priori* identification of urbanism with particular physical locations.

Wirth's analysis of the social effects of *size* closely reflects that of Simmel. Thus he develops the familiar argument that larger size means greater variation, and then draws upon the ecological tradition to suggest that this in turn will be reflected in the spatial segregation of different groups according to ethnicity, race, status, occupation and so on. He also suggests, *pace* Simmel, that an increase in size reduces the chances of any two individuals knowing each other personally, and that this leads to segmentalism in social relationships, an emphasis on secondary rather than primary contacts, and a corresponding indifference towards others:

The contacts of the city may indeed be face to face, but they are nevertheless impersonal, superficial, transitory and segmental. The reserve, the indifference and the blasé outlook which urbanites manifest in their relationships may thus be regarded as devices for immunising themselves against the personal claims and expectations of others. [Wirth 1938, p. 12]

It is important to note that Wirth does not claim that primary relationships disappear in the city; in his earlier study of a Jewish ghetto in Chicago, for example, he concluded that it formed a 'cultural community' with a communal way of life (1927, p. 71). Nor does he suggest that the urbanite knows fewer people than the country dweller; the reverse may well be the case. All that he is arguing here, therefore, is that in a large settlement, the individual will be personally acquainted with a smaller proportion of those with whom he interacts, and that this fact alone explains the development of the social distance that characterizes urban life.

Like Simmel, Wirth recognizes that size engenders a tension between individuality and individual freedom, for a large human group undermines the former while encouraging the latter: 'Whereas the individual gains, on the one hand, a certain degree of emancipation or freedom from the personal and emotional controls of intimate groups, he loses, on the other hand, the spontaneous self-expression, the morale and the sense of participation that comes with living in an integrated society' (1938, pp.12–13). Life in large groups thus tends to become anomic, and moral deregulation is countered by the development of more formal agencies of control and participation such as the mass media.

The effects of *density* on social relationships are a function of the growth of differentiation. Wirth follows Durkheim and the Chicago ecologists in arguing that differentiation is the way in which any population responds to an increase in numbers in a given area. The effects of an increase in density are therefore clearly related to those of size, and Wirth notes that 'Density thus reinforces the effect of numbers in diversifying men and their activities and in increasing the complexity of the social structure' (1938, p. 14).

Complex differentiation of functions within a human aggregate creates forms of interaction in which people relate to each other on the basis of their specific roles rather than their personal qualities: 'We see the uniform which denotes the role of functionaries, and are oblivious to the personal eccentricities hidden behind the uniform' (p. 14). It therefore fosters an instrumental attitude towards others who are treated merely in terms of the role they perform, and the resulting spirit of mutual exploitation has therefore to be regulated by law and other mechanisms of formal control. However, Wirth also notes that homogeneous sub-groups created in the process of differentiation tend to congregate together in different parts of the city, forming what Park and his colleagues termed 'natural areas'. Predatory relationships within the city as a whole may therefore come to be mediated within different parts of the city by the development of more personal and emotional ties: 'Persons of homogeneous status and needs unwittingly drift into, consciously select, or are forced by circumstances into the same area. The different parts of the city acquire specialized functions and the city consequently comes to resemble a mosaic of social worlds in which the transition from one to the other is abrupt' (p. 15).

If Wirth's discussion of density relies heavily on Park, his analysis of the effects of *heterogeneity* leads him to return once again to Simmel. The analysis of social heterogeneity is couched largely in terms of Simmel's geometry of social circles. Individuals participate in many different circles, none of which can command their undivided allegiance. These circles are tangential and intersecting (in contrast to the concentric totality of the rural community), and individuals enjoy a different status, and perhaps even a different identity, in each of them with the result that instability and personal insecurity becomes a norm. The urban personality easily becomes disorganized, and rates of mental illness, suicide and so on increase accordingly.

Heterogeneity also leads to a process of social levelling in which the individual is subordinated to the mass: 'If the individual would participate at all in the social, political and economic life of the city, he must subordinate some of his individuality to the demands of the larger community and in that measure immerse himself in mass movements' (p. 18). Action, to be effective, has to be collective, and political participation is achieved through representation. The individual is 'reduced to a stage of virtual impotence' (p. 22), and official agencies assume responsibility for a wide range of provisions and services on which he increasingly depends.

Wirth's description of urbanism as a way of life, and in particular his diagnosis of the urban personality, is overwhelmingly bleak, yet neither he nor Simmel could be described as rural romantics. Wirth was as aware of the positive aspects of city life as he was of the negative aspects of the countryside. Nevertheless, his work did serve to bring social theory closer to the rural nostalgia and virulent anti-urbanism that has been so characteristic of Western culture, for his description of urban life as anonymous, impersonal, superficial, instrumental and so on was entirely consistent with the imagery portrayed in English novels and poetry for generations. The difference, of course, is that Wirth deduced these characteristics from an analysis of the sociological significance of three variables, and thereby established the traditional imagery of the city in the form of a hypothesis: 'The deductive inferences sound plausible, principally because they point to the characteristics that have for so long been accepted as typically urban' (Reissman 1964, p. 143). As with Simmel's work, Wirth's essay appears intuitively plausible as a description of city life, but the question, as we shall see, is whether his simple explanation in terms of the necessary effects of size, density and heterogeneity does in fact account for the phenomena he describes.

Support for Wirth's thesis came just three years after the publication of his essay from another of Park's students, Robert Redfield. Redfield (1941) studied four communities in the Yucatan peninsula of Mexico, ranging from the small, homogeneous and very isolated settlement at Tusik to the largest town in the region, Merida. On the basis of this study, he argued that the less isolated and more heterogeneous the settlement, the more it became characterized by cultural disorganization, secularization and the growth of individualism. On the basis of this and other studies, Redfield (1947) then proceeded to develop an ideal type of the 'folk society' which complemented Wirth's analysis by identifying the cultural characteristics of communities at the other end of the rural–urban continuum.

According to Redfield, 'Folk societies have certain features in common which enable us to think of them as a type – a type which contrasts with the society of the modern city' (1947, p. 293). He saw the city as a 'vast complicated and rapidly changing world' (p. 306), and contrasted this with the folk society as 'small, isolated, non-literate and homogeneous with a strong sense of group solidarity' (p. 297). The ideal type folk society was small, isolated, intimate, immobile, pre-literate, homogeneous and cohesive. It had only a rudimentary division of labour based mainly on a rigid differentiation of sex roles; the means of production were shared; and economic activity was contained within the community. The culture of the folk society was strongly traditional and uncritical. It was grounded in social bonds based upon kinship and religion, and its internal coherence derived from custom rather than formal law. Patterns of interaction were based on ascribed status, and social relationships were personal and diffuse. In such relationships, added Redfield somewhat wistfully, 'There is no place for the motive of commercial gain' (p. 305).

Taken together, the work of Wirth and Redfield exhibits two main themes. The first is that patterns of human relationships can be conceptualized in terms of a pair of logically opposite ideal types (the contents of which are open to discussion) such that any empirical case can be located at some point between them and compared with other cases against some purely conceived yardstick of urbanism or ruralism. It should be noted that the characterization of the ideal types themselves is variable, for some researchers may choose to emphasize one aspect while others may select other aspects. It is not a valid criticism of Wirth's approach to suggest that cities exhibit certain features that are different from those he identified in his paper, for Wirth's characterization of urbanism is a logical construct, not an empirical description. It is a construct designed to facilitate empirical research on actual cities by providing a conceptual criterion of urbanism, and like all ideal types, it may therefore be evaluated in terms of its usefulness but not its empirical validity.

Wirth's paper, of course, attempts to go beyond a simple exercise in conceptualization and to develop an explanation of empirical variations in ways of life between different settlements. This provides the second theme to emerge out of his and Redfield's work: namely that variations in patterns of human relationships between different communities are to be explained in terms of differences in their size and density, their degree of internal homogeneity, and the extent of their isolation from other centres of population.

The first of these themes is therefore a concern with conceptualization, while the second is an attempt at explanation. It follows that this line of work has to be evaluated on two levels, for the exercise in conceptualization may be assessed only in terms of its logical consistency and its fruitfulness for empirical research, while the attempt at explanation has to be examined in terms of its theoretical adequacy. Unfortunately, as we shall now see, much of the subsequent work that has claimed to refute Wirth has failed to recognize this distinction.

'Real but relatively unimportant'

Just as the critics of the Chicago school in the 1930s were led up an empiricist blind alley by attempting to refute Burgess's concentric zone model of urban growth while ignoring the theoretical adequacy of the ecological postulates that lay behind it, so too much of the debate over Wirth's thesis since the war has been theoretically sterile. There is now, as Pahl points out, 'an almost overwhelming body of evidence that the central areas of cities differ from what Wirth and many others have suggested' (Pahl 1968, p. 267). Yet such evidence is of only marginal relevance to an evaluation of Wirth's theory, for it has generally been cited as part of an ultimately misguided and futile attempt to refute an ideal type with empirical data.

Such evidence falls mainly into two categories. The first concerns those studies (e.g. Young and Willmott 1957, Gans 1962, Abu-Lughod 1961) that have documented the existence of 'rural' ways of life (such as close kinship links or personal friendships among neighbours) in the centre of large cities (in the case of these writers, London, Boston and Cairo respectively). There is now a lot of evidence from a lot of different cities which indicates that what Gans terms 'urban villages' are fairly common, and that Wirth's description of urban ways of life in terms of anonymity, impersonality and so on is not applicable to them.

The second category of evidence concerns studies that have documented 'urban' ways of life in the countryside. Mann (1965, p. 106) provides one such example when he suggests that the residents of the small Surrey village of Forest Row exhibit more 'urban' characteristics in terms of sophistication and a blasé attitude than do the inhabitants of a northern town such as Huddersfield. More pertinently, Lewis (1951) studied the same Mexican village of Tepoztlan that Redfield had studied twenty years earlier (and from which he had derived many of his original conceptions regarding folk society) and found not 'rural' harmony, tranquillity and consensus, but rather a 'pervading quality of fear, envy and distrust in inter-personal relations' (p. 429).

Two points need to be made about these and other similar studies. The first is that, despite the claims often made for them, they are not necessarily inconsistent with Wirth's characterization of urban and rural types. Evidence on the existence of urban villages and what Abu-Lughod terms the 'ruralization of the city' is encompassed by Wirth's argument that one effect of increased density is precisely the creation of a 'mosaic of social worlds' in which groups of similar race, class, status, etc., congregate. Similarly, studies of rural areas that find elements of urban culture can readily be explained in Wirth's approach as the result of the dominance achieved by the city over its hinterland. It is a source of some surprise, therefore, that evidence like this has so often been used in an attempt to counter the description of city life that Wirth provides.

The second point is that, even if such data were not consistent with the image of urban life that Wirth presents, they would not constitute a refutation of his theory, but only a criticism of the usefulness of his concepts. As Sjoberg has recognized, 'We must not confuse an analytical distinction with empirical reality' (1964, p. 131). To repeat once again, Wirth did not argue that ways of life in cities were necessarily anonymous, superficial, transitory and segmental; only that it was in terms of such characteristics that he wished to conceptualize the notion of urbanism. If Bethnal Green is not like that then, from this perspective, Bethnal Green is not highly urban (though from another perspective, such as one that conceptualized urbanism in terms of atmospheric pollution or mileage of made-up roads, it clearly would be).

This, however, does raise the first significant question-mark against Wirth's approach, in that we may validly ask how useful or fruitful such a conceptualization of the urban really is. We cannot disprove an ideal type, but if we doubt its relevance to empirical research we are most certainly justified in ignoring it.

One problem with his conceptualization of the urban, and with the very notion of a continuum between two ideal types of urban and rural, is that it is indiscriminate. This has been recognized both by those who defend an approach based on rural–urban distinctions (e.g. Miner 1952, Jones 1973) and by those, such as Lewis, who attack it. The problem is that many different variables are clustered together at each pole of the continuum, but it cannot be assumed that they are all interdependent and that they will all vary consistently with each other. Lewis, for example, suggests that it is logically and empirically possible for a society to exist with both a high degree of homogeneity and of individualism, and he concludes that 'The concept "urban" is too much of a catchall to be useful for cultural analysis' (1951, p. 434). This argument was subsequently reinforced by Duncan (1957), who showed not only that 'urban' and 'rural' charactertistics did not always vary consistently with each other, but also that they did not even exhibit a continuous gradation.

A second problem with this mode of conceptualization, also noted by Lewis, is that it appears too narrow to be useful. Thus Lewis accounted for much of the difference between his and Redfield's descriptions of Tepoztlan in terms of the limitations imposed upon the scope of Redfield's observation by his commitment to the organizing principle of the folk–urban continuum. According to him, the process of change in Mexican society is far too complex to be reduced to a single principle: 'There is no single formula which will explain the whole range of phenomena' (Lewis 1951, p. 445). Of course, Weber argued when he developed the ideal type as the distinctive method of sociological analysis that an all-embracing view of the social world was impossible, and that it was precisely the function of an ideal type to identify and isolate those aspects of reality that the researcher found most relevant to his concerns. Lewis's argument is that the use of urban and folk types fails to identify the most significant aspects for study.

A third criticism concerns not so much the usefulness of the concepts of urban and rural as their evaluative character. To quote Lewis's critique of Redfield once again, 'Again and again in Redfield's writings there emerges the value judgement that folk societies are good and urban societies bad. It is assumed that all folk societies are integrated while urban societies are the great disorganizing force' (1951, p. 435). This is a common criticism made against those who employ rural–urban contrasts, although it appears less applicable in the case of Wirth (who was careful to point to the positive aspects of urbanism, especially the growth of individual freedom, as well as its negative side) than it does to Redfield. Without wishing to enter the long debate over value-freedom in the social sciences (which I have discussed briefly in Saunders 1979, pp. 338–46), it should nevertheless be noted that the ideal type method is inherently evaluative (see Chapter 1). The decision to emphasize certain aspects of 'urbanism' and to ignore others is a decision that is necessarily grounded in value, and while we may wish to take issue with the values that guide and interpret work such as that by Redfield or Wirth, it is hardly a valid criticism to attack them for an evaluative bias *per se*.

Despite these various criticisms, therefore, it may be suggested that the main problems with Wirth's approach concern not his mode of conceptualization but the adequacy of his theoretical explanation. The problem here is that Wirth fails to demonstrate that size, density and heterogeneity are the key determinants of the ways of life he describes; both Morris (1968) and Reissman (1964) argue that the same characteristics could be deduced from many other variables that are similarly commonly associated with cities (for example technology, economic rationality and so on). This line of criticism has been developed most fully by Gans and Pahl.

Gans levels three fundamental criticisms against Wirth's analysis:

First, the conclusions derived from a study of the inner city cannot be generalised to the entire urban area. Second, there is as yet not enough evidence to prove – nor, admittedly, to deny – that number, density and heterogeneity result in the social consequences which Wirth proposed. Finally, even if the causal relationship could be verified, it can be shown that a significant proportion of the city's inhabitants were, and are, isolated from these consequences by social structures and cultural patterns which they either brought to the city, or developed by living in it. [Gans 1968, pp. 98–9]

Of these three points, the third is ultimately most significant.

Gans illustrates his first point, concerning Wirth's spurious generalization from statements about the inner city to a theory of the city as a whole, by citing evidence on social relationships in outer city and suburban areas which shows that ways of life in these areas, though not entirely intimate, are nevertheless not entirely anonymous and impersonal either. Gans then coins the term 'quasi-primary' to describe these relationships in which 'interaction is more intimate than a secondary contact, but more guarded than a primary one' (1968, p. 104).

His second point, which relates to the dubious adequacy of size, density and heterogeneity as explanatory variables in those cases where ways of life do approximate Wirth's ideal type of urbanism, is developed by arguing that the key characteristic of parts of the inner city is their residential instability, and that this factor (which itself gives rise to heterogeneity) constitutes a more adequate explanation than Wirth's three variables:

Under conditions of transience and heterogeneity, people interact only in terms of the segmental roles necessary for obtaining local services. Their social relationships thus display anonymity, impersonality and super-ficiality. The social features of Wirth's concept of urbanism seem therefore to be a result of residential instability, rather than of number, density or heterogeneity. [Gans 1968, p. 103]

The important implication of this argument is that 'urban' ways of life may be expected to develop wherever there is residential instability, irrespective of whether it occurs in the city or in the countryside. Gans's second point therefore throws into doubt the validity of any attempt to develop a theory of the city in order to account for ways of life found within it, and it is this theme that is developed more fully by his third point.

His third argument is that, even if Wirth's three variables could be shown to affect the quality of social relationships, this can be the case only where certain social and cultural factors obtain. To illustrate this point, he distinguishes between five types of inner city residents, all of whom live in densely populated and socially heterogeneous surroundings. The cosmopolites, such as students, intellectuals and professionals, choose to live in the inner city because of its proximity to the cultural centre. Young unmarrieds and childless couples, on the other hand, tend to live there until they start a family, at which point they remove to the suburbs. Both of these first two groups therefore reside in the inner city by choice but are largely detached from it, either because their interests lie outside their immediate environment, or because they are located there only temporarily. The third group is the urban villagers, who are in, but not of, the city, and who form a relatively self-contained and homogeneous enclave within which ways of life continue relatively unaffected by the surrounding urban environment. Like the first two groups, therefore, they too remain virtually immune from the effects Wirth described. Only the last two groups – the deprived (who are forced by their material circumstances to live in inner-city slum areas) and the trapped (usually elderly people who remain behind in deteriorating inner neighbourhoods) – are susceptible to the sorts of factors Wirth analysed, for they are not detached from their surrounding environment.

What emerges from this argument is that, even in the inner city, many residents enjoy a choice as regards their physical location and the way of life they adopt, and that, the greater the choice available, the less significant do Wirth's three variables become. Gans therefore shifts analysis of social relationships in the city from identification of the determinants of ways of life to the study of choice as a way of life. In this way, he suggests that the most significant factors explaining variations in social relationships are the sociological variables of class and life-cycle: 'If people have an opportunity to choose, these two characteristics will go far in explaining the kinds of housing and neighbourhoods they will occupy and the ways of life they will try to establish within them' (p. 111).

For Gans, then, where people do not enjoy choice their ways of life will reflect the degree of residential instability of their neighbourhoods, and where they do social patterns will be a function of factors such as class and life-cycle. In neither case will size, density and heterogeneity appear as particularly significant explanatory variables. It follows from this that the explanation of social and cultural forms in the city cannot be accomplished through an analysis of inherent characteristics of the city: 'If ways of life do not coincide with settlement types, and if these ways are functions of class and life-cycle stage rather than of the ecological attributes of the settlement, a sociological definition of the city cannot be formulated .... The sociologist cannot, therefore, speak of an urban or suburban way of life' (pp. 114–15).

This conclusion is reasserted by Pahl, who argues that the

explanation of social patterns in any given locality can be achieved only through analysis of social structure. Concepts of urban and rural thus appear of little value as analytical frameworks, and are positively misleading when used as explanatory variables: 'It is clear it is not so much communities that are acted upon as groups and individuals at particular places in the social structure. Any attempt to tie particular patterns of social relationships to specific geographical milieux is a singularly fruitless exercise' (Pahl 1968, p. 293).

Pahl therefore agrees with Gans that social relationships have to be explained with reference to sociological factors, and that geographical and environmental theories are essentially misconceived. However, he also takes Gans's argument several stages further, first by pointing to factors other than class and life-cycle which must be taken into account in any analysis (e.g. divisions between traditional residents and newcomers and the different patterns of social networks between locals and cosmopolitans), and second by indicating the direction in which urban sociology should develop. For Pahl, local social processes are important in affecting people's lives, and what Stacey (1969) later termed 'local social systems' are therefore an important area of study. But both Pahl and Stacey emphasize that the analysis of localities must take into account the relationship that exists between them and the wider society, for 'in any locality study some of the social processes we shall want to consider will take us outside the locality' (Stacey 1969, p. 145). It follows from this that the important distinction around which research should be oriented concerns not whether a particular locality is 'urban' or 'rural', but rather the relationship between the local and the national: 'I can find little universal evidence of a rural–urban continuum, which even as a classificatory device seems to be of little value. Of much greater importance is the notion of a fundamental distinction between the local and the national' (Pahl 1968, p. 285). As we shall see in Chapter 4, this distinction lies at the heart of Pahl's subsequent attempt to specify a distinctive area of interest for urban sociology, for he argues that 'Since people will always have their lives shaped by a combination of national and local influences and processes, a sub-discipline will continue – and this implies a convergence between rural and urban sociology – under whatever name' (p. 287). It is Pahl's view, in other words, that while an urban sociology cannot be founded upon the notion of a distinctive urban culture, there is nevertheless a conceptual space for a sub-discipline which focuses upon the combination of local and national processes and their effects on individuals' life chances.

Before we proceed to consider this claim in the next chapter, we should however pause to consider two final questions regarding the arguments discussed in this. The first is why, if the rural–urban distinction is essentially spurious, it nevertheless occupies such a central place in Western culture? Ideas like this cannot achieve dominance in people's conceptions of their world unless they are in some way related to aspects of their everyday experience of that world. So we must ask to what, if anything, does the urban–rural dichotomy refer? Second, and in part related to this, we should also consider whether physical factors such as the size of human settlements are really totally irrelevant to an understanding of different patterns of social relationships, for there is a danger in following the critiques offered by writers such as Gans and Pahl that we throw the (albeit small) baby out with the bathwater.

On the question of why rural–urban imagery remains so pervasive in Western culture, we can do no better than refer to Williams's argument in the final chapter of *The Country and the City* (1973). Williams suggests that the resilience of this imagery points to a real division in our experience and to a fundamental need which that division creates: 'Clearly the contrast of country and city is one of the major forms in which we become conscious of a central part of our experience and of the crises of our society . . . the persistence indicates some permanent or effectively permanent need, to which the changing interpretations speak' (1973, p. 289). It is through reference to the physical forms of the country and the city that 'experience finds material which gives body to the thoughts' (p. 291).

According to Williams, the experience from which this imagery derives and to which it relates is that of social relationships in a capitalist society. Capitalism divorces a necessary materialism from a necessary humanity, and this division is expressed, not only in the dichotomy of work and leisure, week and weekend, society and individual, but also in that between town and country:

The pull of the idea of the country is towards old ways, human ways, natural ways. The pull of the idea of the city is towards progress, modernisation, development. In what is then a tension, a present experienced as tension, we use the contrast of country and city to ratify an unresolved division and conflict of impulses, which it might be better to face on its own terms. [Williams 1973, p. 297]

Leading our everyday lives in the context of a capitalist mode of production, we come to accept as normal the 'modes of detached, separated, external perception and action: modes of using and consuming rather than accepting and enjoying people and things' (p. 298). Alienation is the accepted condition. Yet elements of the suppressed humanity remain – in childhood memories, in occasional communality when collectively we are threatened, and so on. It is this recurring sense that 'one is not necessarily a stranger and an agent, but can be a member, a discoverer, in a shared source of life' (p. 298) which becomes displaced into the representation of the country and the subsequent antithesis between it and the town: 'Unalienated experience is the rural past and realistic experience is the urban future' (p. 298). The rural–urban contrast is therefore the ideology through which we live and interpret our alienated existence under capitalism. It follows from this, of course, that those sociological theories that are premised upon this contrast are themselves in their function 'ideological' (see Chapter 5).

This need not imply, however, that these theories have no basis in reality. It is one thing to argue that differences in the size and density of human settlements cannot provide an adequate explanation for variations in ways of life, but quite another to conclude from that that they are therefore irrelevant. Simmel's analysis of the changes wrought by an increase in the size of any human aggregate undoubtedly has some validity, and Gans appears to recognize this when he notes that social differences between residents cannot entirely account for variations in social patterns which 'must therefore be attributed to features of the settlement' (Gans 1968, p. 112). Similarly Pahl (1968, p. 273) notes that status group interaction will tend to be more marked in a small settlement, while elsewhere (1975, p. 91) he lists some of the significant differences in life chances (e.g. in terms of availability of local services, the range of occupational choice and so on) between urban and rural areas which follow directly from the differences between them in terms of population density. While we are surely right to reject the division between rural and urban cultures as the basis for an urban social theory, it does nevertheless appear that there are certain differences between them that can be explained in terms of factors such as size and density.

What is basically at fault with the theories of Simmel, Wirth, Redfield and other similar writers is not that they chose to focus their attention on, say, the question of how size affects the pattern of social relationships, but that they failed to recognize the very limited scope of such an approach and in consequence attempted to explain a wide range of culturally variable phenomena through an illegitimate physical reduction. As Dewey recognized some years ago, 'The inclusion of both population and cultural bases in the term "urbanism" renders it useless except for labelling time-bound phenomena' (1960, p. 64).

Dewey argues that, other things being equal, variations in the size of human settlements do tend to be reflected in the degree of anonymity, differentiation, heterogeneity, impersonality and universalism of social relationships within them, but that the sorts of cultural factors that have been identified by various writers as 'urban' or 'rural' have nothing to do with size:

There is no such thing as urban culture or rural culture, but only various culture contents somewhere on the rural–urban continuum. The movement of zoot suits, jass and antibiotics from city to country is no more a spread of urbanism than is the transfer or diffusion of blue jeans, square dancing and tomatoes to the cities a movement of ruralism to urban centres. [Dewey 1960, p. 65]

If Dewey's argument is accepted, then it does seem that we should draw back a little from Pahl's somewhat sweeping assertion that the analysis of social relationships in terms of physical location is a singularly fruitless exercise. The size and density of settlement does have some effect on patterns of social relationships and, indeed, on the distribution of life chances. However, it also follows from Dewey's analysis that the scope of these effects is limited, for it does not take us very far to suggest that anonymity is more characteristic of life in cities than of life in small rural settlements, or that social differentiation tends to be more marked in large towns than in small villages. As Dewey observes, 'No evidence suggests that these concepts can acquire more than incidental importance in the understanding of the complexities of human relations in cities or hamlets' (1960, p. 66). Furthermore, 'It may occur to one that, if this be all that there is to the rural–urban continuum, it is of minor importance for sociology. He would be quite correct' (p. 66).

The most judicious conclusion, then, would appear to be that, while there is no distinctively urban culture and thus no basis in the work of Simmel or Wirth for development of a specifically urban social theory, it is nevertheless possible to identify a small range of questions in which the issue of population size and density remains pertinent. It is, however, doubtful whether such questions can constitute the basis for a specific theory or sub-discipline, for not only are the social implications of size very limited, but it may also be suggested that any attempt to analyse them will involve not an urban theory but a social–psychological theory in which spatial factors are taken into account as one among several variables. In other words, the size of human settlements is just one factor among many which may have some effect on the pattern of social relationships, and there appears little justification for isolating it as the object of intensive and specialized study. It is for this reason that we may endorse Dewey's argument that the effects identified by cultural theories of urban–rural differences are 'real but relatively unimportant'.

4   The urban as a socio-spatial system

For many years following the Second World War, urban sociology was unmistakably in decline as it became increasingly isolated from developments within the discipline as a whole. Following the demise of Chicago ecology and the lingering but finally inevitable collapse of the rural–urban continuum, urban sociology staggered on as an institutionally recognized sub-discipline within sociology departments, yet its evident lack of a theoretically specific area of study resulted in a diverse and broad sweep across a range of concerns that shared nothing in common save that they could all be studied in cities. Urban sociology became the study of everything that happened in 'urban' areas – changing patterns of kinship, political controversies over land use, educational deprivation among the working class, social isolation in council tower blocks – and it therefore became indistinct from the sociological analysis of advanced, industrial capitalist societies. The 'urban' was everywhere and nowhere, and the sociology of the urban thus studied everything and nothing. As Pahl observed, 'It is as if sociologists cannot define urban without a rural contrast: when they lose the peasant they lose the city too' (1975, p. 199).

Given this context, it is not surprising that urban sociologists (in Britain at least) reacted with considerable enthusiasm and not a little gratitude to the publication in 1967 of a book that aimed partly to contribute to the sociology of race relations, but which also set out to develop a new sociological approach to the analysis of the city. *Race, Community and Conflict*, written by John Rex and Robert Moore, reported a study of housing and race relations in an inner-city area of Birmingham called Sparkbrook. In it they developed a theoretical framework which represented a fusion between Burgess's work in Chicago on the zone of transition and Weber's sociological emphasis on the meaningful actions of individuals, and in this way they laid the foundations for an urban sociology which could retain its distinctive concern with the spatial dimension to social relationships while at the same time drawing upon a body of theory located within mainstream sociology in order to analyse such relationships.

Spatial structure and social structure

For Rex and Moore, the significance of the Chicago school in general, and of the work of Burgess in particular, lies in their recognition that, in the course of its historical development, the city becomes differentiated into distinct sub-communities which are spatially segregated into various zones or sectors, and which are associated with particular types of residents who collectively exhibit particular kinds of culture. Rex and Moore take this insight as the starting-point for their theory of the city, and they suggest that 'In the initial settlement of the city, three different groups, differentially placed with regard to the possession of property, become segregated from one another and work out their own community style of life' (1967, p. 8). These three groups are, first, the upper middle class, who own relatively large houses located near the cultural and business centre but away from the factories and other negative urban amenities; second, the working class, who rent small terraced cottages and whose common experience of economic adversity generates a strong sense of collective identity and mutual support; and, third, the lower middle class, who rent their houses but who aspire to the way of life of the bourgeois home-owners.

Like Park and Burgess, Rex and Moore suggest that the process of city growth involves the migration of population from central to outlying areas. In part this is due to the expansion of the central business district, but it is also due to the widespread pursuit of a middle-class way of life which becomes associated with the newly developing suburbs. Thus, while the professionals and the 'captains of industry' move out to detached houses in the inner suburbs, the lower middle class (who can gain access to credit for house purchase) move further out to semi-detached suburbia, and the working class (whose growing political muscle comes to be reflected in the provision of state housing) similarly relocate to a 'new public suburbia' (p. 9). As a result of this 'great urban game of leapfrog' (Rex 1968, p. 213), the various types of nineteenth-century housing around the city centre are abandoned to new users. The imposing homes of the bourgeoisie become swallowed up by the encroaching central business district, while the houses once occupied by the lower middle class are bought up and sublet as lodging houses accommodating new migrants into the city. In this way, inner-city zones like Sparkbrook are gradually transformed into 'twilight areas', characterized by physical decay of short-life properties and by growing concentrations of immigrant population.

Central to Rex and Moore's theory is their assertion that 'the city does to some extent share a unitary status-value system' (1967, p. 9) in the sense that the move to the suburbs is an aspiration that is general among all groups of residents: 'The persistent outward movement which takes place justifies us in saying and positing as central to our model that suburban housing is a scarce and desired resource' (Rex 1968, p. 214). If suburban housing is widely desired, however, it is clear that it is not widely available. It is a scarce resource, and access to it is unequally distributed among the population. Two key points follow directly from this. First, if desirable housing is in short supply, then the means whereby it is allocated to different sections of the population become crucial to an understanding of the distribution of life chances in the city. Second, it is clear that the pattern of housing distribution constitutes the basis for at least potential conflict between different groups demanding access to the same resource. It was by pointing to the significance of these two questions of access and conflict that Rex and Moore provided urban sociology with a new orientation to the analysis of urban processes; an orientation that was inherently political in the fundamental concerns it raised.

Their analysis of the question of access to scarce and desirable housing indicated the importance of two principal criteria. The first was size and security of income, for it was largely on this basis that those institutions (e.g. the building societies) that controlled the allocation of credit for house purchase determined whether or not individuals could achieve access to the private owner-occupied housing sector. In general, the income criterion could be expected to operate in favour of middle class and relatively well paid skilled manual workers. The second criterion related to 'housing need' and length of residence, for need and residence qualifications were laid down by local authorities as conditions of access to good standard public housing. Thus, in Birmingham at the time of the research, the housing department operated a five-year residence rule which effectively rendered recent immigrants from the West Indies and the Indian sub-continent ineligible for council housing. Furthermore, even those immigrants who could satisfy the local authority's criteria then had to negotiate a further hurdle represented by the housing visitor whose job it was to grade applicants according to their suitability for different qualities of council accommodation, and this often resulted in black families being offered sub-standard short-life housing in inner-city clearance areas. The only other means of access to council housing was by being rehoused as part of a local authority slum clearance programme, and even this channel was often closed off to immigrants as a result of the council's apparent policy of clearing predominantly white areas while leaving areas of black concentration to continue deteriorating.

Rex and Moore's analysis of access to desirable housing thus suggested that, while the white middle class could generally gain entry to the owner-occupied sector in the suburban areas through the market mode of allocation, and while the white working class could usually secure access to council housing on suburban estates via the bureaucratic mode of allocation, there was nevertheless a residual group in the population (in which immigrants were heavily over-represented) that was effectively deprived entry to either of these desirable housing tenures. This third category could not therefore fulfil the general aspiration for suburban life, and was instead obliged to seek accommodation in the inner-city zone of transition.

According to Rex and Moore, the first cohort of immigrants to arrive in the city, faced with their effective exclusion from both the owner-occupied and local authority sectors, were forced either to seek private rented accommodation or to purchase the large deteriorating houses in areas like Sparkbrook which had been vacated owing to the middle-class flight to the suburbs. Because such purchases could not be arranged through building societies, however, they had therefore to turn to alternative sources of finance which entailed their accepting short-term loans at high rates of interest. The high repayments on such loans in turn necessitated sub-division and multi-occupation of the houses: 'Buying a house of this kind was possible only if the owner proceeded to let rooms. Once he did this he found himself meeting a huge demand from other immigrants' (1967, p. 30). Certain areas thus soon became characterized by multi-occupation, and the housing stock began to deteriorate even more quickly. Furthermore, as more immigrants moved into an area, so more indigenous families moved out. In Birmingham, as elsewhere, particular inner-city areas thus swiftly became associated with large concentrations of minority groups living in poor quality lodging houses.

In contrast to suburban owner-occupation, which is legitimated by the core values of a 'property-owning democracy', and purpose-built council housing, which is legitimated by values of welfare statism, such lodging house areas are, according to Rex and Moore, deemed to be illegitimate forms of tenure by radicals and conservatives alike: 'Both unite . . . in condemning the "bad landlords" who operate the system, and also the tenants for their failure to obtain better housing' (p. 40). The response of the local authority is therefore to insulate such areas in an attempt to stop them spreading into surrounding neighbourhoods, and thus to consolidate the formation of ghettos. The local authority therefore acts against the very group – the lodging house landlords – who provide housing for those (like themselves) who fall between the two stools of market and bureaucratic allocation: 'The city, having failed to deal with its own housing problem, turns on those upon whom it relies to make alternative provision, and punishes them for its own failure' (p. 41). Immigrant landlords, who were forced into landlordism because of the lack of alternative strategies for achieving accommodation, thus become convenient scapegoats for the inadequacies of the housing system.

It follows from Rex and Moore's analysis that the twilight zones of the city come to be populated by four distinct housing groups: tenants of nineteenth-century working-class housing, inhabitants of short-life slum property (often owned by the local authority) awaiting demolition, lodging-house landlords, and lodging-house tenants. While there are obvious sources of conflict between these groups (for instance between tenants and landlords over rents, repairs, etc.), all four appear disadvantaged as compared with suburban owner-occupiers and council tenants on purpose-built estates. All four are frustrated in their general desire for suburban living. The effect of local authority planning and public health policies, which are designed to restrict the growth of the twilight areas, and of its housing policies, which function to prevent certain groups from gaining access to more desirable forms of housing, is to exacerbate this comparative disadvantage and to foster the conditions for more intense conflict over the housing issue: 'Any attempt to segregate the inhabitants of this area permanently is bound to involve conflict. The long term destiny of a city which frustrates the desire to improve their status by segregationist policies is some sort of urban riot' (Rex and Moore 1967, p. 9).

The basic social processes within the city therefore relate to the allocation of scarce and desirable housing, both through the market and by bureaucratic means, and to the resulting struggle over housing by different groups located at different points in the housing hierarchy. As we shall see later, Rex and Moore suggested that this struggle over housing could be analysed as a class struggle over the distribution of life chances in the city. In other words, just as class struggles occurred in the world of work with respect to the distribution of life chances, so too they occurred in the realm of consumption of housing.

The significance of Rex and Moore's study is two-fold. First, by emphasizing housing as an important, and analytically distinct, area in which individuals' life chances were determined, they located the theoretical concerns of urban sociology firmly within the traditional concerns of mainstream sociology with the sources of inequality and class conflict (see Harloe 1975, p. 2). Second, they showed how the spatial structure of the city articulated with its social organization through the system of housing allocation: 'The housing market represents, analytically, a point at which the social organisation and the spatial structure of the city intersect' (Haddon 1970, p. 118). In this way they laid the foundations for a new approach to urban sociology, although it was left to Pahl to draw out a conceptualization of the urban system which remained largely implicit in their study.

Like Rex and Moore, Pahl argues that the city is a source of new inequalities over and above those generated in the world of work, although like them he also recognizes that wage inequalities are an important factor determining urban inequalities. His argument is that individuals' life chances are affected by their relative access to sources of indirect, as well as direct, income; those who have to travel long distances to work (such as central city service workers who cannot afford to live in central areas) are therefore worse off than those who can choose to live near their employment, just as those who live near to positive public resources such as shops, parks and so on are better off than those who live near to negative ones such as gasworks or motorways. While high wages enable people to buy privileged access to positive urban resources, it is also the case that, in a country like Britain, allocation of public resources by the state is also important in distributing life chances. The task of urban sociology, therefore, is to study the distributional patterns of urban inequalities as these are affected by both market and bureaucratic processes: 'Urban sociologists are concerned with the basic constraints which affect people's life chances in urban areas, in so far as these fall into a pattern' (Pahl 1970, p. 53).

For Pahl, as for Rex and Moore, the city can be conceptualized as a relatively discrete local social system (see Elliott and McCrone 1975, p. 32). This does not imply that the city can be studied independently of the wider society of which it forms a part (the fact that Pahl recognizes that people's position in the occupational structure strongly influences their position in the urban system indicates his awareness of the need to understand the relationship between city and society). Indeed, Pahl has criticized traditional urban sociology for making precisely this assumption: 'Paradoxically, the fundamental error of urban sociology was to look to the city for an understanding of the city. Rather, the city should be seen as an arena, an understanding of which helps in the understanding of the overall society which creates it' (1975, pp. 234–5). Like Stacey, therefore, Pahl's position is that, while the urban system cannot be divorced from the wider society, there are nevertheless important processes within it which can be identified and analysed in their own right (see page 105).

The most fundamental of these processes concerns the distribution of scarce urban resources. Thus Pahl defines the city as 'A given context or configuration of reward-distributing systems which have space as a significant component' (1975, p. 10). There are three main implications of this approach.

First, space remains an important factor in Pahl's analysis. It has consistently been a basic feature of his approach that space is inherently unequal since no two people can occupy the same location in relation to the provision of any facility. This is why, according to his definition, an urban resource must have a spatial component. Urban sociology does not, therefore, study all allocative or distributive systems: 'Housing and transportation are elements in my view of the city; family allowances and pension schemes are not' (p. 10). The specificity of urban sociology lies in its concern with the patterns of distribution of those resources that are inherently unequal owing to their necessary location in a spatial context.

Given that inequalities in the distribution of urban resources are inevitable, it follows that spatial constraints on life chances will always operate to some extent independently of the mode of economic and political organization in society: 'It is central to my argument that these spatial constraints on the distribution of resources operate to a greater or lesser degree independently of the economic and political order. . . . These constraints can be ameliorated by political intervention but such intervention cannot totally negate their effects' (Pahl 1975, p. 249). Both capitalist and socialist societies are confronted with the operation of this spatial logic, and both may therefore encounter similar problems with regard to the distribution of urban facilities: 'The process of resource allocation has certain common elements no matter what the scale of organization or the specific mode of production with which we are concerned' (Pahl 1979, p. 34). It is for this reason that the results of state intervention in the urban system may be similar in very different types of society, and that the actual effects of policies may fall far short of the original intentions behind them' (see Pahl 1977a, p. 154).

Pahl does not, however, argue for a spatial or ecological determinism, for the second implication of this approach is that, although urban resources will always be unequally distributed, the question of *how* they are distributed is largely a function of the actions of those individuals who occupy strategic allocative locations in the social system. A pattern of social distribution is thus superimposed upon an underlying spatial logic. In the urban system, there are various 'gatekeepers' whose decisions determine degrees of access of different sections of the population to different types of crucial urban resources, and the task of urban sociology is therefore to study their goals and values in order to explain resulting patterns of distribution: 'We agree that certain urban resources will always be scarce and that social and spatial constraints will mutually reinforce one another whatever the distribution of power in society may be. However, given that certain managers are in a position to determine goals, what are these goals and on what values are they based?' (Pahl 1975, p. 208).

The third implication of Pahl's approach is that conflict over the distribution of urban resources is inevitable in any society. This is because such resources are crucial in the determination of individuals' life chances, yet are inevitably scarce and unequally distributed: 'Fundamental life chances are affected by the type and nature of access to facilities and resources and this situation is likely to create conflict in a variety of forms and contexts' (Pahl 1975, p. 204). Whether or not this conflict becomes manifest through conscious and politically organized struggles is for Pahl an open question, for distinct patterns of urban inequalities are not always immediately visible, and different groups may appear to be relatively more privileged in respect of the allocation of one type of resource and less privileged in relation to another. However, Pahl does suggest that, in future years, consciousness of common urban deprivations may develop, in which case conflicts between the managers and the managed in the urban system will increase: 'I am not certain whether a distinctive class struggle over the means of access to scarce urban resources and facilities could emerge . . . but increasingly political pressure may be less to reduce inequalities at the work place than to reduce inequalities at the place of residence' (1975, p. 257).

These three elements – spatial constraints on, social allocation of, and conflict over, the distribution of life chances in the urban system – together constitute Pahl's framework for urban sociological analysis. For Pahl, the urban is to be conceptualized as a socio-spatial system which generates patterns of inequality in the distribution of life chances over and above the inequalities generated in the sphere of production. He summarizes his perspective in the following terms:

(a) There are fundamental *spatial* constraints on access to scarce urban resources and facilities. Such constraints are generally expressed in time/cost distance. (b) There are fundamental *social* constraints on access to scarce urban facilities. These reflect the distribution of power in society and are illustrated by: bureaucratic rules and procedures [and] social gatekeepers who help to distribute and control urban resources. (c). . . . The situation which is structured out of (a) and (b) may be called a socio-spatial or socio-ecological system. Populations limited in this access to scarce urban resources and facilities are the *dependent* variable; those controlling access, the *managers* of the system, would be the independent variable. (d) Conflict in the urban system is inevitable. [Pahl 1975, p. 201]

Taken together, the work of Rex and Moore and Pahl provides a distinctive focus for urban sociology which combines an emphasis on the sociological significance of spatial distribution of population and resources with the familiar Weberian concerns with the goals and values of individual actors and the distribution of life chances in society. In particular, this body of work has served to focus attention within urban sociology on two questions: first, the significance of urban managers as allocators of life chances, and, second, the significance of patterns of urban resource distribution for the development of new forms of class struggle. It is to an examination of these two themes that the remainder of this chapter is devoted.

Urban managers: independent, dependent or intervening variables?

We have seen that, in his original conception, Pahl saw urban managers as the independent variables of analysis. In other words, the explanation of any given pattern of resource distribution could be achieved through analysis of the goals and values of strategically placed allocators and controllers of the stock of scarce and desired urban facilities. Thus: 'A truly *urban* sociology should be concerned with the social and spatial constraints on access to scarce urban resources and facilities as dependent variables and the managers or controllers of the urban system, which I take as the independent variable' (Pahl 1975, p. 210). This position was, of course, entirely consistent with that of Rex and Moore, who identified the actions of housing managers, housing visitors, planners, building society managers and so on as the source of the inequalities of opportunity in Birmingham's housing system.

As regards the identification of crucial urban managers, Pahl's original work suggested that a wide range of individuals, working in both the private and the public sectors, controlled access to key urban resources such as housing, and that the task for research was to discover the extent to which these different gatekeepers shared common ideologies and therefore acted consistently with each other in generating and perpetuating definite patterns of bias and disadvantage in respect to different sections of the population:

The crucial urban types are those who control or manipulate scarce resources and facilities such as housing managers, estate agents, local government officers, property developers, representatives of building societies and insurance companies, youth employment officers, social workers, magistrates, councillors and so on. These occupations and professions should be studied comparatively to discover how far their ideologies are consistent, how far they conflict with each other and how far they help to confirm a stratification order in urban situations. [Pahl 1975, p. 206]

This perspective stimulated and encompassed much fruitful research (see Williams 1978 for a brief summary). Some studies focused on gatekeepers in the private sector; Ford (1975), for example, showed how building society managers were socialized into a value system that defined certain types of applicants for mortgages as bad risks; Elliott and McCrone (1975) analysed the motives and values of private landlords in Edinburgh; and so on. Other research concentrated on the actions of political leaders and state employees in local government; Davies (1972), for example, showed how planners in the Rye Hill area of Newcastle imposed their values in the name of the client population; Young and Kramer (1978) showed how the ideologists of suburban political elites in London led them to frustrate attempts by the Greater London Council to decentralize council housing; and so on. Some research (notably that by Harloe,

Issacharoff and Minns, 1974) took up Pahl's call for comparative research and engaged in analysis of both private and public sector gatekeepers in order to discover how far a comprehensive housing policy was possible.

Increasingly, however, such research encountered two problems on which Pahl's urban managerialism thesis provided little effective guidance. The first concerned the identification of urban managers. Should research address itself to the values and goals of those in the top positions in bureaucratic hierarchies who were formally responsible for deciding policies, or should it focus instead on lower-level employees who actually worked at the interface with the client population? Furthermore, should studies of urban managerialism consider the actions of public sector gatekeepers as more significant than those of individuals in private sector agencies or vice versa? What such problems pointed to was the fact that, although he had urged sociologists to consider the actions of crucial urban managers, Pahl had failed to provide any theoretically rigorous criteria by means of which the relative significance of different types of managers could be assessed. As Norman (1975) pointed out, his identification of urban managers was achieved descriptively rather than analytically. Research grounded in this perspective could thus easily degenerate into mindless empiricism, studying one set of empirically determined urban managers after another with no coherent theoretical rationale other than some vague recognition that they all appeared to enjoy some degree of control over allocation of some resource.

The second problem concerned the autonomy of those managers who were selected for study. Pahl did, of course, recognize that, although they could be treated as independent variables in analysis, urban managers were nevertheless constrained to some degree by the operation of a spatial logic which contained its own inherent inequalities. Later research, however, indicated that the context of constraint was much broader than this. Harloe *et al.* (1974), for example, found that, while the ideologies of those involved in the supply of housing were important in determining their actions, so too were the organizational constraints upon them, in terms both of the availability of resources such as land and finance, and of the limitations imposed on their choice of action by other organizations with which they interacted. What this and other studies tended to suggest, therefore, was that urban managers in the public sector at least were restricted in their actions by the operation of market processes in the private sector (for example, land for public housing had to be purchased at current market prices, finance for such schemes had to be raised from the private capital market at current rates of interest, and so on), and by the organizational structure in which they were located (for example, many areas of policy were strictly regulated by higher-level governmental agencies). Given such constraints, the designation of urban managers as independent variables began to look somewhat dubious.

These two problems of identification and autonomy led Pahl to introduce two important refinements in his later work on urban managerialism. First, he distinguishes between managers in the private sector and those in the local state sector and restricts his definition of urban managers to those in the latter category. Second, he recognizes that local state bureaucrats have to operate under the constraints imposed by their relations with the private sector and central government. In this way, he moves from an analysis of urban managers as independent variables to one that conceptualizes them as intervening variables mediating between, on the one hand, the contradictory pressures of private sector profitability and social needs, and on the other the demands of central government and the local population:

It seems to me that one set of urban managers and technical experts must play crucial *mediating roles* both between the state and the private sector and between central state authority and the local population. Another set of private managers control access to capital and other resources. . . . The attempt to focus on the relationship between market distributive systems and 'rational' distributive systems, seeing the urban managers as the essential mediators between and manipulators of the two systems, is extremely interesting. [Pahl 1977c, p. 55]

This shift in Pahl's approach is a significant one, for while he continues to see the analysis of the goals, values and actions of local state employees as a valid and useful area of research, he does so only in so far as such an analysis is situated in a broader theoretical framework in which the key variables are the state and the capitalist economy. Thus he criticizes his own earlier formulation for its focus on the 'middle dogs' to the exclusion of the 'top dogs', and for its neglect of the constraints imposed upon public policy by the operation of national and international capitalism. At best, he suggests, local authority officers 'only have slight, negative influence over the deployment of private capital, and their powers of bargaining with central government for more resources from public funds are limited' (Pahl 1975, p. 269). To locate responsibility for urban inequalities and the urban crisis in the actions of local state employees is, he argues, 'rather like the workers stoning the house of the chief personnel manager when their industry faces widespread redundancies through the collapse of world markets' (1975, p. 284). Clearly we have moved a long way from an analysis of urban managers as the independent variables of the subject.

In this revised formulation, therefore, urban managers are significant as allocators of resources, but it is recognized that the initial availability of such resources depends upon decisions made by central government and by those who control investment in the private sector. It follows from this that an adequate explanation of the distribution of life chances in the urban system can be achieved only by combining an analysis of the process of allocation at the local level with an analysis of the production of resources in society as a whole. Put another way, if urban managers are no longer the independent variables, then it is necessary to identify those individuals or groups that are. For Pahl, this entails analysis of the changing role of the state in an advanced capitalist society like Britain.

Pahl's argument is that, in Britain at least (for he denies the possibility of developing a single theory of *the* capitalist state given the wide variations between different capitalist societies), lack of investment in the private sector, coupled with the growing intensity of international competition, has increasingly resulted in a qualitative change in the relation between the state and private capital. Britain, he suggests, is developing into a corporatist society:

In general it could certainly be argued until fairly recently that the state was subordinating its intervention to the interests of private capital. However, there comes a point when the continuing and expanding role of the state reaches a level where its power to control investment, knowledge and the allocation of services and facilities gives it an autonomy which enables it to pass beyond its previous subservient and facilitative role. The state manages everyday life less for the support of private capital and more for the independent purposes of the state. . . . Basically the argument is that Britain can best be understood as a corporatist society. [Pahl 1977a, p. 161]

His discussion of the role of the state in the new corporatist society is located firmly within the Weberian tradition of political sociology. In particular it reflects three basic themes in Weber's writings: namely, a conceptualization of the state as an apparatus controlled by individuals with definite aims and motivations; a view of the state's mode of operation in which officials and technical experts are deemed to prevail against elected political leaders; and a commitment to a theory of politics as a realm autonomous of economic class relations.

We saw in Chapter 1 that Weber's approach to sociological explanation rests on the analysis of the goals and values that guide individuals' actions in relation to others. We also noted his ontological commitment to a view of the social world as a moral realm in which individual actors are constantly confronted with choices between irreconcilable values (Weber's 'warring gods'). From these two basic orientations, it is clear that the question of power was central to Weber's entire sociology, for as soon as individuals attempt to achieve transcendent goals (that is, to impose their objectives against those of others), conflict becomes inevitable and power becomes crucial. Thus in Weber's view, power involves the ability of any one actor within a social relationship to realize his will, if necessary against the opposition of others. It is, in other words, a function of the relationship between individuals. When the power of one actor in relation to others becomes sufficiently well established that there is a recurring probability that his commands will be obeyed by them as a matter of course, Weber identifies a relationship based on domination.

Domination over others may be achieved on the basis of economic power (through control of goods and services in demand by others) or of political power. Weber insisted that these two spheres of domination in society were analytically distinct. He denied the Marxist claim that there was a necessary correspondence between them, for although he recognized that historically those who controlled economic resources often also controlled the instruments of state power, he argued that this did not reveal any historical necessity. While economic power is achieved through control of commodity or labour markets, political power is achieved through control of the state and therefore refers to 'the leadership, or the influencing of the leadership, of a political association, hence today of a state' (Weber 1948b, p. 77). Political power, in other words, entails the pursuit of given goals or values by those individuals who are in a position to control or influence state policies. Thus we arrive at the first of Weber's key principles that is carried over into Pahl's analysis: political domination is autonomous of economic class domination.

The second principle develops directly out of this, for it is apparent that, for Weber, the state is a 'thing' to be controlled by individuals.

More accurately, it is a particular type of political association which is characterized by a legally sanctioned monopoly over the use of physical coercion:

Ultimately one can define the modern state sociologically only in terms of the specific means peculiar to it, as to every political association, namely the use of physical force. . . . Of course, force is certainly not the normal or the only means of the state – nobody says that – but force is a means specific to the state . . . a state is a human community that (successfully) claims the monopoly of the legitimate use of physical force within a given territory (1948b, pp. 77–8).

Political domination is therefore achieved by individuals through privileged access to the instruments of state power. In order to understand state policies, therefore, it is necessary to understand the goals and values of certain key individuals. This is reflected in Pahl's argument that the state today manages society according to its own independent purposes. It is also, of course, the logic behind his search for crucial urban managers.

The third aspect of Weber's work that recurs in Pahl's analysis concerns the role of state officials. We saw earlier that, in his reformulation of the concept of urban managers, Pahl came to focus exclusively on the actions of bureaucrats and technical experts who are in the employment of the state. Similarly in his discussion of corporatism, it is clear that Pahl traces the 'independent purposes' of the state to the objectives set by the state bureaucracy through the establishment of various agencies of social and economic planning. This emphasis on the role of the bureaucracy reflects Weber's argument that the growing rationalization and complexity of modern capitalist (or socialist) societies must increasingly be reflected in the rationalization of the state's administration of these societies: 'The question is always who controls the existing bureaucratic machinery. And such control is possible only in a very limited degree to persons who are not technical specialists' (Weber 1968, p. 224).

Weber is resolutely sceptical as regards the claims made on behalf of modern representative democracy, for he argues that direct democratic control over a large and complex state is impossible. Representative assemblies perform just two functions: they are the means for mobilizing the consent of the masses to their own subordination, and they provide the means whereby new political leaders can emerge. Weber therefore rejects the notion of parliaments representing the 'will of the people', and argues instead that the masses vote for leaders rather than policies, and out of emotion rather than calculation. The most successful political leaders are those who have mastered the art of demagogy: 'Democratisation and demagogy belong together' (1968, p. 1450). Elected on the basis of plebiscitary democracy, it is then the task of strong political leaders to attempt to counter the deadening hand of bureaucracy by introducing a spark of creativity into the political process. Political administration in modern society thus exhibits a recurring tension between the official and the charismatic leader, the ethic of responsibility and the ethic of conviction, bureaucracy and democracy, rational administration and value-commitments, in which the power of expertise generally prevails over the power of ideals.

The picture that emerges from Weber's political writings is that of a centralized state imposing goals of efficiency in its administration of ever-widening areas of social and economic life. It is precisely this picture that is developed in Pahl's work on the development of a corporatist society in Britain and which underpins his more recent discussions of the role of urban managers.

Pahl's work on corporatism is contained mainly in two articles (Pahl 1977a, b), although it is carried over into much of his recent work (e.g. 1977c, 1979) and is complemented by papers by Winkler (1976, 1977), who has been mainly responsible for elucidating the basic elements of the theory to which Pahl refers. Taking all this work together, we may discuss the corporatism thesis in terms of the three questions of the causes, functions and mode of operation of the new corporatist state.

There are basically four factors that explain the increased role of the state in managing the British economy. The first is the growing concentration of capital into a small number of large oligopolies such that the fate of the economy as a whole is now bound up with the fate of a handful of companies. The state must therefore act to ensure that these companies continue to generate an adequate rate of return on investment, but in underwriting their profits it must also ensure that it does not create a 'licence to plunder'. Profits, in other words, must be both guaranteed and regulated. Second, the falling rate of profit in the economy as a whole (which the theory does not itself explain) has resulted in private companies seeking state financial aid as alternative sources of investment dry up. In providing capital (for example through the National Enterprise Board), the state has therefore been able to exert its influence over patterns of investment in the private sector. Third, new technological developments, which have themselves spurred on the process of industrial concentration, have generated new problems which have necessitated further state regulation of, and participation in, the private sector. Research and development costs, for example, have escalated to a point where even the largest companies require state aid, while the social implications of new technology in terms of pollution, public safety, levels of employment and so on have necessarily led to increased state involvement. Finally, as we have already seen, the growing intensity of international competition has led private sector firms to seek the support and protection of the state in their search for new markets and their need to consolidate existing ones.

These four factors have not only resulted in a quantitative increase in state economic activity, but have provoked a qualitative shift in its role in relation to the private sector: 'Stripped to its essentials, corporatism is principally defined by one particularly important qualitative change, the shift from a supportive to a directive role for the state in the economy' (Winkler 1976, p. 103). It is fundamental to Pahl's and Winkler's position that the developing corporatist society represents a mode of political and economic organization that is different from that of both capitalism and socialism: while capitalism entails the private control of private property, and socialism entails state control of collective property, corporatism 'is an economic system of private ownership and state control' (ibid., p. 109).

The change in the state's role from the support to the direction of the private sector thus involves a new set of state functions which to some extent challenge some of the basic principles of capitalism. Corporatism replaces the anarchy of the free market with the order of the rational plan; it substitutes predictability for profit maximization; and it undermines traditional elements of capitalist property rights by dictating uses (such as investment) and restricting benefits. In place of the principles of free enterprise and competition, the corporatist state imposes four principles of its own: unity (collaboration and co-operation between the functional interests of capital and labour), order (stability and discipline in, for example, industrial relations), nationalism (defence of the national interest both domestically, against sectional interests, and internationally, against foreign competitors) and success (the dominance of the principle of means by the pragmatism of ends – notably in ensuring efficiency). Not only, therefore, does the state extend its sphere of economic influence and control, but it increasingly directs the economy according to its own non-capitalist criteria.

The mode of corporatist control is hierarchical but essentially non-bureaucratic in the sense that a premium is placed upon flexibility of administration. The state dictates policy but attempts to find others to carry it out, preferably on a 'voluntary' basis. Thus, for example, agreements are reached with the trade union leadership over wages policy, and it is then left to the union bureaucracies to impose or sell the policy to the rank-and-file. Similarly, planning agreements are secured with the largest companies as the means of controlling the economy as a whole. As Winkler puts it,

What appears to be happening is a formalisation of interest group politics; an institutionalisation of pluralism. And, indeed, within co-optive institutions, the state will have to bargain and make compromises. But the ultimate purpose of such institutions is to give the state some measure of control over what were previously autonomous private organisations. [Winkler 1977, p. 54]

The corporatist state is therefore centralized, hierarchical and co-optive.

It is in this context that the role of urban managers – local state officials – has to be analysed. On the one hand, they are agents of a centralized corporatist state, and this leads Pahl to reject the view that they are responsible for the policies that they carry out: 'The previous work on local decision-makers "running" a town overtly or covertly seems curiously inadequate and dated' (Pahl 1979, p. 42). On the other hand, however, it is in his view inevitable that the peripheral agents of a centralized state must enjoy a certain degree of discretion in determining how policies are to be carried out: 'Those who administer these systems of allocations we may term the managers, and generally they have considerable discretion either in determining the rules or in administering the rules determined elsewhere' (1979, p. 39). It follows from this that, while they are certainly not the independent variables in any analysis of the pattern of urban resource distribution, they must be taken into account as significant intervening variables: 'The urban managers remain the allocators of this surplus; they must remain, therefore, as central to the urban problematic' (1975, p. 285).

The argument that Pahl continually emphasizes is that the state, both at national and local levels, cannot be studied merely in terms of the 'needs' of capital. In other words, state policies do not always or necessarily reflect the interests of capital but are rather the outcome of 'managerial bargaining' between agents representing different types of organizations. Like Weber, therefore, he is concerned to stress, first, that political power is not simply a reflection or derivation of economic power but can be and is used to direct, control and influence key economic interests, and, second, that such power has ultimately to be analysed as a function of relationships between individuals: 'Specific *agents* ultimately control and allocate resources' (1979, p. 43). Analysis of political outcomes must therefore begin with the goals, values and practical purposes of those individuals who control access to key resources, and then must attempt to identify the constraints that limit the potential scope of their actions.

In the case of urban managers, this necessitates carrying the analysis beyond and outside the urban system: 'It is no longer possible to consider "urban" problems and "urban" studies separately from the political economy of the society as a whole' (Pahl 1975, p. 6). Thus, by arguing that urban managers perform a dual mediating role between the private sector and the welfare sector on the one hand, and between the central state and the local population on the other (see page 121), Pahl identifies the context of political and economic constraints within which the allocators of resources within the urban system must operate. In other words, not only are their actions limited by the operation of an inequitable spatial logic within the urban system (for throughout his work Pahl has consistently reiterated his argument that territorial inequalities are inevitable in any society), but they are also constrained by the power of a centralized interventionist state and by decisions taken by private sector firms outside it. None of these three factors – ecological, governmental and economic processes – can be said to *determine* the pattern of urban resource distribution (theories that deny the relevance of urban managers are therefore every bit as inadequate as those that assert their autonomy), but all three together constitute the system of constraints within which the actions of urban managers must be studied and understood.

Williams has pointed out that 'Urban managerialism is not a theory, nor even an agreed perspective. It is instead a framework for study' (1978, p. 236). The question, therefore, is how useful this framework appears for empirical study.

The first point to note is that Pahl's recent work on corporatism and on the mediating role of urban managers has overcome the two main weaknesses of his earlier formulation. The problem of identification has been resolved by situating urban managerialist analysis within a broader analysis of the changing role of the state in Britain, and thus by providing a coherent theoretical rationale for limiting the application of the concept to local state officials. Similarly, the problem of autonomy has been overcome by theorizing the external political and economic constraints on these officials, thereby avoiding what Pahl himself terms the 'managerialist heresy' (1975, p. 7).

Second, this recent work goes some way to answering or encompassing some of the criticisms and refinements of the concept that have been made by subsequent researchers. It is no longer the case, for example, that, 'The managerial approach, in concentrating on studying the allocation and distribution of "scarce resources", fails to ask why resources are in scarce supply' (Gray 1976, p. 81), for urban managers are no longer taken as the independent variables, but are rather analysed in the context of the wider political economy. Similarly, the argument developed by Lambert *et al.* (1978) to the effect that the importance of urban managers lies not in the content of their policies but in the style with which they allocate resources is not entirely inconsistent with Pahl's view of the role of managers in mediating between the demands of the local population and the policies imposed by central government, although Lambert and his co-authors do also take issue with Pahl's theory of the corporate state and with his assumption of the inevitability of scarcity and inequality in the system of resource distribution.

It is, in fact, the work on corporatism that now attracts most criticism. In effect, what Pahl has done in response to the attacks on his earlier work is to retain a Weberian perspective which asserts the autonomy of politics and identifies actors rather than classes as the basic units of analysis, but to shift the application of this perspective from the local to the national level. The result is that criticisms of his basic approach, which were formerly directed at his conceptualization of urban managers, are now directed at his conceptualization of the state. While some of these criticisms appear valid, others are essentially misplaced or else derive from little more than doctrinal assertions.

One type of criticism, for example, seeks to equate Pahl's work in particular, and Weberian political sociology in general, with largely discredited theories of democratic pluralism. Lambert *et al.*, for example, write: 'The state is represented as the arbiter of competing or more truly contradictory interests and will itself impose its own will and purpose. ... such a conceptualization begs, it would seem, all the questions of the pluralist model of political power of which it is a variant' (1978, p. 11). Such a charge, however, simply cannot be sustained, for the differences between the work of those such as Dahl who have developed liberal theories of democratic pluralism, and the work of Weber and Pahl are so great as to deny any approach that seeks to criticize the latter as a variant of the former.

I have discussed the basic principles and fundamental weaknesses of pluralist theories elsewhere (Saunders 1979, chs. 1 and 4), so my discussion here will be brief. Basically, pluralist theory conceives of the state as a forum within which the political demands of different groups with different interests come to be represented. It rests on three fundamental principles. First, the state is independent of any one section of the population and its policies reflect a relatively open, though not necessarily equal, competition between different groups organized loosely into shifting coalitions which attempt to assert their preferences against those of others. State policies, in other words, are determined by the relative political strength of competing groups in relation to any given issue. Second, those who control state policy-making are elected by the masses at periodic elections and are therefore accountable to the population as a whole for their actions while in office. This ensures that the wishes of the majority cannot systematically be ignored in favour of privileged minorities. Third, the political power of those elected to state office is exercised on the basis of a fundamental value consensus in society, and political disputes are therefore generally limited to disagreements within a context of a widely accepted political framework. There is, in other words, rule by consent, for if this were not the case, no political regime could survive for very long.

This perspective has been widely and, more often than not, justifiably criticized, mainly on the grounds that it ignores the fact that political bias may be perpetuated merely as a result of routine administration, and that it misleadingly equates the lack of political opposition to policies and to powerful groups with the existence of value consensus among the masses. Similar criticisms have been levelled against Pahl's Weberian analysis of the state on the grounds that it is essentially a pluralist theory and that it too assumes the neutrality of the state and the existence of widespread consensus regarding the use of state power. Hill, for example, suggests that 'The state appears to embody purposes independent of class interests in Pahl's framework because state power (at least in formal democracies) derives from the consent of the governed' (1977, p. 42). Such criticisms rest on a fundamental misinterpretation of

Weberian political analysis. Two points are significant here. First, the assertion of the autonomy of politics (which is characteristic of both Pahl's and Weber's work) does not imply the assumption of the neutrality of the state. To deny that the state necessarily reflects, in one way or another, the interests of the capitalist class or of some dominant section of it is not to argue that the state is the representative of the popular will. As we saw earlier (page 124), Weber is in fact highly critical of those theories that argue for the democratic accountability of the modern state, and his analysis of the limited role of elected assemblies and of the virtual impotence of elected leaders in relation to the power of the bureaucracy is sufficient to demonstrate that his is not such a theory. Similarly, there is nothing in Pahl's analysis to warrant the charge of pluralism, and he has himself expressed his exasperation with critics such as Hill who assume that, if an analysis is not Marxist, then it must be 'some naive end-of-ideology logic-of-industrialism position'. As Pahl asks, 'Cannot Hill and others accept that some of us may try to be a little more subtle than that?' (1977d, p. 342).

Second, it is a complete inversion of the Weberian position to suggest, as Hill does, that it rests upon an assumption of value consensus. This charge appears to derive from a cursory reading of Weber's definition of the state as a political association with a monopoly over the use of *legitimate* force. This cannot be taken as indicative of a presumption of value consensus, however; for as we have seen, Weber's analysis of values led him to the conclusion that the *most fundamental* conflicts in society were irresolvable since they derived from incompatible moral positions. For Weber, state power is exercised on the basis of consensus only in the sense that it rests on widespread agreement as to the facts of power, but not necessarily as to its use: 'Of course, persistent dissatisfaction endangers the stability of a coercive regime, but it does not invalidate the consensus as long as the powerholder can objectively count on the adequate execution of his commands' (1968, p. 1378). It follows that obedience may result from the moral endorsement of state power by the masses (in which case Weber speaks of authority), but it may equally reflect their awareness 'of the probability of physical coercion backing up such obligations' (1968, p. 903). The use of state power, in other words, is not necessarily seen as legitimate, but it is widely recognized as legally enforceable.

The important point about all this is that Weber's concern lies not in the reasons for obedience but in the fact of obedience. As Hirst argues, this follows directly from his concern with the purposive goals of individual actors, for once a subordinate obeys a command he becomes, for sociological purposes, the instrument of another's will, and therefore ceases to be an acting subject: 'In the economy and in domination, only those who can entertain ends or give commands are subjects' (Hirst 1976, p. 87). There is, therefore, some truth in the charge that Weberian political sociology is 'elitist' (a criticism that Harloe (1975) makes against the urban managerialist perspective) in that its focus lies on those who control the state rather than those who obey it. It does not however imply any assumption about the existence of popular consent or the responsiveness of the state to popular demands and interests. Indeed, Pahl's emphasis on 'managerial bargaining' would hardly make sense if he assumed that the different interests between which managers mediate were essentially compatible.

A second type of criticism that has been made against the corporatism thesis is that the new 'corporatist' society appears little different from the old capitalist one. Westergaard (1977), for example, points to the continuing inequalities based on the distribution of property, while Hill (1977) argues that the increased intervention of the state has done nothing to change underlying class relations based upon the appropriation of surplus value. Both authors conclude from this that the society is still capitalist. As Hill puts it,

The key issue is not whether the state has become progressively more involved in the accumulation process, of course it has, but whether and to what extent state involvement has fundamentally altered the class relations of capital accumulation through the production and appropriation of surplus value. In sum, why call Britain corporatist rather than state capitalist? [Hill 1977, p. 42]

Pahl's answer to this is to point to the differences between a society like Britain on the one hand, and one such as the United States on the other (1977d, p. 342). What is basically at issue here is a fundamental difference of methodology, for while Pahl (following Weber) denies the possibility of developing a single theory to account for the observable diversities between different Western societies and is concerned to analyse these differences by means of ideal type constructs such as corporatism, Hill, writing from a Marxist perspective, claims to be able to discover underlying uniformities behind the differences and is therefore concerned to develop a realist theory that can identify these latent forces and structures. While Pahl addresses his work to differences in phenomenal form, Hill addresses his to similarities in underlying structure. Hill therefore criticizes Pahl's ideal type formulations as superficial, while Pahl criticizes Hill's assertions regarding 'real' (but unobservable) structures as doctrinaire and unfalsifiable. This debate (or perhaps non-debate) between advocates of ideal type and realist methodologies is one to which we shall have cause to return in later chapters. Suffice it to say here that criticisms of corporatist theory that are developed on the basis of an alternative Marxist paradigm do nót so much articulate with the work of writers such as Pahl and Winkler as develop alternatives to it. What we are faced with is not critique but divergence. As Hill himself observes, 'Proponents of alternative theories of the state are likely to be often concerned with different problems and divergent questions even when they seemingly employ the same concepts to depict social reality' (1977, pp.37–8).

Pahl's conceptualization of corporatism can, however, be criticized on its own terms. Of particular relevance in this respect is a paper by Panitch (1978), who argues, first, that the ideal type of corporatism is internally incoherent and illogical, and, second, that it is of dubious empirical use in research.

The basis of Panitch's charge of internal inconsistency lies in Winkler's statement that 'Surplus value, exchange value and accumulation would not be significantly altered by a move towards corporatism. The law of value, commodity production, appropriation, entrepreneurship and freedom of contract would' (1976, p. 114n). Yet as Panitch argues, it is difficult to see how it is possible to have surplus value without the law of value, exchange value without commodity production, and accumulation without appropriation. At best, the analysis of the corporate economy as a new mode of production and a new organization of political economy appears hopelessly muddled.

The second problem is that the empirical evidence on which both Pahl and Winkler draw in order to support their argument appears very weak. Pahl, for example, suggests that 'The corporatist strategy is to manipulate tax concessions and price controls in return for the power to control and to channel investment' (1977b, p. 14), while Winkler similarly emphasizes the significance of prices and incomes policies and planning agreements as indicative of a developing and irreversible tendency for the state to direct the economy. As Panitch points out, however, the planning agreements system introduced by the Labour government in 1974 never got off the ground, while price controls have tended to be more symbolic than real. Thus Panitch concludes that the Pahl–Winkler conceptualization of corporatism is virtually useless, even as an ideal type, since it has gone too far in generalizing from a few recent changes in the relation between the state and the private sector to the construction of a model of a qualitatively new mode of production. Clearly, if the concept of corporatism is to provide a fruitful framework for research, a rather more modest approach is called for (see Chapter 8).

To these two basic criticisms may be added a third, which goes to the heart of the problem with Pahl's recent work, and this concerns the problem of autonomy and discretion. As we shall see in Chapter 6, where we consider the difficulties that recent Marxist work has encountered in attempting to theorize the relationship between the state and capital, there are good grounds for accepting the Weberian assumption of a necessary non-correspondence between economic classes and political domination. However, as Pahl himself recognizes, the state at both national and local levels is nevertheless hedged in by constraints, many of which derive from the operation of a capitalist market system in land, financial resources, labour and so on. The analytical autonomy of politics does not mean that the state can do whatever it wants. The problem then becomes how to theorize these constraints. This is a problem which, from our present perspective, is particularly significant as regards the level of urban management.

The problem with Pahl's view of urban managers as mediators between the central state authority, the private capitalist sector and the social needs and demands of the local population for state services is that it remains unclear how far managers enjoy some discretion in discharging their role. That they enjoy *some* autonomy from the dictates of central government and the constraints imposed by the operation of the process of capital accumulation is taken as axiomatic, but how far and in which situations does this autonomy extend? Pahl's answer appears to be that this is an empirical question, but such an answer is inadequate given that empirical research, even if conducted comparatively across different types of local authority (or even different types of society), will be unable to identify the sources of particular policies unless it is grounded in a theoretical framework that specifies the sorts of situations in which managers are able to exercise discretion as opposed to those in which they are not. If we start out merely on the assumption that they are constrained to some extent, then we lack any theoretically informed criteria for determining where in the economic and political organization of society to begin looking for the explanation of any given policy. Quite simply, Pahl's recent work leads empirical research into the familiar problem of the receding locus of power; the actions of urban managers can be understood only in the context of national state policy; national state policy can be understood only in the context of the operation of a complex mixed economy; the operation of the economy can be understood only in the context of the crisis of the capitalist world; and so on. Thus the researcher who starts out by attempting to understand, say, the patterns of housing inequalities in Birmingham ends up by trying to analyse the oil policies of the Middle Eastern states or the impact of American fiscal policy on the international balance of trade.

The point of these comments is not to suggest that such factors are not important – of course they are – but to show how, in an attempt to meet the criticisms made against his original formulations, Pahl's later work has effectively undermined the possibilities for research into the urban question. As we saw in Chapter 1, it was precisely these sorts of problems that led Weber to argue that total sociological explanations were impossible, and that research must progress by selecting partial aspects of the social world for study on the basis of ideal type constructions. This was the logic behind Rex's reformulation of the sociology of the city and Pahl's conceptualization of a socio-spatial system, for this work identified the specific aspects of social reality (namely the articulation of a spatial logic with the local political process) with which they, as urban sociologists, chose to be concerned. That these formulations proved to be of less heuristic value than had originally been asumed is undeniable, but instead of attempting to develop a more fruitful conceptualization of the urban, Pahl abandoned the project altogether and embarked upon an analysis of political economy which, irrespective of the validity of the theory of the growing corporatism, destroyed the basis for a viable urban sociology.

The result is that we are left with a central body of theory concerned with the role of the state in the contemporary British economy, and with a residual 'urban' element comprising a vague and ill-defined concept of managers as mediators together with a continuing belief in the inevitability of territorial inequalities. The concern with the state then leads us to consider all aspects of state policies including, for example, prices and incomes regulation, British membership of the EEC, trade union reform and so on, none of which is specifically 'urban'. The concern with managers as mediators and with spatial inequalities, on the other hand, leads us to a very narrow range of questions which explicitly exclude those distributional policies that do not have a spatial component yet are obviously crucial in the determination of life chances (most aspects of the welfare state, for example, would seem to fall into this category). The concern with the state results in too broad a range of questions while the concern with space results in an unnecessarily restricted perspective for which there is little theoretical rationale (indeed, if the significance of local state officials lies in the fact that they stand at the interface between the political economy of the society and the needs and demands of the local population, then there would appear no good reason for studying only those policies that involve the spatial location of some facility). If we are to study the state, then why retain the lingering commitment to spatially relevant policies, and if we are to study spatial distribution, then why the new commitment to political policies, which have nothing to do with spatial location?

We search in vain through Pahl's recent work for a coherent framework for urban analysis, for the specificity of the urban has collapsed into the intellectual minefield of political economy. His work has in this sense met the same fate as that of Park and McKenzie, Simmel and Wirth, before him. However, the concern with urban management was only one of the themes to have developed out of the new approach to urban sociology proposed by Rex and Moore. If analysis of the process of resource allocation was one aspect of their work, analysis of the struggle among different groups in the city to achieve access to such resources was the other. If urban sociology can no longer be defined by its concern with the former, can it nevertheless still be defined in relation to the latter?

Housing distribution and class struggle

We saw in the first section of this chapter that the fundamental argument developed by Rex and Moore in their attempt to reformulate a sociology of the city was that the distribution of scarce and desired housing resources created new patterns of inequality of life chances that were analytically separate from those arising out of the occupational system. Drawing on Weber's analysis of class and class conflict, they then suggested that, just as struggles over access to wages could be seen in terms of class struggle, so too could competition over access to housing. The central principle of their urban sociology, therefore, was that

There is a class struggle over the use of houses and that this class struggle is the central process of the city as a social unit. In saying this we follow Max Weber who saw that class struggle was apt to emerge wherever people in a market situation enjoyed differential access to property, and that such class struggles might therefore arise not merely around the use of the means of industrial production, but around the control of domestic property. . . . There will therefore be as many potential housing classes in the city as there are kinds of access to the use of housing. [Rex and Moore 1967, pp. 273–4]

For Weber, the concept of class, like any other collective concept in sociology, can be understood only as referring to an aggregate of individual subjects. Class is a sociological construct which is imposed upon reality in order to clarify analysis – in reality there are only individuals, not classes, who act – although Weber did recognize that class may, in certain situations, become a meaningful concept for groups of individuals who may therefore come to designate themselves as a class and act accordingly. For Weber, therefore, it is fallacious to argue that classes exist and that 'the individual may be in error concerning his interests but that the "class" is "infallible" about its interests' (1968, p. 930), and this is the first of two crucial differences between his and Marxist approaches. Marx's distinction between a class in and for itself is alien to Weber's sociology; for Weber, class is ultimately only an idea, whether it be an idea used in sociological analysis or one to which groups of individuals orient their actions.

The second major difference between Weber's and Marx's analysis is that for Weber, the concept of class may usefully be applied to the analysis of any situation in which groups of individuals share roughly common life chances as a result of their economic power in labour or property markets. The relationship between employer and employee was therefore only one among several different class situations in which individuals may find themselves, and Weber drew a basic distinction between commercial classes, which referred to groups of individuals who typically shared common life chances as a result of their possession or non-possession of marketable skills, and property classes, which could be identified among groups whose life chances were a function of the ownership or non-ownership of resources that could be used to generate income. Unlike Marx, who analysed classes in terms of the relationship between those who owned and controlled the means of production in society and those who did not, Weber therefore located class analysis in the sphere of distribution rather than production relations, in the market rather than in the mode of production.

In arguing that competition over housing could be conceptualized in terms of a class struggle, Rex and Moore thus drew upon Weber's distinction between commercial and property classes by suggesting that, while power in the labour market was clearly an important factor in determining an individual's power in the housing market (including the mode of bureaucratic allocation), the distribution of housing nevertheless created a situation in which an individual could occupy one class situation in respect of his power to command a wage and another in respect of his power to command access to a desirable house. The formation of commercial classes in the world of work would not therefore necessarily be reflected in the formation of property classes in the city, in which case the task for urban sociology was, first, to analyse the distribution of life chances consequent upon the differential power of different groups in the housing system and, second, to study the extent to which these groups come to recognize their common market situation and to mobilize politically in order to defend or improve it.

There was, however, a problem with this approach which was apparent from the outset and which derived directly from Rex and Moore's commitment to Weber's view of classes as distributionally defined aggregates of individuals. This concerned the identification of the main types of access to housing, and thus of the major housing class categories. It is an inescapable implication of Weber's formulation that, if classes are to be defined in terms of common degrees of market power among different individuals, then the number of potential classes that may be identified is almost infinite since no two individuals will ever share an exactly identical market situation. As Weber recognized, 'A uniform class situation prevails only when completely unskilled and propertyless persons are dependent on irregular employment' (1968, p. 302). The problem is thus to construct ideal types of different class situations which are mutually exclusive and relatively unambiguous. This was what Weber attempted to achieve with his concept of 'social class' which referred to a cluster of different market situations between which individuals could move relatively easily. As Giddens (1971) shows, he was then able to develop a model of the class system in which three main social classes were identified, consisting of an upper class with privileged access to property and skills, a lower class with little or no property and skills, and a middle class, comprising those with property but few skills and those with marketable skills but little property. Quite apart from the question of the usefulness of such a formal taxonomy in empirical research where the allocation of different individuals to different class categories is likely to remain a hazardous and somewhat arbitrary process, this mode of conceptualizing the class structure also left unexamined the problem of how the three social classes related to one another. Weber's work on class is descriptive rather than analytical, static rather than dynamic, positional rather than relational.

The same problems recur in the work of Rex and Moore (1967). For a start, it is never clear how the different housing classes are to be identified. At the beginning of *Race, Community and Conflict*, they suggest that the system of housing allocation gives rise to five housing classes: owner-occupiers, council house tenants, tenants of private landlords, owners of lodging houses and lodging house tenants (p. 36). By the end of the book (p. 274), however, they have added a sixth, namely those buying a house on mortgage, and have sub-divided the 'class' of council tenants into those in long-life accommodation and those in slum stock. This sub-division was then subsequently represented as a distinct class division (Rex 1968, p. 215), bringing the total number of housing classes to seven, and in his latest study Rex has elaborated on this schema to identify four more classes or sub-classes, thereby bringing the grand total to eleven (Rex and Tomlinson 1979, p. 132). Yet there is no reason why taxonomic innovation should end there; for Moore (1977, p. 106) has suggested that two more classes could have been analysed in the Sparkbrook study, Rex (1977, p. 21) has argued that any group (such as one-parent families) that is discriminated against in housing may constitute a housing class, and Pahl (1975, pp. 242–3) has pointed out that the framework fails to take account of large landowners or of local authorities (who are, after all, more significant providers of housing than lodging house owners), both of which could, given the logic of Rex and Moore's approach, be included. There are, it seems, dozens of potential housing classes.

Part of the problem here derives not so much from the inherent pluralism of any Weberian class analysis as from a confusion, noted by Haddon (1970), between the conceptualization of housing classes and their empirical identification. While Rex and Moore's conceptual model stresses inequalities in *access* to scarce housing resources, their various taxonomies all refer to differences in current housing tenure:

'They equate this typology of housing with "housing classes" assuming that, analytically at least, people who are *at the present moment* in the same type of housing accommodation constitute a housing class' (Haddon 1970, p. 128).

In one sense, this criticism does not appear particularly cogent, for although there undoubtedly are some people who continue to live in relatively undesirable housing despite their ability to gain access to a more favoured type (for example the inner-city intellectuals and urban villagers identified by Gans – see page 103), these would appear to be in a small minority, in which case current housing situation may be taken as a reasonable indicator of potential power in the system of housing allocation. This, in fact, is how Rex and Tomlinson counter Haddon's criticism: 'This seems on reflection to be an unreasonable criticism since the type of housing occupied is a very good indicator of the strength of its occupants in the housing market' (1979, pp. 20–1). Yet in another sense the criticism is highly pertinent, and Rex and Tomlinson's response to it misses the significant point. This is that the theoretical emphasis on inequalities of access to housing should lead in empirical research not to a concern with housing groups as the units of analysis, but rather to a concern with different types of social groups. When Rex, for example, argues that fatherless families may constitute a housing class, he is clearly resorting to a very different mode of conceptualization from that employed when he identifies, say, council tenants in slum property as a housing class; single-parent families may be found in owner-occupied housing, on council estates, in rented rooms in the inner city and so on, and they cannot therefore be equated with a particular type of housing in the way in which council tenants obviously can be. Rex and Moore's application of the housing class concept is therefore confused. Indeed, it may be argued that their theoretical concern lies not with *housing* classes, but with different groupings within *social* classes (for instance, blacks, women, one-parent families, etc.) who, because of their peculiar *status* characteristics, experience greater difficulty in achieving access to certain types of housing than do other people who are in a similar market position with regard to the distribution of other types of resources in society. This is a crucial point, for it suggests that analysis of differential access to housing does not involve a sociology of the city at all, but rather entails analysis of the sources of inequality in society as a whole, in which case the distinctiveness of urban sociology disappears. This is the point to which we shall return at the end of this chapter.

A second problem with Rex and Moore's analysis concerns their assumption of a unitary value system in the city in which owner-occupation is valued above renting, council tenancies are valued above private tenancies, and suburban locations are valued above inner-city locations. This assumption was, it will be recalled, central to their theory of the city, since it was the foundation of their argument that the basic urban process was one of conflict between different classes desiring the same type of housing.

Subsequent research has, however, called this assumption into question. Davies and Taylor (1970), for example, report that in Newcastle ownership of lodging houses is positively desired by many Asians as a means of upward social mobility through property ownership. Indeed, no less than 75 per cent of the Asian population who owned the property in the Rye Hill area were landlords, and most of these were absentee landlords (indicating that, far from being pushed into lodging house ownership through lack of alternatives, many recent immigrants were opting for it as a means of capital accumulation). Furthermore, Davies (1972) went on to show that rented accommodation was generally despised by Asians to the extent that none of those interviewed had made any attempt to gain access to council housing and many had resisted attempts by the local authority to move them from inner-city clearance areas into council accommodation. He suggested that renting was rejected as a vulnerable form of tenure and that property ownership was embraced because of the security and opportunities for capital gains that it offered. He also claimed that few immigrants experienced unusual difficulties in gaining access to funds for house purchase: 'I have no evidence at all that the question of colour intruded into the economics of house buying in such a way as to *force* the immigrant into unwanted and oppressive methods of finance' (p. 32).

Further evidence against Rex and Moore's assumption is provided in a study of housing in the city of Bath by Couper and Brindley (1975). They show that one-third of all applicants for council housing in Bath would prefer a central to a suburban location, that one-quarter of all tenants in the city were in privately rented accommodation and would not apply for a council tenancy under any circumstances, and, perhaps most surprisingly of all, that 'There appear to be many people, not necessarily on low incomes, who prefer renting to owning' (p. 567) – indeed, one-half of all tenants in unfurnished accommodation said that they preferred to rent rather than to buy.

Such evidence appears very damaging to Rex and Moore's thesis, although, as Couper and Brindley themselves recognize, there is a methodological problem in such research in that the preferences that people articulate may reflect their (scaled-down) realistic aspirations as much as their ideal choices. Rex (1971), for example, criticizes the Davies and Taylor findings by suggesting that immigrant landlords may claim to have chosen this form of tenure even though they were in fact forced into it, although in the same article he concedes that 'multiple value systems do exist' (p. 297). He then argues, somewhat obscurely, that there may be a dominant value system among the competing value systems in the city, but this does little to rescue the original analysis since it appears that it is precisely those groups living in the supposedly 'undesirable' housing who do not subscribe to the dominant value system on which Rex and Moore founded their hierarchy of desirable housing types. Indeed, in his later research in the Handsworth area of Birmingham, he and Tomlinson have recognized that the desire to move to the suburbs is not prevalent among blacks living in the inner city, and they argue (rather lamely) that this 'does not alter the fact of the existence of housing classes (at least in themselves) since access is in effect denied to those who do wish to move' (Rex and Tomlinson 1979, p. 132). The point is however that, while this may not invalidate an ideal type model of housing classes, it does remove the very factor – competition over scarce resources desired by virtually all city dwellers – that made this model useful in urban research. By conceding that many of those in apparently disadvantaged housing conditions do not aspire to suburban living, Rex has therefore removed the grounds for arguing that the housing classes he identifies are in conflict with one another. As with Weber's ideal types of social classes, we are therefore left with a static positional description rather than a dynamic relational analysis.

In their Handsworth study, Rex and Tomlinson have effectively attempted to rectify this by shifting the emphasis of their analysis of distribution of life chances in the city from an exclusive focus on access to housing to one that encompasses education and employment as well as housing opportunities. Their argument is that blacks in areas like Handsworth constitute a distinct 'underclass' in British society owing to the systematic inequalities they experience in competition with whites for jobs and for educational success, and that it is this broad area of disadvantage rather than discrimination in housing *per se* that creates the conditions for conflict. The significance of discriminatory housing policies is that they have created black concentrations in particular inner-city areas which enable the development of political organization separate from the white labour movement. In other words, the process of segregation in housing has produced the conditions – neighbourhood-based ethnic and kin ties – by means of which blacks can mobilize as an 'under-class-for-itself':

Just as exploitation in industry gave rise to the trade union movement and more widely to the Labour movement amongst native British workers, so the fact of discrimination in housing has given rise to partially segregated areas, and to locally-based and relatively effective communal and ethnic organisa-tions which are useful as a means of protecting the rights of minority groups. [Rex and Tomlinson 1979, p. 157].

In this later study, therefore, Rex and Tomlinson argue that situations of common housing deprivation are the means rather than the cause of conflict, and they document the growth in militancy of the West Indian organizations that are based in neighbourhoods like Handsworth. However, although this argument provides a convincing explanation of the sources of conflict, it does so largely at the expense of the housing class concept, for when Rex and Tomlinson discuss housing class mobilization, they are in fact referring to the mobilization of a black underclass on the basis of neighbourhood organization. Indeed, their emphasis on the common situation of disadvantage experienced by blacks in Handsworth in the job market and the educational system leads Rex and Tomlinson to deny the significance of tenure divisions among them, yet such divisions were the very basis of Rex's original housing class concept. Thus they write: 'Private property owners and renters on the one hand, and immigrant council tenants on the other, have tended to be much the same sort of individual and, to all intents and purposes, we found very little differences in the observed attributes of those housed in the public and private sectors' (p. 144). The key factor, then, is not housing but race, and the focus of concern turns out not to be urban inequality but racial inequality. Once again, therefore, we find that the housing class concept does not constitute the basis for urban analysis but rather points to the need to understand sources of inequality in the society as a whole.

The third major criticism that can be levelled against Rex and Moore's discussion of housing classes is that it rests on a misinterpre-tation of Weberian class analysis. As we have seen, Weber applied the concept of class to the analysis of groups of individuals who share roughly common life chances as a result of their power in labour or commodity markets (that is, as a result of their ability to realize income from the sale of their skills or their property). He then distinguished between classes and status groups, defining the latter in terms of the distribution of social honour or prestige in society as reflected in different styles of life, and he argued that, while social honour (like political power) was often empirically closely related to patterns of economic inequality, it was nevertheless analytically separated and 'need not necessarily be linked with a class situation' (Weber 1968, p. 932). It followed from this that groups of individuals may come to act either as classes or as status groups, and that collective action on the basis of shared status characteristics could cross-cut class divisions.

Weber summarized the distinction between classes and status groups as basically that between the situation of individuals with respect to the distribution of life chances through the market, and their situation with respect to the distribution of life-styles through the process of consumption of goods and services. Seen in this way, it is clear that the groups that Rex and Moore identify as 'housing classes' are not classes at all but housing status groups. Different types of housing tenure are simply different modes of consumption of housing which may be differently evaluated according to the life-styles associated with them. The class situation of the council tenant with respect to the ability to realize returns in the housing market is the same as that of the private tenant, for both are, in Weber's terms, 'negatively-privileged' in the sense that neither owns property that can be used to generate income. The difference between them is a difference in their style of life – in other words, a status difference – rather than a difference in their market power. As Haddon puts it, 'Use of housing is an index of achieved life chances, not primarily a cause' (1970, p. 132).

This does not mean that a Weberian analysis of housing classes is not possible – Weber himself sees the ownership of domestic buildings as one type of property that may differentiate the market situation of various property classes (1968, p. 928) – but it does mean that Rex and Moore's emphasis on forms of tenure has to be replaced by an analysis grounded in the question of ownership and non-ownership of those types of housing that, potentially at least, may generate economic returns. This is the logic behind Pahl's reconceptualization of housing classes in which he distinguishes between large property owners (public or private), smaller landlords, owners of capital sufficient to buy their own houses, and those who lack property and are obliged to rent (Pahl 1975, p. 245). Similarly, I have suggested that the application of a Weberian framework leads to the identification of three housing classes, namely those who live off the economic returns from house ownership (such as landlords and private developers), those who use housing purely as a means of consumption (tenants in the private and public sectors), and those who, in the process of consuming housing, typically enjoy a return on capital (most owner-occupiers, who achieve considerable capital gains from their ownership of housing) (see Saunders 1978; 1979, ch. 2). In Weber's terms, these three groups represent positively privileged, negatively privileged and middle property classes, and their conflicting property interests can be shown to lie behind many political struggles over housing issues (e.g. see Saunders 1979, ch. 6).

We shall see in Chapter 8 that an analysis of the different economic interests that derive from these different types of relationship to the ownership of domestic property may constitute one important aspect of a distinctively urban sociology, although as Dunleavy (1979) has argued, it does not necessarily follow from this that a Weberian class model is the most appropriate tool for analysing these interests. The basic problem is that even a reformulated Weberian framework fails to explain the relationship between housing classes and social classes (for example, how does the class situation of a manual worker who owns his house differ from that of one who does not?), in which case it may be more fruitful to abandon the housing class concept altogether and to employ some other concept such as 'consumption sectors'.

Rex, however, remains resolutely sceptical about any attempt to reformulate the housing class concept around the question of property ownership, for, as we have seen, in his work with Tomlinson he argues both that owner-occupation among immigrants in the inner city may be no less a disadvantaged form of tenure than renting, and that the original conception of housing classes, suitably expanded to encompass groups such as homeless families and tenants of housing associations, remains a useful framework for analysis.

Such an assertion, however, simply ignores Haddon's argument that the housing class concept derives from a misreading of Weber and that the various groups that Rex identifies are in fact differentiated by status rather than by class situation. Rex has never answered this most fundamental criticism, yet it is crucial since it leads to the conclusion that housing struggles between different tenure groups can be understood only as status group conflicts, which may cross-cut and obscure more basic economic class divisions. It is but a short step from here to much of the contemporary Marxist literature on housing, which argues that divisions grounded in different forms of housing consumption are important only at the level of ideology in that the working class is fragmented by different types of provision, none of which alters the basic underlying class division between wage labour and capital (see Chapter 7). If this kind of analysis is followed through to its conclusion, then it becomes apparent that the analysis of 'housing classes' involves an analysis of modes of class control in a capitalist society, in which case the task is not to study struggles over housing between different groups in the city, but rather to understand how dominant ideologies in the society as a whole function to divide the working class against itself. By his refusal to reconceptualize the problem of housing classes and his failure to recognize that property ownership rather than tenure is the basic element in the model, Rex therefore lays himself open to a Marxist critique which denies the economic relevance of housing divisions and substitutes a theory of ideology for a sociology of the city.

The inescapable conclusion that suggests itself as a result of our discussion of the three major problems with Rex and Moore's work on housing classes is that the attempt to found a sociology of the city on this concept has now collapsed. Rex virtually admits as much in his book with Tomlinson, when he suggests that 'It was never claimed that the housing classes which seemed more relevant to explaining ethnic political conflict in Sparkbrook in the mid-1960s could be taken as a kind of inductive generalization covering all cases at all times' (Rex and Tomlinson 1979, p. 128). In other words, he now suggests that housing class is not a generic concept, yet this is clearly a retreat from his earlier position, in which he suggested that 'The *basic process* underlying urban social interaction is competition for scarce and desired types of housing', and that 'What is *common to all urban situations* is that housing, and especially certain kinds of desirable housing, is a scarce resource', for which different groups are in competition (Rex 1968, pp. 214 and 216; emphases added). In his work with Moore (1967) Rex clearly saw the concept of housing classes as the basis for a new approach to the sociology of the city; in his work twelve years later with Tomlinson (1979) he equally clearly does not.

We have seen that there are three main reasons why a specifically urban sociology cannot be based upon the concept of housing class. First, the focus on access to housing means that housing classes cannot be equated with housing tenure groups and that analysis must focus not on a theory of the city but on a theory of social stratification which explains why different groups enjoy different degrees of access to the housing system. Second, the work by Rex and Tomlinson (1979) clearly demonstrates that the lack of a common value system with respect to desirable types of housing undermines an analysis of housing class conflict unless the application of the concept is restricted to particular groups (i.e. the black 'underclass') whose situation in other areas of life (namely the occupational and educational systems) creates the potential for conflict. In other words, the analysis of housing class struggles becomes merely a part of a sociological theory of race relations rather than the basis for a distinctive urban sociology. Third, the fact that, even from a Weberian perspective, the housing classes that Rex and Moore identify are not classes but status groups indicates that the analysis of housing divisions can be accomplished only through the attempt to theorize the significance of patterns of consumption for class relations, in which case what is called for is a theory of class structure or a theory of ideology rather than an urban theory. In all three cases, therefore, we see that what appears to be the concern of urban sociology with housing class conflict is in fact the concern of a sociology of stratification, and that urban research premised upon this concept collapses into an analysis of questions of class structure, the relation between ethnicity and class, and the problem of consumption divisions and ideology.

Taking together the related concepts of housing class and urban managerialism, we can only endorse the conclusion reached by Lambert *et al.* (1978) in their study of housing allocation in Birmingham that we should 'reject the former notion and substantially redefine the latter' (p. 171). As they stand, neither concept provides a satisfactory foundation for a specifically urban sociology. This does not, however, necessarily imply that the search for a Weberian urban sociology is futile, for as we shall see in Chapter 8, it is possible to develop an ideal type conceptualization of the urban which takes account of the issue of housing consumption sectors without falling into the problems of housing class analysis, and which identifies the significance of urban managers without losing the specificity of the urban in an analysis of the political economy of advanced capitalism. Before we go on to consider how this might be achieved, however, we must first consider the various Marxist alternatives to Weberian analysis which have developed over the last decade in order to show why a Weberian urban sociology remains not only feasible but worthwhile.

5 The urban as ideology

Since the late 1960s, there has been a tendency for Western Marxist theory to broaden its traditional horizons in order to take account of various radical movements that have developed outside the process of production and which cannot simply be analysed in terms of the wage labour–capital relation. The growth of the feminist movement, for example, has spawned a considerable literature on the role of women and the family in capitalist societies and on the relationship between the women's movement and the labour movement. Similarly, the rise of black movements in the West and in the Third World and (to a lesser extent) the explosion of student radicalism in the 1960s both helped to undermine narrow conceptions of Marxist theory and political practice which sought to reduce all political struggles to that between bourgeoisie and proletariat.

It is in this context that Marxist theory has rediscovered the problem of the city, a problem that has been posed by the development of radical movements in the cities addressed to issues such as the decline of urban public services, environmental desecration and so on. The argument of Marx and Engels (discussed in Chapter 1) to the effect that the capitalist city is not in itself theoretically significant has therefore been reconsidered in recent years.

This reconsideration has involved two steps. The first is the critique of existing urban theories (such as human ecology) and urban practice (for instance, planning) as 'ideological'. The term 'ideology' has, however, meant different things for different writers, and this reflects two distinct (though related) meanings of the concept in Marx's work. Thus some writers have emphasized the notion of ideology as a means of legitimating class domination, and in this they have taken their cue from arguments such as that advanced in the *Communist Manifesto* that 'The ruling ideas of each age have ever been the ideas of its ruling class' (Marx and Engels 1969, p. 125). Current conceptions of urbanism and current explanations of urban problems are then termed ideological on the grounds that they reflect and are subordinated to the class interests of the bourgeoisie. Other writers, however, have seen this as too limited a conception of ideology and have attempted to develop a conception (also found in Marx) that contrasts 'theoretical ideologies' with 'scientific practice'. In other words, current theories are criticized on the grounds that they fail to break with the ideological appearances of material reality and thus reproduce ideological modes of thought in an elaborated theoretical form which is justified by a spurious claim to scientific status.

√   Having established the critique of existing conceptions of urbanism as ideological, the second step is to develop a theory that is not subordinate to dominate class interests or does not simply formalize existing ideological representations. Again, however, there are intense disagreements between different writers, and these tend to reflect a major division between humanist and determinist interpretations of Marxism. Thus, while one approach addresses the urban question in terms of the limitations and potential of 'urban society' for human liberation and individual self-realization, another is openly contemptuous of socialist humanism and rejects notions of the individual human subject as metaphysical. While the first conception sees the 'urban crisis' as central to advanced capitalism, the second sees it as secondary to the basic class struggle in industry. And while the former focuses on the question of the production of space (that is, on the way in which capitalist organization becomes extended and imprinted upon all aspects of everyday life), and hence on the need to develop new forms of struggle against capitalist domination of space, the latter sees the urban question as significant only in so far as urban crisis enables an extension of the traditional struggle against capitalist domination of industrial production.

It should be noted that these disagreements are not merely academic but reflect very different views regarding Marxist political strategy. As we shall see, the humanist approach seeks fundamentally to reorientate the workers' movement towards what it sees as the central question of the quality of everyday life, while the determinist approach seeks rather to encompass urban struggles within the existing workers' movement. The theoretical gulf between these two approaches cannot therefore be fully understood except in the context of recent debates within the European (and notably the French) communist parties regarding socialist strategy in the conditions of advanced capitalism. It is, in other words, no accident that the literature that we shall be discussing in this and the following chapter is almost entirely French and Italian in origin, for it is precisely in these countries that the question of communist strategy has been posed in its most practical terms since 1968.

In this chapter we shall focus on the work of two writers – Henri Lefebvre and Manuel Castells – in order to illustrate the different ways in which recent Marxist theory has attempted to take account of the urban question while rejecting existing non-Marxist approaches as ideological. The next two chapters will then consider the subsequent development of these different approaches in order to assess their contribution to a theoretical understanding of urbanism in advanced capitalist societies.

Henri Lefebvre: the humanist critique of urbanism

Lefebvre's work on urbanism is not widely known in the English-speaking world. In part this appears to be due to the relative inaccessibility of his relevant work, for little of it exists in English translation. It is also due in part to the fact that Castells's text, *The Urban Question*, has been widely read and discussed, and this includes a heavily critical chapter on Lefebvre's theories. In other words, not only have the terms of academic Marxist debate (in Britain at least) been set largely by reference to Castells's framework, but also there has been little stimulus to examine Lefebvre's ideas since these were apparently demolished and transcended by Castells's work. To the extent that Lefebvre has had an impact on British urban studies, it has been through the mediation of the work of David Harvey (see Chapter 7). But even where his work has been made available and has been read, it has still failed to provoke much interest or debate, and this is probably due to its highly speculative, self-consciously 'utopian' character. Lefebvre's writings appear lively but also (sometimes at least) lacking in academic rigour. In places he clearly contradicts himself; the development of his argument often seems more arbitrary than logical; and the sense of spontaneity that pervades his writing stands in stark contrast to the painstaking formalism of a text such as *The Urban Question*. It is perhaps this difference in style (which itself clearly reflects a difference in their approaches to Marxism) that more than any other factor explains the differential response in Britain to Lefebvre and Castells, for the British intellectual tradition within and outside Marxism is one that has bred an extreme suspicion of academic speculation and spontaneity.

Lefebvre's critique of existing urban theories is premised on the argument that any theoretical system that guides human actions in such a way that they serve to maintain the existing system of social relations may be termed ideological: 'Any representation is ideological if it contributes either immediately or "mediately" to the reproduction of the relations of production. Ideology is therefore inseparable from practice' (1976, p. 29). He cites as an example the traditional ideology in capitalist societies that the system reproduces itself naturally, without the purposive interventions of human agents, for this not only serves to legitimate the system (what is natural is acceptable), but also denies the possibility of radical interventions to change it (what is natural is inevitable). Already, therefore, we see here the basis of Lefebvre's rejection of deterministic Marxist as well as of 'bourgeois' theories, for both have the practical effect of stunting the development of revolutionary action (that is to say, a deterministic Marxism that denies the effectivity of conscious human subjects denies also the potential for radical action and thus performs the same function as 'bourgeois' theories in undermining the practical struggle against capitalist domination).

Ideologies, therefore, are general social theories that have the practical effect of maintaining the dominance of particular class interests: 'It is the role of ideologies to secure the assent of the oppressed and exploited' (1968a, p. 76). This is achieved by masking the true interests of the dominated classes and thus curtailing their political struggle against the source of their domination. Marxism is not therefore ideological in this sense since it enables and facilitates such struggles; in other words, it is revolutionary in its practical effects: 'It discloses – not by some power of "pure" thought but by deeds (the revolutionary praxis) – the conditions under which ideologies and works of man generally . . . are produced, run their course and pass away' (1968a, p. 86).

In arguing that Marxism is not an ideology, Lefebvre does not seek to imply that it is therefore a science with a privileged insight into 'truth' and 'reality'. Far from it; for all theory, he suggests, is a mixture of truth and error, and there is no sharp distinction between science and ideology, truth and falsity. His discussion of ideology is not premised on the science/ideology distinction but on the distinction between those theories that have revolutionary practical effects and those that secure political consensus and containment. Lefebvre's views are echoed by Harvey, who criticizes 'the rather trivial view that there is one version of some problem that is scientific and a variety of versions which are purely ideological', and who asserts on the contrary that 'The principles of scientific method (whatever they may be) are normative and not factual statements. The principles cannot therefore be justified and validated by appeal to science's own methods . . . the use of a particular scientific method is of necessity founded in ideology' (Harvey 1974, p. 214). This reveals a crucial distinction between Lefebvre's view of Marxism and that of Castells, since for Lefebvre Marxism is not a science but a political theory of socialist practice. This is a view that the argument developed in the final section of this chapter will strongly endorse.

Given this view of Marxist theory, it follows that the development of radical ideas is crucial, not because ideas can wish away the material reality of capitalism, but because practical activity by individuals is guided and informed by the ideas that they have of that reality. This leads Lefebvre to designate himself as a 'utopian' on the grounds that 'Today more than ever there are no ideas without a utopia. Otherwise a person is content to state what he sees before his eyes' (1977, p. 349). Lefebvre's project, therefore, is to develop a set of ideas about urbanism that can stimulate radical action against what he sees as a new and all-embracing mode of capitalist domination of everyday life.

It is in this context that he develops his critique of urban planning and of the theory that underpins it. This is a theory that represents space as a purely scientific object and gives rise to a planning 'science' that claims to be as precise and objective as mathematics. It is a technocratic theory, in that spatial forms are taken as given and planning is conceived as a technical intervention which can bring about particular effects on the basis of a scientific understanding of a purely spatial logic. Urban theory and planning practice are thus premised on a denial of the inherent political character of space – politics are conceived as an irrational element that intrudes upon the spatial system from outside it rather than as an essential element in the constitution and perpetuation of spatial forms. This theory is thus ideological, for it sustains the *status quo* by depoliticizing the question of space and its use, and as an ideology it permeates throughout the society with the effect that political struggles over the use of urban space are defused:

Urbanism, almost as a system, is now fashionable. Urban questions and reflections emanate from technical circles, from specialists and intellectuals who think of themselves as *avant garde*. They pass to the public sphere via newspaper articles and writings with various aims and objectives.

Simultaneously, urbanism becomes ideology and praxis. Yet questions concerning the city and urban reality are not yet well understood or recognized, they have not yet assumed a *political* importance in the same way as they exist in *thoughts* (in ideology) or in *practice*. [Lefebvre 1968b, p. 9]

The politicization of space is dependent upon the critique of the apolitical theory of space and hence on the recognition that spatial forms are politically created and serve political functions:

Space is political. Space is not a scientific object removed from ideology or politics; it has always been political and strategic. . . . Space, which seems homogeneous, which seems to be completely objective in its pure form such as we ascertain it, is a social product. The production of space can be likened to the production of any particular type of merchandise. [Lefebvre 1977, p. 341]

It is precisely because space is a product of capitalism, and that it is therefore infused with the logic of capitalism (production for profit and exploitation of labour), that the urban ideology of space as a pure and non-political object is so crucial.

What is required, according to Lefebvre, is not therefore a science of space *per se,* but rather a theory of how space is produced in capitalist societies and of the contradictions that this process of production generates: 'We are not speaking of a science of space, but of a knowledge (a theory) of the production of space' (1976, p. 18). Such a theory will involve not a logical and physical theory of structures and systems, but rather a dialectical theory of contradictory processes which provide the basis for political struggle over the urban question. The basic contradiction in the production of space is that between the necessity for capital to exploit it for profit and the social requirements of those who consume it; in other words, the contradiction between profit and need, exchange value and use value. The political expression of this contradiction is found in the constant political struggle between individualistic and collectivistic strategies. It is this contradiction and this struggle that lies at the heart of Lefebvre's concern with the urban question.

Lefebvre argues that the contradiction identified by Marx between the forces and relations of capitalist production has been overcome in the advanced capitalist societies by urban growth. The development of capitalism, in other words, has not encountered its limits because capital has transformed space itself into a commodity: 'We now come to a basic and essential idea: capitalism is maintained by the conquest and integration of space. Space has long since ceased to be a passive geographical milieu or an empty geometrical one. It has become instrumental' (1970, p. 262). From a system where commodities are produced in a spatial setting capitalism has evolved into a system where space itself is produced as a scarce and alienable resource. Space, that is, is created as an homogeneous and quantifiable commodity:

Space, e.g. volume, is treated in such a way as to render it homogeneous, its parts comparable, therefore exchangeable. . . . The subordination of space to money and capital implies a quantification which extends from the monetary evaluation to the commercialization of each plot of the entire space. . . . Space now becomes one of the new 'scarcities', together with its resources, water, air and even light. [Lefebvre 1970, pp. 261–2]

In this new era of capitalism, manufacturing industry is replaced by the construction and leisure industries as the pivotal points of the capitalist system of production:

Capitalism has not just integrated existing space, it has extended into completely new sectors. Leisure is becoming an industry of prime importance. We have conquered for leisure the sea, mountains and even deserts. The leisure industry and the construction industry have combined to extend the towns and urbanization along coastlines and in mountain regions . . . this industry extends over all space not already occupied by agriculture and the traditional production industries. [Lefebvre 1970, p. 265]

In this way, the capitalist production of space has become integral both in generating surplus value (for these industries employ an immense and low-paid labour force and are characterized by a low organic composition of capital) and in realizing profits (since the commodification of space has created vast new markets). It is this gradual transition from an industrial to an urban base of modern capitalist production that Lefebvre refers to as 'the urban revolution', and he likens it to the earlier industrial revolution in which the main basis of production shifted from agriculture to manufacturing.

It is apparent from Lefebvre's concept of an urban revolution that he does not intend to equate the concept of the urban with the physical object of the city. It is precisely his argument that the urban revolution creates an urban society, in which case the physical separation of city and countryside becomes of less and less significance. Rather, the urban for Lefebvre consists of three related concepts, namely space, everyday life and reproduction of capitalist social relations. The urban, that is, is the global spatial context through which the relations of production are reproduced in people's everyday experience. Capitalist social relations are reproduced through the everyday use of space because space has itself been captured by capital and subordinated to its logic:

The reproduction of the relations of production cannot be localized in the enterprise. . . . Reproduction (of the relations of production, not just the means of production) is located not simply in society as a whole but in space as a whole. Space, occupied by neo-capitalism, sectioned, reduced to homogeneity yet fragmented, becomes the seat of power. [Lefebvre 1976, p. 83]

Because space bears the imprint of capitalism, it imposes the form of capitalist relations (individualism, commodification, etc.) on the whole of everyday life. The architecture of our cities symbolizes capitalist relations ('The Phallic unites with the political: verticality symbolizes power' – (1976, p. 88), our leisure space reflects capitalist relations (since it commercializes our non-work lives in line with our working lives), the dispersal of our homes in far-flung suburbs is a product of capitalist relations (central areas are taken over by commercial functions while residential use of space is relegated to the periphery), and so on. The logic of capitalism is the logic of the social use of space is the logic of everyday life. The class that controls production controls the production of space and hence the reproduction of social relations.

Lefebvre's analysis is by no means inherently pessimistic, however, for he argues that the urban revolution that overcomes one set of problems for capital gives rise to another. This is because the colonization of space by capital can proceed only by fragmenting and decentralizing the population: 'The centre attracts those elements which constitute it (commodities, capital, information, etc.) but which soon saturate it. It excludes those elements which it dominates (the "governed", "subjects" and "objects") but which threaten it' (1976, p. 18). This creates a political problem in so far as the city has traditionally been the cultural centre of the society – the principal source and location of the reproduction of social relations. If the city is fragmented and dispersed leaving only the economic and political offices of administration at the centre, then, while political power becomes centralized, cultural hegemony will necessarily become weakened:

The spread of urban tissue is accompanied by the fragmentation of the town. And it is this that gives rise to one of the deepest contradictions of space. For the town not only represents a colossal accumulation of wealth, it is also the centre of birth and learning, the point of reproduction of all social relations. But it also becomes the place where these relations are threatened. . . . Should it be sacrificed, letting the urban tissue proliferate in disorder and chaos but thereby strengthening the decision-making centres? It is an unsettling contradiction for the reproduction of social relations. [Lefebvre 1976, p. 28]

The effect of the progressive extension of the capitalist production of space is therefore to concentrate the decision-making centre while creating dependent colonies on the periphery: 'Around the centres there are nothing but subjugated, exploited and dependent spaces: neo-colonial spaces' (1976, p. 85). In France, for example, Paris presides over a system of internal colonialization in which the disparities between the underdeveloped regions of Brittany and the south and the over-urbanized metropolitan centre become ever more stark (see 1970, p. 258). Thus, while capitalism is consolidated through the exploitation of space, this very process engenders at the same time a contradiction which threatens to undermine capitalist domination: 'If space as a whole has become the place where reproduction of the relations of production is located, it has also become the terrain for a vast confrontation' (1976, p. 85). The political power of the centre is strengthened as key decision-making functions become concentrated there, yet at the same time the cohesion of the society is weakened as everyday life becomes dispersed to the periphery: 'Power suffers, as in Shakespearian tragedy: the more it consolidates, the more afraid it is. It occupies space, but space trembles beneath it' (1976, p. 86). The result, potentially at least, is a crisis of the reproduction of capitalist social relations.

This is a crisis that the bourgeoisie attempts to regulate and mediate by means of its control of the decision-making centres, and notably the state. Yet it is ultimately an irresolvable crisis, since the more capitalism becomes extended in space, the more it undermines the reproduction of the social relations on which its continuation depends. Lefebvre neatly summarizes the paradox by distinguishing between the extension of capitalist organization and the fragmentation of the organization of capitalism that results from it. The capacity of the productive forces to produce space on a large scale, and thus to extend capitalist organization into every corner of life, increasingly confronts the need to reproduce the relations of production, and thus to maintain the organization of capitalism. The hegemony of the bourgeoisie is threatened by the growing fragmentation of space and of everyday life, and the increasing power of the centre is challenged by the reaction of the periphery. It is in this way that Lefebvre explains the trend towards regional devolution in the advanced capitalist countries, for such a strategy involves the attempt by the ruling class 'to offload some of their responsibilities on to local and regional organisms while preserving the mechanisms of power intact' (1976, p. 87).

This basic contradiction in the new urban society is not only revealed in political struggles between centre and periphery, however, but is also expressed in a broadening concern with the quality of life. The traditional assumption that the development of the productive forces of capitalism would automatically involve an improvement in the qualitative conditions of everyday life has been undermined:

This is what is new . . . that economic growth and social development can no longer be confused, as they have been before, by thinking that growth would bring development, that the quantitative would sooner or later bring the qualitative. . . . The ideology of growth has been mortally wounded. The vast ideological construct crumbles slowly but surely. Why? Because of the urban malaise, of the destruction of nature and its resources, because of blockages of all kinds which paralyze social development while enabling economic growth. [Lefebvre 1970, p. 260]

The penetration of everyday life by capitalist organization has therefore revealed more clearly than before the contradiction between private profit and social need, between capitalist domination and social life. It is for this reason that Lefebvre sees the urban crisis as the central and fundamental crisis of advanced capitalism, for the struggle over the use of space and the control of everyday life goes to the heart of the conflict between the requirements of capital and social need.

The practical political implications of Lefebvre's analysis are clear; the workers' movement must organize in order to harness the productive forces to social needs, and this will involve a strategy that links the periphery (meaning not only the regions, but also 'urban peripheries' such as black city ghettos and migrant worker shanty towns, and international peripheries in the Third World) to the labour movement and organizes both production and everyday life in terms of self-management. However, he recognizes that the existing strategies of the French Communist Party represent the very antithesis of such a programme. This is because, first, the party is still waging the industrial battle in the urban era; that is, it interprets all political struggles in terms of a basic economic orientation to questions of the workplace, and thus fails to address the fundamental issue of advanced capitalism concerning the control of space and everyday life. The result is that it lacks a strategy for confronting the bourgeoisie over the most crucial question of advanced capitalism, and it approaches urban struggles armed with only the most 'infantile' concepts which seek to reduce such struggles to the traditional and superseded categories of the Marxist analysis of a century ago.

The second source of divergence between Lefebvre's position and that of orthodox Marxism is that he totally rejects the Leninist view of the role of the party and criticizes the Communists for their inherent conservatism in seeking merely to 'take over the baton' from the bourgeoisie. Against their orientation towards an appropriation of the power centres of the existing society, Lefebvre asserts the need for self-management which necessarily entails the abolition of central domination altogether. As Castells (1977a, p. 89) suggests, Lefebvre's position thus appears not only humanist but anarchist.

For Lefebvre, then, the critical struggle in the urban phase of capitalist development is the struggle to free everyday life from capitalist organization and to bring about the management of space by and for the masses. This is what he means by the title of one of his books, *The Right to the Town* (1968b), for the concentration of the power of capital in the centres and the consequent expulsion of the people to the periphery most vividly symbolizes the subordination of need to profit in the contemporary period. The potential offered by urban society for human liberation is immense, but this potential can be realized only through the struggle against the capitalist domination of space, and hence by transcending the technocratic ideology of space of the bourgeoisie and the narrow economistic ideology of the existing Marxist parties.

Manuel Castells: science, ideology and the urban question

Like Lefebvre, Castells has developed a critique of existing theories of urbanism as ideological. Unlike Lefebvre, however, he does not rest this argument on the identification of the functions of such theories in sustaining capitalist class relations, but rather explains this functional aspect of 'theoretical ideologies' as itself due to the failure of existing theories to transcend the ideological relations through which individuals live their relation to the real world. In other words, existing theories (and Castells includes Lefebvre's work in this category) are ideological in that they merely elaborate rather than break with the ideological forms of capitalist society, and therefore fail to establish the basis for a scientific analysis of the reality of that society. As Walther suggests, 'In Castells, the fact that urban sociology and its dispersed fields had bowed to social demand is hardly criterion enough to refute it as ideology. His critique of ideology in urban sociology delves to a more subtle level; it is essentially an *epistemological critique*' (1978, p. 5). Castells's critique of existing theories as ideological is thus premised on the argument that there is a scientific mode of analysis by means of which it is possible to identify ideological discourses.

It should be noted at the outset that, in the course of the development of his work, Castells had cause to amend his initial epistemological position quite considerably. In this section, however, we shall be concerned principally with his earlier work, since it is here that he develops his critique of urban sociology as ideological. The subsequent revisions to his epistemology were developed as a result of his attempt to apply his approach in empirical research, and this experience appears to have led him to reconsider his earlier conceptions of science and its relation to ideology. As we shall see, this reconceptualization has the effect of undermining any attempt at maintaining such a distinction and thus throws into question his earlier critique of alternative theories, yet Castells has continued to refer to such theories as ideological despite his rejection of the very epistemology that originally sustained this critique.

The original critique of urban social theories was grounded in a relatively uncritical application of the Marxist philosophy of Louis Althusser to the urban question. Of particular significance was Althusser's argument that science develops out of an 'epistemological break' with existing ideological discourses – in other words that science involves a theoretical transformation of ideological concepts into scientific ones – for it was this that led Castells to engage in a critique of existing theories as the first step in developing a framework through which the 'real' question to which such theories were oriented could be identified and explored. As Althusser put it, 'The theoretical practice of a science is always completely distinct from the ideological theoretical practice of its prehistory: this distinction takes the form of a "qualitative" theoretical and historical discontinuity which I shall follow Bachelard in calling an "epistemological break" ' (1969, pp. 167–8).

According to Althusser, the procedure whereby scientific practice comes to transcend prescientific ideological theories is implicit in

Marx's own work, but is only ever made explicit in the 1857 Introduction in the *Grundrisse*. His argument is that Marx succeeded in breaking with ideology and founding a science of social formations when he developed his method of dialectical materialism, but that he never actually came to write the theory of this method. This is the task that Althusser takes upon himself and which he designates the Theory of Theoretical Practice.

The argument, which is derived mainly from a reading of the 1857 Introduction, begins by suggesting that the production of theory takes the same form as material production in society – that it involves the 'transformation of a determinate given raw material into a determinate product, a transformation effected by a determinate human labour, using determinate means (of production)' (Althusser 1969, p. 166). What this means is that scientific practice begins with certain raw materials of thought which it sets out to transform. These raw materials are existing general concepts, which may themselves be ideological or the products of earlier scientific practice. Althusser therefore endorses Marx's argument in the *Grundrisse* that science begins with abstractions, not with concrete reality itself: 'A science never works on an existence whose essence is pure immediacy and singularity ("sensations" or "individuals"). It always works on something "general" . . . a science always works on existing concepts. . . . It does not "work" on a purely objective "given", that of pure and absolute "facts"' (1969, pp. 183–4). This is because Althusser denies that reality is ever known through experience; knowledge is conceptual, not experiential. Science must therefore start out from existing abstract concepts (which Althusser terms 'Generalities I').

These general concepts are transformed through the application of theoretical means of production (Generality II). Just as production in society involves the application of certain tools to certain raw materials, so too theoretical production involves the application of theoretical tools to prescientific concepts. It is important to recognize that for Althusser this process does not entail the imposition by the theorist of his own ideas, for the theorist is merely the agent by means of which theoretical tools come to be applied, just as the worker is the agent of the means of production which he operates. Althusser is as opposed to idealism (the view that knowledge is a product of the individual human consciousness) as he is to empiricism (the view that knowledge is a reflection of concrete reality on to consciousness). Science involves neither the direct analysis of a given reality, nor the imposition of subjective constructs on to reality: 'The act of abstraction whereby the pure essence is extracted from concrete individuals is an ideological myth' (Althusser 1969, p. 191).

What this means, of course, is that the product of scientific practice (Generality III, knowledge) is the result of a theoretical transformation of existing concepts rather than of any direct articulation with the reality it claims to explain. For Althusser, it seems, there are two 'realities'; the reality that exists outside of thought, and remains unaffected by theoretical practice, and the reality that exists as a product of theoretical practice. There are, he says, 'two different concretes: the concrete-in-thought which is a knowledge, and the concrete-reality which is its object. The process which produces the concrete-knowledge takes place wholly in the theoretical practice' (1969, p. 186).

At this point, the obvious question concerns the relationship, if any, between the concrete reality and the concrete in thought. Althusser, however, rejects the premise on which such a question is based since the question makes sense only if we hold to an epistemology that distinguishes a knowing subject from the object of knowledge. His epistemology rejects this dualism since it rejects the notion of the knowing subject; as we have seen, the theorist is merely an agent of the theoretical transformation that takes place in scientific practice. This practice is itself *real* in that it involves a real transformation of ideology into knowledge:

The critique which, in the last instance, counterposes the abstraction it attributes to theory and to science and the concrete it regards as the real itself, remains an ideological critique since it denies the reality of scientific practice, the validity of its abstractions and ultimately the reality of that theoretical 'concrete' which is a knowledge. [Althusser 1969, p. 187]

In other words, Althusser defines scientific knowledge as the product of theoretical practice since it cannot be the product of pure experience, and further suggests that to deny the validity of such knowledge is to deny the validity of science itself and thus to collapse into ideology. As we shall see later, however, this all too neat solution to the problem still begs the question as to why dialectical materialism should provide the only correct guide to scientific practice – that is, why we should accept Althusser's epistemological legislation of scientific investigation in the first place.

It will be clear from this short exposition that, when Althusser turns to consider the question of ideology, his epistemology obliges him to reject the traditional argument that ideology involves the distortion of reality through ideas, since to argue thus would be to accept that knowledge is the product of the consciousness of human subjects (idealism), or to accept that reality is reflected in some way in our ideas about it (empiricism). Ideology is no more capable of distorting concrete reality than science is of representing it. Ideology, therefore, is not an ideal representation of reality, but is rather the way in which individuals relate to reality in their everyday lives: 'It is not their real conditions of existence, their real world, that "men represent to themselves" in ideology, but above all it is their relation to those conditions of existence which is represented to them there' (Althusser 1971, p. 154). Because the real relations in which individuals enter cannot themselves be directly known, individuals relate to their world by means of an imaginary relation. Thus, just as the product of scientific practice (the 'concrete-in-thought') is distinct from the concrete-reality, so too is the product of ideological practice (the 'imaginary lived relation'.)

One implication of this argument is that, although particular ideologies may change through history, ideology in general remains ever-present. Even in a communist society ideology would remain essential as the means whereby individuals lived their everyday lives, since reality itself will never become apparent. Ideology, therefore, is an inherent feature of social organization: in Althusser's terms, it is one 'instance' of the social totality (the concept of the social totality is considered in Chapter 6). It is also important to emphasize that, like science, ideology is a practice since it refers not to ideas about reality but to the very way in which we live that reality. Put another way, ideology is not ideal but material: 'Men "live" their ideologies as the Cartesian "saw" or did not see – if he was not looking at it – the moon two hundred paces away: not at all as a form of consciousness, but as an object of their "world" – as their "world" itself' (Althusser 1969, p. 233).

The most significant function of ideology, and one that serves to illustrate Althusser's argument, concerns what he terms the 'interpellation' of concrete individuals as subjects. By this he means simply that it is through our imaginary lived relation to the real world that we come to recognize ourselves and others as acting human subjects. In everyday life we act towards others, and others act towards us, as if we were subjects; that is, it is through ideological practices that we become constituted as subjects. The notion of the human subject, generating his own ideas from his own unique consciousness and imposing these ideas on the external world, is therefore a product of ideological practice in that subjects are constituted only through such practice: 'All ideology has the function (which defines it) of "constituting" concrete individuals as subjects. . . . Like all obviousnesses . . . the obviousness that you and I are subjects – and that that does not cause any problems – is an ideological effect, the elementary ideological effect' (Althusser 1971, pp. 160–1).

If the very notion of human subjectivity (with its related notions of human consciousness, human essence and so on) is a product of ideological practice, of our *imaginary* lived relation to the world, then it follows, of course, that scientific practice must involve a break with the category of the subject if it is to produce a knowledge that transcends ideology. For as long as theory retains the ideological concept of the human subject, it will remain incapable of developing a scientific knowledge of real, as opposed to 'imaginary', relations. Put somewhat crudely, such a theory will fail to see the wood (the totality of objective social relations) for the trees ('human subjects' constituted by such relations). Such a theory will be 'closed' in the sense that it will fail to open up the question of how the imaginary relation is itself constituted and is therefore destined merely to reproduce ideology in elaborated form. It is only when science breaks with ideology and becomes autonomous from it that it becomes possible to recognize ideology for what it is:

Those who are in ideology believe themselves by definition outside ideology: one of the effects of ideology is the practical denegation of the ideological character of ideology by ideology: ideology never says, 'I am ideological'. It is necessary to be outside ideology, i.e. in scientific knowledge, to be able to say: I am in ideology (a quite exceptional case) or (the general case): I was in ideology. [Althusser 1971]

It is now possible to understand the Althusserian critique of humanism as ideology, for it is not that humanist theories (that is, those that set 'man' at the centre of the theoretical stage and endow him with consciousness and effectivity) are in some way false, but rather that they take categories constituted through ideological practice as the basic and unquestioned categories of analysis and thus preclude the possibility of explaining them: 'When I say that the concept of humanism is an ideological concept (not a scientific one), I mean that while it really does designate a set of existing relations, unlike a scientific concept it does not provide us with a means of knowing them' (Althusser 1969, p. 223). It is precisely this argument that Castells employs against Lefebvre.

Castells levels a number of criticisms against Lefebvre's analysis, most of which are aimed at demolishing his concept of an urban society that has gone beyond the classic period of industrial capitalism. The main thrust of his critique, however, is epistemological, not theoretical, for Castells takes issue with Lefebvre's assumption that space is produced through the conscious activity of human subjects (capitalists, politicians or whatever). This analysis, he suggests,

indicates that space, like the whole of society, is the ever-original work of that freedom of creation that is the attribute of Man, and the spontaneous expression of his desire. It is only by accepting this absolute of Lefebvrian humanism (a matter of philosophy or religion) that the analysis might be pursued in this direction: it would always be dependent on its metaphysical foundation. [Castells 1977a, p. 92]

Lefebvre's analysis is therefore little more than a theoretical ideology, since it is grounded in ideological (or 'metaphysical') categories which it simply elaborates. The consequence of this is that it prevents any break-through to science through its failure to recognize the determinate conditions of social life. Despite its radical flavour, therefore, it effectively hinders rather than aids scientific critique: 'This new urban ideology may thus serve noble causes . . . while masking fundamental phenomena that theoretical practice still finds difficult to grasp' (Castells 1977a, p. 94).

Castells develops much the same argument against other, less radical, urban theories which similarly seek to explain urban processes in terms of the actions of individual subjects. The (mainly American) community power literature, which is concerned to trace which individuals or groups at the local level enjoy the greatest power to determine policies, is one obvious example, since for Castells power cannot be conceptualized in terms of individual attributes or individual relationships (see Chapter 6). Another equally obvious example concerns the urban managerialist literature discussed in Chapter 4:

This perspective which, by virtue of the ease with which it responds to the concrete problems that face the 'decision-makers', is assuming increasing importance . . . rests entirely on an ideological base, for it is based on a meta-physical postulate, without which it becomes purely empirical description. This postulate is that 'ultimately one must place the accent on the freedom of man who remains, whatever his situation, an autonomous agent capable of negotiating his cooperation'. [Castells 1977a, p. 250]

As we saw in Chapter 4, the basic problem encountered but not resolved in the urban managerialism approach concerns the need to theorize the limits on the autonomy of significant actors. Castells's analysis suggests that this problem must necessarily remain unresolved for as long as theory begins with the (ideological) category of individual subjects rather than with the question of the social totality that constitutes them as subjects: 'It is by situating the elements of social structure in a prior theoretical context that one will succeed in making significant the practices concretely observed and then, and only then, can one rediscover this supposed "autonomy" of the "actors" ' (p. 251). For as long as analysis retains the actor as its focus of concern, it is doomed merely to reproduce but never to explain the imaginary relation of individuals to the real world:

The analysis that sets out from the concrete actors and their strategies necessarily ends up in an impasse: if these actors are simply empirical objects, the analysis becomes a mere description of particular situations; if they are first realities, therefore essences, the analysis is dependent on a metaphysics of freedom. [Castells 1977a, p. 251]

For Castells, as for Althusser, the notion of the human subject consciously constituting his world must therefore be abandoned to the realm of pre-science. He states his position most clearly in one of his earlier essays where he writes,

To identify the production of forms with their origin in action presupposes acceptance of the notion of actor-subjects, constructing their history in terms of their own values and aims. . . . This requires that one take as a starting point actors and combinations of actors, and thus that one accept the existence of primary essences, not deduced from social structures. . . . The theoretical issue is this: historical actors founding society through their action, or support-agents expressing particular combinations of the social structure through their practice. We will take for granted that the first approach belongs to the philosophy of history, and that only the second is capable of founding a science of society. [Castells 1976b, pp.77–8]

The practices of individuals thus can be explained only through a scientific theory of structure.

This emphasis on a theory of structure and of its elements explains the ironic feature of Castells's critique of urban sociology; namely that he is most implacably opposed to the most radical theories (for example those of Lefebvre and the elite theorists of community power) while finding much that is commendable in the most conservative theory (namely human ecology) and its later derivatives (mainly Wirth's theory of urbanism). As regards the ecological approach he writes, 'The attempt to explain territorial collectivities by the notion of an ecological system constitutes the most serious attempt to give urban sociology a specific theoretical field in conjunction with the functionalist approach' (1976b, p. 71); and he later extended the compliment to Wirth's work, which he sees as 'the most serious theoretical attempt ever made within sociology to establish a theoretical object (and consequently a domain of research) specific to urban sociology' (1977a, p. 77). The significance of Park and Wirth is that they not only avoided explanations couched in terms of human subjects (neither Park's biotic forces nor Wirth's size, density and heterogeneity made reference to the purposive actions of individuals in bringing about certain effects), but they also attempted to explain urban reality by developing a theory of determinate processes. In other words, their theoretical practice sought to identify a theoretically specific problem (what Castells terms a 'theoretical object') as the precondition for developing a scientific explanation of a concrete reality (the 'real object'). For them, as for Castells, the city or space cannot be known and explained directly but must be analysed in terms of a theoretically produced object. Park's theoretical object was integration (that is, the urban system was theorized in terms of the biotic forces operating to bring about social and system integration), while Wirth's was a specific cultural content (the urban was theorized in terms of the causal effect of demographic factors in bringing about anonymity, superficiality, etc.).

The problem with both of these theories, however, was that their theoretical objects, while valid in themselves, could not provide the basis for a distinctively urban theory that could be applied to the empirical study of the city. The problem of integration, for example, necessarily involved analysis of factors that bore no necessary relationship to urbanism: 'As soon as the urban context is broken down even into such crude categories as social class, age or "interests", processes which seemed to be peculiar to particular urban areas turn out to be determined by other factors' (1976a, p. 40). This resulted in the tension diagnosed in Chapter 2 between human ecology as a theory of the city and human ecology as a theory of adaptation, for there was no reason why the theoretical object of biotic processes of integration and adaptation should be confined to analysis of the city. Similarly, Wirth's problem of urban culture turned out on closer inspection to be a theory of the cultural forms of capitalism, for not only did research demonstrate that the cultures of pre-industrial and non-capitalist cities differ from that identified by Wirth, but the sorry history of the rural–urban continuum demonstrated that the factors that he took as adequate for explaining cultural differences between town and country in capitalist societies were in fact inadequate.

Neither of these theories therefore succeeded in producing a theoretical object by means of which the real object (urbanism, space) could be analysed. Rather, by equating a concept of urbanism with what was in fact a theorization of capitalism, they succeeded only in representing capitalist processes (competition, individualism, etc.) as inherent to the nature of cities: 'An urban sociology founded on urbanism is an ideology of modernity ethnocentrically identified with the crystallization of the social forms of liberal capitalism' (1976b, p. 70). In this way, these theories served an ideological function by providing a naturalistic explanation for people's everyday experiences: 'Such a "theory" is extremely useful to ruling political elites inasmuch as it conceptualizes social organization as depending less on social data, in particular class relations, than on natural, spatial, technical and biological data' (1977b, p. 62).

By this stage of his argument, Castells has effectively demolished the whole of urban sociology as ideological. The problem with previous work is two-fold. First, theories such as those developed in the urban managerialist literature or that advanced by Lefebvre are grounded in the ideological category of the human subject and are therefore incapable of sustaining a scientific analysis (since such an analysis must be derived from a theory of the system and of its interrelated elements). Second, theories such as human ecology that avoid such categories have failed to develop a means of relating their real object of study (urbanism) to their overall theories of adaptation, and have therefore resulted in ideological effects (since they equate the effects of overall social processes within capitalism with the specific effects of urban processes). What is required, therefore, is a radical reformulation which can identify what is to be studied (the real object) and can provide a theoretical framework by means of which this real object can be studied in the context of its relationship to the system as a whole (a theoretical object).

As the first step towards such a reformulation, Castells suggests that, among the plurality of real objects which urban sociology has studied in the past, it is possible to identify two that, when taken together, constitute a legitimate focus for scientific concern. The first of these is space: 'The sociological analysis of space appears to us to be a quite legitimate field of study. However, it is not a theoretical object but a real object, since space is a material element and not a conceptual unit' (1976b, p. 70). Concern with space is, of course, the common feature of all previous approaches, but none of them has succeeded in demonstrating the coincidence of spatial units with social units. Thus spatial units do not coincide with distinctive cultural units (Wirth), with distinctive political units (Pahl), and so on, and this is why previous approaches have collapsed into a non-specific concern with culture in general, politics in general or whatever. It is therefore a precondition for any scientific reformulation of the 'urban question' that we establish the coincidence of a real spatial unit with a real social unit: 'What we would like to examine . . . is under what conditions a sociology could be defined as urban from the point of view of its scientific object. In our opinion this possibility exists when there is a coincidence between a spatial unit and a social unit' (1976a, p. 57).

The only candidate among the various social phenomena that have been studied by urban sociologists which can fulfil this requirement is what Castells terms 'collective consumption' units. As we shall see in the next chapter, his definition of collective consumption is by no means clear, and it undergoes various metamorphoses as his work develops, but in the early essays this term refers simply to 'consumption processes whose organization and management cannot be other than collective given the nature and size of the problems' (1976b, p. 75). The examples provided by Castells include housing, social facilities and leisure provisions. The basic assertion in his reformulation of the urban question is that, unlike units of production, which are organized on a regional (or even national or international) scale, units of consumption are socially organized and provided within the context of a spatially bounded system. The coincidence between a spatial unit and a social unit which has so often eluded urban sociology is therefore identified as that between spatial organization and the organization of collective consumption facilities. This is a relationship that has often been implicit in urban analysis but has never before been made explicit as the definition of the urban real object: 'Urban sociology has in fact tended to tackle two types of problem: (1) relationships to space and (2) what may be termed the process of collective consumption. . . . Thus, as well as ideological themes and highly diverse real objects, the urban sociology tradition includes a sociology of space and a sociology of collective consumption' (1976b, pp. 74–5).

Having identified the real object as a (spatial) unit of collective consumption, Castells has prepared the ground for the rise of a new theoretical Phoenix with a secure scientific foundation from the ashes of the old urban sociology. It only remains for him to apply his ready-constituted theory of the total social system (a theory that he finds in Althusserian Marxism) in order to identify the theoretical element in that system to which collective consumption corresponds. As we shall see in Chapter 6, this is a relatively simple process since the theory breaks down the social totality into three analytical levels (the economic, the political and the ideological), and further breaks down the economic level into its constitutive elements of production, consumption and exchange. Each of these elements is defined through its functions within the system as a whole such that production entails the application of human labour to the material environment in order to create commodities; exchange involves the circulation of these commodities and thus (in capitalism) the realization of exchange value; and consumption involves the final utilization of these commodities by individuals as their means of life and sustenance. It is through the process of consumption, in other words, that individuals reproduce their labour-power (for example by consuming food, housing, recreation, education and so on) which then re-enters the system as a resource to be used in the process of producing new commodities. Consumption is therefore defined within this theoretical system in terms of its function in reproducing labour-power, and in this way its relation to the other elements (production, exchange) and levels (political and ideological) of the total system is established.

Castells, therefore, is now in possession of both a real object (the concrete reality of spatial units of collective consumption) and a theoretical object (the process of consumption as a functional element within the total social system involving the reproduction of the most fundamental resource in that system – labour-power). He is then in a position to analyse the real object by analysing the role of the theoretical object to which it corresponds within the total theoretical system. But before we consider the analysis that he offers, it is necessary to examine critically his claim that this new approach to the urban question is set upon a secure scientific basis which distinguishes it from the ideological character of all previous theories.

Epistemological imperialism and the new urban sociology

In rejecting existing theories as ideological while setting up his own approach as scientific, Castells has clearly engaged in a very dangerous game, for as we shall see in Chapter 6, other theorists may equally lay claim to the 'correct' mode of analysis and reject his formulations as ideological. As Lebas (1979) has noted, much of the current Marxist literature is marked by what she terms 'theoretical terrorism' as each new combatant defends his own approach as scientific (invariably through selected textual references to the holy grail of *Capital*) while dismissing all alternatives as 'bourgeois', 'empiricist', 'ideological' or any other equally pejorative term taken from the expanding litany of academic abuse. Castells appears particularly vulnerable in this respect since (a) his application of the Althusserian schema appears somewhat inconsistent, (b) the Althusserian distinction that he employs between science and ideology can and must be rejected, and (c) in rejecting certain key aspects of Althusser's work in his later writings, he has himself undermined the basis on which his original critique and reformulation was developed. The remainder of this chapter is devoted to an elaboration of these three points.

The inconsistency in Castells's early work concerns his discussion of the real and the theoretical object. The latter appears relatively unproblematic within the context of the Althusserian schema, for it evidently refers to Althusser's notion of the 'concrete-in-thought' or scientific knowledge (which does not imply some 'final' state of knowledge or some absolute truth, but rather means that it is the foundation for the further development of scientific, as opposed to ideological, discourse). But what of the 'real object'? There appear to be two possibilities.

The first is that Castells intends this term to refer to what Althusser calls the 'concrete reality'. In this sense, spatial units of collective consumption exist in the real world but can never be directly known, either through experience or through ideal abstractions. But if this is what Castells means by a real object, then it would appear illogical to suggest, as he does on several occasions, that a science may be said to exist if it possesses *either* a real *or* a theoretical object: 'A scientific discipline is built either by a certain conceptual cutting up of reality, i.e. through the definition of a *scientific object*, or by a specific field of observation, i.e. through the choice of a *real object*' (Castells 1977b, pp. 61–2). Yet it is precisely Althusser's argument that the concrete reality can never itself be known, and Castells echoes this view when he warns that 'There is no such thing as a direct relationship between researcher and real object. All thought is more or less consciously shaped by a pre-existing theoretico-ideological field' (1976b, p. 83). The necessary consequence of this argument is that a science cannot be constituted through its possession of a real object, a 'specific field of observation', but rather constitutes itself through its theoretical practice. If we assume that Castells is following Althusser in his early work, then we must assume that the real object does not refer to the concrete reality, since for Althusser a science cannot be defined in terms of its empirical concern with some aspect of reality. Thus it will be recalled that he argues explicitly that 'The act of abstraction whereby the pure essence is extracted from concrete individuals is an ideological myth' (Althusser 1969, p. 191).

The second possibility is that Castells intends the real object to refer to the ideological raw materials of thought (Generalities I) which scientific practice transforms into theoretical knowledge. In this sense, the real object is not the concrete reality itself but the existing representations of the imaginary relation to the concrete. This is the interpretation of Castells offered by Pickvance when he suggests that 'The real object refers to some aspect of reality, ready-wrapped in preconceptions which are usually "ideological", while the science seeks knowledge in the form of a theoretical object' (Pickvance 1976a, p. 4). But if this is indeed what Castells means by the term, then it follows that spatial units of collective consumption are merely existing categories through which urban sociologists have conceptualized the real world, and that science will involve the transformation of these categories and hence their supersession. Clearly this is not what Castells intends, for he claims to have identified both a theoretical and a real object for his new scientific approach. His aim is not to transcend the real object but to study it. Collective consumption is not a pre-scientific category in his analysis but a constitutive category of his analysis.

We are forced to the conclusion that Castells's notion of the real object has no reference in Althusser's philosophy of scientific practice. Indeed, despite his protestations to the contrary, it is apparent that the whole thrust of Castells's critique of human ecology and of his subsequent reformulation of the field is premised upon an epistemology that Althusser himself rejects. Put simply, when Castells criticizes human ecology for failing to develop a theory specific to an urban real object, he has to assume that such a real object exists and can be known outside of theory, for how else can the lack of correspondence between the theory and the object be established? Similarly, when he sets out to identify a new real object (the coincidence of units of collective consumption with spatial units), he has first to assume that this can be identified unproblematically through observation before he can go on to show how it can be studied by means of his theoretical object. In short, both the critique and the reformulation are based on the argument that there must be a *correspondence* between some aspect of reality termed 'urban' and the theory that relates to it. Castells, in other words, has effectively reintroduced the knowing subject/object of knowledge dichotomy which Althusser sought to reject. By defining his science in terms of the relation between theory and reality, a theoretical object and a real object, he has fallen into what Althusser sees as the ideological trap of empiricism–humanism and has thereby reopened the question of how a correspondence can be demonstrated between them. As we shall in Chapter 6, Castells can therefore be criticized on precisely the same grounds as he criticized others; namely that his conceptualization of the urban does not 'fit' the reality observed. Thus Harloe has rightly noted the 'remarkable similarity between Castells's actual approach, as opposed to his intentions, and that of the bourgeois theorists he has criticized', for he ends up by imposing his theoretical categories on to reality in an attempt to relate the reality of the city to his pre-existing conceptual system (see Harloe 1979, p. 128).

This procedure of 'cutting up reality' conceptually in order to isolate and analyse its theoretically significant aspects clearly bears more approximation to Weber's ideal type method than it does to Althusser's scientific practice, and this is an argument we shall pursue in more detail in the next chapter. For the moment, we may merely note that the reason why Castells disguises what is basically a Weberian method in Althusserian clothing is that there is no basis in Weber's sociology for the distinction he wishes to draw between scientific and ideological discourses. This is why Castells resorts to the formal structure of Althusserian scientific practice in his critique of urban sociology, even though his own method has little relation to this practice. Thus he begins with a critique of current conceptions of urbanism (the 'ideological' raw materials of thought); he then applies the theoretical tools of Marxist analysis to these conceptions (the theory of structure); and he ends up by producing a new scientific knowledge of the urban question (in terms of the function of collective consumption in reproducing labour-power). The move from

Generalities I to Generalities III is reproduced in formal terms in his work, for it is only by means of this schema that he can claim to have developed a scientific knowledge that transcends ideological conceptions through an epistemological break with them.

There is, however, an irony in this attempt to hang on to the appearance of an Althusserian method, for even if Castells's approach had been consistent with that of Althusser, we should still have to reject the claim that it can distinguish between scientific and ideological theories. The reason for this, quite simply, is that no epistemology can legislate on the question of correct scientific method *per se*. The role of epistemology (as Castells was later to recognize in his article written jointly with Ipola) is to aid the clarification and subsequent resolution of problems confronted *within* particular discourses, not to referee what are basically irresolvable disputes over method *between* different discourses. It can, for example, point to obstacles of empiricism that may arise within approaches that seek to reject empiricism, but it cannot lay down with any final authority that empiricism is itself an 'incorrect' or 'invalid' approach to scientific knowledge (still less that it is inherently ideological).

My argument here closely reflects that developed in the recent work of Paul Hirst (1979). He has provided a detailed critique of Althusser's theory of ideology (including its later revisions) in the course of which he emphatically restates the critique of epistemological imperialism which he first developed in his work with Hindess. Basically, his argument is that no epistemology can establish a general principle, to be applied to all discourses, regarding the relation between theory and reality. This is because the relationship of any discourse to reality is defined within the discourse itself: 'Outside of epistemology what it is discourses and practices construct and refer to has no necessary common attributes; equally these constructions and referents are unintelligible except in and as discourse . . . we deny any non-discursive level of "experience" or "consciousness"' (p. 20). It follows that epistemological principles that lay down the means of developing scientific knowledge cannot exist outside the theories that adopt and apply them, in which case Althusser's epistemology is applicable only within Althusser's theory (or, to put the same point in a different way, it has no general applicability and is not therefore an epistemology, in the sense of a general theory of the production of knowledge, at all).

If we abandon epistemology, then it follows that criteria of valid knowledge are always internal to theoretical systems:

> We would argue that discourses and practices *do* employ the criteria of
> appropriateness or adequacy (not of epistemological validity) but these are
> specific to the objectives of definite bodies of discourse and practice. None
> will pass muster as a general criterion of validity, but there is no knowledge
> process in general and, therefore, no necessity for such a criterion. [Hirst
> 1979, p. 21]

This argument does not represent a collapse into relativism, both
because relativism itself is only a problem within debates over general
epistemological principles, and because different discourses may
share common criteria of adequacy (in other words, criteria may be
dependent upon, but not exclusively determined by, specific theories
– see Andrew Sayer (1979, p. 9).

The effect of this argument is to undermine any claim to
epistemological privilege on the part of Marxist theories, and thus to
demolish the division between science and ideology that such theories
assert: 'Marxism is not a "science" (equally it is not a "non-science",
science-ideology is an epistemological distinction), it has no
privileged knowledge' (Hirst 1979, p. 6). This conclusion, of course,
relates back to the discussion of Marx's method in Chapter 1, for
there we noted that Marx has no privileged starting-point for
analysing reality and that his method consists in hypothesizing
certain relations as a means of providing a plausible explanation for
the phenomena he identified in the real world. This is a perfectly
acceptable method on its own terms, but it contains no means for
asserting itself as the general and only scientific method for analysing
social reality, nor does it establish any general criteria of scientificity
against which other approaches may cavalierly be dismissed as
ideological.

Even if Castells had remained faithful to the Althusserian position,
therefore, there would be no warrant in his work for his
epistemological distinction between scientific and ideological
theories of the urban question. Yet, as we have already noted, in his
later work he came to reject certain crucial elements of that position
and thereby himself to undermine his original critique.

Of considerable significance here was a joint article originally
published in 1972 and translated into English four years alter. In this
paper, Castells sought to retain Althusser's critique of humanism and
subjectivism and his concept of the epistemological break while
rejecting any general theory of science and ideology: 'We do refuse

the abstract general thesis of an absolute and universal opposition between science and ideology and the consequences such a distinction entails' (Castells and Ipola 1976, p. 117). The authors went on to suggest that epistemology is limited in the scope of its intervention in scientific practice to clearing obstacles that are themselves epistemological; that is, it cannot determine the principles of scientific practice themselves but is rather an aid to clear analysis: 'A materialist epistemological intervention cannot be reduced to the application of pre-established rules according to a theoretical system: its relevance must be assessed after its effects and not after its ability to conform to any "principle" whatsoever' (p. 139). It followed from this that, rather than looking to epistemology to determine criteria of scientific truth, Marxism should develop its theories through concrete political struggles as the means of elaborating and realizing them.

The Castells and Ipola paper appears somewhat ambivalent towards Althusser's position (it is by no means clear, for example, how the epistemological break can be retained without a general theory of science and ideology), but Castells's drift away from Althusser became more marked in later work. The experience of applying the method in empirical research in the Dunkerque region was undoubtedly a chastening one, for in their theoretical and methodological introduction to this study he and Godard recognize the dangers of applying a preconstituted theoretical system to particular concrete cases: 'To fix a certain mode of theoretical analysis and to hold on to its internal logic and to the validity of the social laws already established by the general theoretical framework from which this mode of analysis derives is a considerable risk or, if you like, a gamble on its applicability' (Castells and Godard 1974, p. 14). Such a method would result simply in an unfounded attempt to reduce the complexity of the observed reality to the pre-existing system of concepts, and the authors reject such a sterile approach in favour of one that attempts to establish a correspondence between theory and reality:

We have not 'operationalized' each concept as an indicator, following a one-to-one correspondence which would be perfectly illusory in the analysis of dynamic social processes, but we have traced the correspondence between a 'theoretical chain' and an 'observation chain', through their logical articulation, such that the totality of facts becomes illuminated and interpreted in a coherent and theoretically significant way. [Castells and Godard 1974, pp. 15–16]

Empirical research, in other words, is guided by and interpreted through theory, but theory is in turn itself developed and amended in the course of such research.

One year later, in his Afterword to *The Urban Question* (1977a), Castells underlined the significance of this break with Althusser's theoretical practice by explicitly rejecting the argument that knowledge involves a movement from the abstract to the concrete and arguing instead that the development of theory must be grounded in analysis of concrete cases from the very outset:

What is involved is the very style of the theoretical work, the epistemological approach in question. One must choose between, on the one hand, the idea of a 'Great Theory' (even a Marxist one) which one then verifies empirically, and, on the other hand, the proposition of a theoretical work that produces concepts and their historical relations within a process of discovery of the laws of society given in their specific modes of existence. It is not only a question of 'carrying out empirical research'. It is a question rather of the fact that *'theory' is not produced outside a process of concrete knowledge.* [Castells 1977a, p. 438; emphasis added]

He then goes on to criticize his own earlier theoretical work as formalistic, suggesting that, by developing his theoretical system separately from empirical research in concrete cases, it resulted in a process of merely coding rather than analysing reality. This 'autocritique' is then summarized in one of his most recent essays:

Because there was an immediate need for a theory, it was applied too mechanically. . . . Generally researchers applied established theories without modifying them to the reality observed. In some cases it was Althusserian theory (Castells) . . . the theoretical coding has been too rapid, too formal, the reality analyzed was more complex than the models used. [Castells 1978, pp. 11–12]

There is certainly room for debate over whether Castells has broken with his earlier commitment to the Althusserian approach or whether his early work was ever really Althusserian in the first place (in which case the later discussions can be seen as a tightening up of earlier methodological principles rather than a rupture with them – for instance see Walther 1978). But from our present vantage point such a debate is unimportant, for there can now be no doubt that Castells is committed to a view of Marxist method that is in most important respects the antithesis of Althusser's and is broadly consistent with that outlined in Chapter 1. This being the case, what is the status now of his initial rejection of urban sociology as ideological?

We saw in Chapter 1 that Marx's method of 'retroduction' claims no privileged insight into reality. It generates more or less plausible explanations of phenomenal forms by positing the operation of essential relations, but there is not and never can be any compelling reason to accept these explanations to the exclusion of others. In this chapter we have drawn out the necessary implications of this: namely that no theory can lay exclusive claim to knowledge; that there can be no general epistemological principles outside of specific theoretical approaches; that theoretical pluralism is thus inherent to social science; and that, in the absence of general criteria of scientific and ideological theories, the epistemological division between science and ideology must be rejected.

This need not lead to the rejection of the concept of ideology *per se*, for as we noted at the start of this chapter, it has been applied both as an epistemological category and as a functional one. There is no reason why the latter sense of the term should not be retained; that is the sense of ideology as a set of ideas, realized through action, with specific effects for particular sections of society. The analysis of ideology then becomes a question of political theory, not epistemology (see Giddens 1979, ch. 5, for a similar argument). From this perspective, to argue that a particular theory (say, human ecology) is ideological is to argue that, according to our own theory, it has certain practical political effects for definite social interests (such as that, by representing urban processes as natural, it serves to legitimate the position of those groups whose interests are served by such processes). This, of course, is precisely the way in which Lefebvre uses the term, and it is a perfectly valid usage provided we remember that the identification of different social interests is itself dependent upon particular political theories (see Saunders 1979, ch. I).

Having himself rejected a general theory of science and ideology, Castells has never explicitly readdressed the question he posed in his early work regarding the scientific status of urban sociology and the ideological concept of urbanism. Clearly, however, the logic of his later position must entail a rejection of any monopolistic claim to scientific knowledge and an amendment of his critique of earlier theories. Of course, we may still choose to designate these theories as 'ideological', but this must be seen in terms of their practical political effects rather than their mode of explanation. Similarly, we may still choose to adopt Castells's own approach to the analysis of the urban question, but such a decision will be determined not by its epistemological claims but in terms of its fruitfulness for our own interests and purposes. As Castells recognizes, 'The force of our analyses must come from their explicative capacity', and they can be justified 'only by the fecundity of the research results acquired as a result of these new bases' (1977a, pp. 454, 450). It is to a consideration of precisely these questions that we now turn.

6 The urban as a spatial unit of collective consumption

Althusser's influence on Castells's reformulation of urban sociology was both epistemological and theoretical. We saw in the preceding chapter that the epistemological inheritance that provided the basis for Castells's critique of previous theories must be rejected on the grounds that no epistemology can be self-evident and self-justifying. We also saw that Castells himself was in any case never fully committed to this epistemology and that, as his work developed, so the separation between his and Althusser's method became increasingly explicit. The consequence of this is that the philosophical foundation of his work is now far from clear (for example, the notion of establishing a correspondence between 'chains of observation' and 'chains of theory' begs many familiar questions), and that his early critique of urban sociology as ideological has been undermined.

The rejection of Althusserian epistemology, however, does not in itself entail a rejection of the theoretical framework that Castells derives from Althusser and from other theorists (notably Nicos Poulantzas) influenced by his writings. This follows from the argument developed in the last chapter that theories must be evaluated on their own terms and cannot be upheld or rejected by reference to some set of external and eternal epistemological principles. Thus, while the critique of Althusser's attempt to legislate science and ideology necessarily leads us to reject the basis on which Castells attacked previous theories, it leaves open the question of the theoretical fruitfulness of Castells's own approach to the urban question.

Just as in the last chapter we saw how Castells moved away from his initial (half-hearted) endorsement of Althusser's method, so too we shall see in this chapter that his work has involved a progressive shift away from an initial commitment to Althusser's theoretical framework. Nevertheless, many of the fundamental elements of this framework have been retained, even in his latest writings, and in this sense it may be suggested that the Althusserian theory of structures has retained a central significance in Castells's work in a way in which the Althusserian method for analysing such structures has not. The first step in understanding Castells's theory must therefore involve a discussion of the Althusserian framework from which it derives.

The urban system and the capitalist mode of production

Althusser's single most important contribution to the development of Marxist theory is arguably his critique of traditional interpretations of Marx's dialectic. Basically he suggests that the orthodox view that Marx 'inverted' Hegel's dialectic, thereby substituting a materialist theory of social development for an idealist one, is a gross over-simplification and misunderstanding of Marx's approach. Such a simple inversion would have led Marx to develop a theory of historical change based entirely on the development of the economic forces and relations of production and on the contradiction between them, just as Hegel's dialectic resulted in a theory based entirely on the development of a universal idea or spirit embodied in the state. Such an economist theory does not, according to Althusser, bear any approximation to the theory of historical materialism that Marx did actually produce (although many later Marxist theorists have themselves interpreted Marx in such a way).

According to Althusser, Marx argued that the economic contradiction between the forces and relations of production (which in capitalism takes the form of the contradiction between capital and wage labour) was a necessary but not sufficient condition for historical transformations from one mode of production to another. What was necessary in addition was the development of other, secondary contradictions within the 'superstructure' of political and ideological relations, contradictions that could then act back upon the basic contradiction. In other words, although political and ideological relations derived out of the mode of economic organiza-tion, they developed to some extent independently of economic relations and generated their own effects within the system as a whole. The development of the economic contradiction thus takes place within the context of a unified system of contradictions and cannot be isolated from this system as a single motive force in history, for its development and effectivity is contingent upon the autono-mous and uneven development of secondary contradictions elsewhere in the system (and, indeed, on the international context within which the system as a whole is situated). In Althusser's terminology, the basic economic contradiction is 'overdetermined' by contradictions developing at other points or 'instances' of the system, and the transformation from one mode of production to another is dependent upon the development of a 'ruptural fusion' of these different contradictions at a particular point in time ('historical conjuncture'). It is in this way that Althusser explains the revolution in Russia in 1917, although it should be noted in passing that such a theory will always be *a posteriori* since, as Walton and Gamble (1972, p. 133) point out, it lacks any criteria by means of which we can identify a ruptural fusion of contradictions before a revolution takes place.

Althusser's theoretical framework constitutes a rejection of traditional Marxist concepts of an economic base determining a political and ideological superstructure. In its place he conceptualizes a complex system of three levels – the economic, political and ideological – in which contradictions develop both within and between each level. The system as a whole represents a specific mode of production in its pure form (that is, existing societies or 'social formations' always involve elements of different pure modes of production with the result that further contradictions develop between as well as within the different modes). Within any given mode of production, one of the three levels will perform the dominant role (for example, in a feudal mode of production the dominant level is the ideological, since religion performs the crucial function in maintaining the unity of the whole; in competitive capitalism the dominant level is the economic, because of the self-perpetuating character of commodity production; in ancient societies such as Rome the dominant level was the political, for the state was the crucial factor in maintaining the unity of the system as a whole). The system as a whole is thus termed by Althusser a 'structure in dominance' since it is a system that achieves its (contradictory) unity by means of a dominant level: 'The unity discussed by Marxism is the unity of the complexity itself . . . the complex whole has the unity of a structure articulated in dominance' (1969, p. 202).

The question of which of the three levels is to perform the dominant function in any particular mode of production is determined by the nature of the economic relations pertaining in that mode (feudal economic relations, for example, necessitated a dominant role for religion in maintaining the unity of the system; capitalist economic relations necessitate a dominant role for the economy itself; and so on). In other words, although the economic is not always dominant, it is always determinate in the sense that it determines the nature of the relations between the three levels and hence which is to perform the dominant role. This is what Althusser means by economic determinacy 'in the last instance'.

It is important to recognize that this ambiguous term should be understood analytically rather than temporally. Thus, when Althusser writes that 'From the first moment to the last, the lonely hour of the "last instance" never comes' (1969, p. 113), he does not mean (as some interpreters have suggested) that economic determinacy never actually asserts itself, but rather that, while the economic *always* determines which level is to be dominant, it *never* determines how this level (or the other levels) is to develop. In other words, within a structure of dominance, the different levels develop in different ways and at different rates, and in the process they each affect the development of the others. Each level, that is, is *relatively autonomous* of each other level (only relatively so, since each level is necessarily affected by the specific effects of each other level; they exist only within a unified system, in which case total autonomy clearly becomes impossible). As we shall see later, this concept of relative autonomy has become crucial for Castells's application of the Althusserian system in his own theory.

Both in his early essays and in *The Urban Question*, Castells makes clear his theoretical debt to Althusser (e.g. Castells 1976c, pp. 149–50; 1977a, p. 125), and the development of his theory is premised upon a prior acceptance of Althusser's theory of the structure in dominance. Castell's starting point is therefore given in a theory of which the key elements are (a) the distinction between mode of production and social formation; (b) a concept of mode of production as constituted by three relatively autonomous levels; (c) a recognition of the dominance of one level, this being determined 'in the last instance' by the economic; and (d) an explanation of system change in terms of the identification of structural contradictions which are expressed in and through class practices. Taking this theory of structure as given, Castells then confronts the question of how the urban system relates to this structure.

He begins by arguing that the urban system is not something separate from the total system but is one aspect of it. It is, in other words, the specific expression of that system within a spatial unit of collective consumption: 'We shall use the term spatial structure (or "urban system" to conform to tradition) to describe the particular way in which the basic elements of the social structure are spatially articulated' (1976b, p. 78). The way in which the different levels of the total system articulate with one another must therefore correspond to their articulation in the urban system, and any change in the total system must be reflected in a similar change within the urban system: 'The urban system is not external to the social structure; it specifies that social structure, it forms part of it' (1977a, p. 263).

The first step in Castells's analysis therefore involves the application of the theory of the total system to the urban system. The urban system is thus said to be constituted by three levels – the economic, the political and the ideological. The political level corresponds to urban administration (local government and other locally based agencies of the state) which performs the dominant function within the urban system of regulating the relations between the different levels in order to maintain the cohesion of the system. The ideological level corresponds to the 'urban symbolic' (the meanings emitted by socially produced spatial forms). Finally, the economic level is broken down into its three elements of production, consumption and exchange, each of which corresponds to different elements in the urban system (such as factories and offices, housing and recreation facilities, and means of transportation respectively).

The urban system thus contains all the levels and elements of the social system of which it forms a part, and these levels and elements are all structured in the same way as in the wider system. However, as we saw in Chapter 5, Castells argues that this system within a system is a theoretically significant object of study; it is not merely a microcosm of the total system but performs a specific function in relation to that system. As he puts it, 'It is necessary to refer back to the overall social structure (as a concept) to be able to define the urban system and give it a historical content' (1976b, p. 79). The way in which he identifies the theoretically important specific function that the urban system performs within the total social structure is by a process of elimination.

The urban system cannot be specified as a cultural unit (that is, with reference to the ideological level of the social structure), for as Castells's critique of Wirth demonstrated, there is no urban culture as such. Nor can it be specified as a political unit, for although (as we saw in Chapter 1) the medieval city was indeed a unit of political organization, the capitalist city cannot be so defined since political boundaries appear somewhat arbitrary and do not correspond to the contours of social units. It follows that its specific function within the total system must be economic.

As we have seen, the economic level consists of two main elements, production and consumption, which are mediated by a third, exchange. Castells argues that the urban system cannot refer to the production element since capitalist production is organized on a regional scale (for example, different stages in the production process may be located at different centres, factories in one town are administered from offices in another, and so on). It follows from this that it cannot be a specific system of exchange either. The function of the urban system must therefore lie in the process of consumption. Consumption, of course, performs a number of functions within the total capitalist system. It is, for example, the necessary end point of commodity production: 'Without production, no consumption; but also, without consumption, no production; since production would then be purposeless' (Marx 1973, p. 91). However, the principal function of consumption is that it is the means whereby the human labour-power expended in the production of commodities comes to be replaced. In other words, it is only by consuming socially necessary use values (housing, food, leisure facilities, etc.) that the work-force is able to reproduce its capacity for labour which it sells afresh each day.

The specific function of the urban system thus lies in the reproduction of labour-power. This is performed on a daily basis (through the reproduction of the labour-power of existing workers) and on a generational basis (through the production of new genera-tions of workers to replace the existing one), and it entails both simple reproduction (recreation of expended labour-power) and extended reproduction (development of new capacities of labour-power). The means whereby such reproduction is realized are the means of consumption – housing and hospitals, social services and schools, leisure facilities and cultural amenities, and so on. Unlike the means of production, these means of consumption are specific to urban spatial units: ' "The urban" seems to me to connote directly the processes relating to labour-power other than in its direct application to the production process. . . . The urban units thus seem to be to the process of reproduction what the companies are to the production process' (Castells 1977a, pp. 236–7).

Castells's justification for identifying the consumption process through which labour-power is reproduced as 'urban' is two-fold. First, he suggests (somewhat tentatively) that the growing concentration of capital in advanced capitalist societies is paralleled by a growing concentration of the labour force, with the result that the processes of everyday life through which labour-power is reproduced (eating, sleeping, playing, etc.) are spatially delimited. Second, he argues that such spatial units of everyday life are increasingly structured by the requirements for the reproduction of labour-power within the capitalist system as a whole. For reasons that we shall consider in the next section, the provision of necessary means of consumption within advanced capitalist societies is a contradictory process, and the state has increasingly intervened and then taken responsibility for such provision upon itself. The result is that the means of consumption have not only become concentrated within specific spatial units, but have also become more and more collectivized, and it is this growing significance of the collective provision of the means of consumption that enables Castells to equate the urban system with the process of consumption since it gives rise to increased concentration and centralization:

The organization of a process will be all the more concentrated and centralized, and therefore structuring, as the degree of objective socialization of the process is advanced, as the concentration of the means of consumption and their interdependence is greater, as the administrative unity of the process is more developed. It is at the level of collective consumption that these features are most obvious. [Castells 1977a, p. 445]

Castells's argument may therefore be summarized as follows. (a) The urban system is an expression of the total system of which it forms a part, and it therefore consists of the same levels and elements, interrelated in the same way, as in the total system. (b) It nevertheless performs a significant and specific function within the total system, namely the reproduction of labour-power through the process of consumption. (c) The reproduction of labour-power within the social system as a whole is increasingly achieved within specific spatial units. (d) This is because the process of consumption is becoming concentrated as the population itself becomes concentrated, and as the state assumes increasing responsibility for the provision of crucial consumption facilities. (e) Urban space and the reproduction of labour-power are thus increasingly dependent upon and influenced by the level and form of state provision of necessary means of consumption. It follows from this that, to the extent that consumption becomes collectivized, the urban question becomes a political question.

Urban politics and the crisis of collective consumption

We have seen that Althusser's concept of a 'structure in dominance' indicates the potential development of a multitude of contradictions within any given capitalist society – contradictions internal to each of the three levels of the capitalist mode of production, contradictions between each of these levels, and contradictions between overlapping modes of production within the same society. Given Castells's argument that the urban system is a part of this social structure, it follows that the contradictions that develop in the whole will also develop in the part. To the extent that this is the case, they become manifest as 'urban problems' such as disjunctures between local labour availability and local labour requirements, planning failures, traffic congestion, shortages of building land and so on (see Castells 1976c, pp. 152–3).

For Castells, however, the urban system is not simply one part of the total social structure but is also a specific functional unit within it; it is the sub-system within which labour-power is reproduced. This means that, in addition to reflecting the contradictions within the system as a whole, it is the locus of a specific contradiction or set of contradictions that develops between the process of consumption and other key processes within the total system. Of particular significance here, according to Castells, is the contradiction between consumption and production; that is, between the need to reproduce labour-power and the need to produce commodities at the maximum possible profit.

The argument, quite simply, is that, although the capitalist system must secure the adequate reproduction of labour-power as a prerequisite of continued production and accumulation, individual capitalist producers find it less and less profitable to invest in the production of those commodities that are necessary for such reproduction to take place. The reason for this concerns not the inherent nature of the products concerned (housing, hospitals, educational facilities, etc.) but rather the peculiar character of the firms and industries involved. As one example, Castells cites the French house-building industry (1977a, pp. 149–69).

According to Castells, French capital has found it increasingly unprofitable to invest in the production of low-cost working-class housing, even though there is a desperate need for such housing from the point of view of both workers and industrial capital as a whole (the former because they need somewhere to live, the latter because labour-power must be reproduced cheaply and efficiently). Part of the reason for this is that this widespread need cannot be translated into 'solvent demand' (in other words, housing is an extremely expensive commodity which most workers cannot afford to buy), and to build housing to rent involves a long-term commitment of capital (and firms cannot afford to wait for many years before getting a return on capital). In addition to these problems of realizing profits, there are also problems of generating surplus value through house production. This is because the building industry is fragmented among many small producers, each employing only a few workers, and because of the lack of technological innovation in the industry as a whole. (These problems are discussed in more detail in Chapter 7.)

Castells recognizes that the French case cannot be generalized across all capitalist societies at all points in time. He notes, for example, that the inadequate provision of working-class housing by the private sector is less marked in the United States than it is in France because of a more advanced level of building technology (for instance, factory-based prefabrication), easier availability of building land, a higher level of solvent demand (owing to the higher standard of living), and so on. Nevertheless, he does suggest that the French case is by no means unique: 'The housing question in France is not an exception, but a typical case, within the developed capitalist economy, at a certain phase of its evolution' (1977a, p. 158).

As Duncan (1978) has suggested, there is clearly a danger of drawing unwarranted generalizations from particular cases. Historical and comparative evidence suggests that different types of consumption facilities may fall short of social requirements in different societies at different points in time, and the question of whether and how such situations occur is necessarily contingent upon a range of specific factors which cannot be encompassed within a general theory. However, what is implicit in Castells's argument is that the *potential* for a crisis in the provision of commodities necessary for the reproduction of labour-power is inherent in the nature of capitalist commodity production. The reason for this is simply that production is concerned with exchange values while consumption is concerned with use values. There is, in other words, no necessary reason why what it is most profitable to produce should coincide with what is most socially necessary to consume, since the investment of capital is dictated by rates of return rather than need.

It is Castells's argument that this potential disjuncture between profit and need, exchange value and use value, production and consumption, has become increasingly manifest in different ways throughout the Western capitalist world, and that this has resulted in 'lacunae in vast areas of consumption which are essential to individuals and to economic activity' (1978, p. 18). Left to itself, in other words, private capital has shown a marked inability to produce socially necessary facilities.

If this growing contradiction, which becomes manifest in housing shortages, inadequate medical care, lack of social facilities and so on, is not regulated in some way, then it must necessarily create new sources of political tension and strife. Resorting to Althusserian terminology, Castells suggests that 'Any fundamental contradiction unregulated by the system leads finally to an overdetermined contradiction within the political system' (1977a, p. 270). The regulation of system contradictions is, as we saw earlier, the function specific to the political level. It therefore falls to the state as the agency of social cohesion and the regulator of the total system to intervene in the process of reproduction of labour-power in an attempt to plug the gaps. This is why consumption becomes more and more collectivized and why the urban system as a whole is increasingly structured by state intervention.

Such an explanation for state intervention and the growth of collective consumption does, of course, appear strongly functionalist (system needs provoke system responses), although it is a central feature of this analysis that, while state intervention may overcome one set of contradictions, it necessarily generates another (i.e. the system is not a dynamic equilibrium, as in Parsonian sociology, but is inherently contradictory – see below). Nevertheless, the functionalist assumptions on which this analysis rests have clearly disturbed Castells as his work has developed over the years, and in his later writings he has tended to place more emphasis on the question of the causes of state intervention (which he locates in the development of class struggle) than in the teleological question of the necessary functions that it is deemed to perform. The important point about this shift (which undoubtedly represents a move away from Althusser at the level of theory just as the shift documented in the previous chapter represents a move away from Althusser at the level of epistemology) is that the theory of the state that Castells employs itself contains both aspects. In other words, it is a theory that locates explanations both in the efficacy of class struggle (practices) and in the functional requirements of the system (structures). In his later work, Castells has not so much changed his theory of the state as changed his emphasis on the two aspects of this theory. As we shall see, however, the theory is itself flawed since it fails to relate these two aspects to each other in any coherent way. It fails, that is, to relate structures to practices and the functional requirements of the system to the effects of class struggle, and this means that the shift in emphasis from the former (functions and structures) to the latter (class struggle and practices) merely reproduces the problem and does not resolve it.

The theory of the state that Castells employs draws heavily on the attempt by Poulantzas (1973) to develop what he terms a 'regional theory' (that is, a theory of one level within the capitalist mode of production as conceptualized by Althusser) of the political instance. In the process he attempts to modify the functionalism of Althusser's theory of structures by introducing class struggle into the analysis as a relatively autonomous agency of system change. As Clarke suggests,

The originality of Poulantzas's work lies in his attempt to transcend the integrationist perspective of functionalist sociology. He does this by trying to graft the Marxist proposition that the class struggle is the motor of history onto Althusser's structural-functionalist conception of society. The theory of class is inserted between the structure and the state, so that the state is subject to a double determination. In the first place, it is determined directly by the structure as a specific functional level of that structure. Secondly, its functioning in practice, within limits determined by its place in the structure, is subject to the conditions of the class struggle, which are in turn determined, at least partially, by the structure. [Clarke 1977, p. 11]

In terms of its *structural determination*, Poulantzas analyses the function of the state as its role in regulating the articulation of the different levels of the system as a whole: 'Inside the structure of several levels dislocated by uneven development, the state has the particular function of constituting the factor of cohesion between the levels of a social formation' (1973, p. 44). In other words, its location in the system is such that it must perform this function of system regulation. On the other hand, as a part of the system, it must also necessarily reflect the contradictions that develop within and between the other levels; indeed, it is precisely within the state (namely at the political level) that these contradictions come together and are manifested and 'condensed'. As Castells (1977a, p. 243) suggests, it is therefore at the political level that 'one may map the indices of change'.

In terms of its *determination by class struggle*, Poulantzas argues that the state is a condensation of the class struggle. In other words, while it is certainly not a neutral instrument of political administration as pluralist theory suggests, it is not a tool of any one class as is often claimed by economist Marxist theories. Poulantzas's argument is basically that contradictions within the system give rise to class struggles, and that the state's response to these contradictions through its interventions is determined by such struggles. Thus, while its function is necessarily to maintain the system in the interests of dominant class interests, the way it achieves this is by responding to the political balance of class forces at any one time. Quite simply, the state cannot possibly perform its (structurally determined) function of maintaining system cohesion without responding to the political pressures exerted upon it from dominated as well as dominant classes, for to remain aloof from working-class claims would be to fail to intervene on the contradictions that have provoked such claims.

It follows from this argument that the state does not itself have power, but rather reflects through its interventions the political relations between different classes. Power, in other words, is a function of class relations and is revealed through class practices: 'The concept of power is constituted in the field of class practices.... Class relations are relations of power' (Poulantzas 1973, p. 99). The various institutions of the state are merely the organizations that express the relative power of different classes in any given 'conjuncture'. It also follows from the argument that class practices are constituted at all three levels of the social formation; Poulantzas is heavily critical of the familiar dichotomy in Marxist analysis between classes in and for themselves, arguing instead that classes are constituted through their practices and that such practices develop (albeit unevenly) through economic, political and ideological struggles simultaneously. Political struggles are thus an inherent aspect of class practices (that is, classes do not first constitute themselves as economic categories and then engage in political struggles), although the political groupings (for example, parties) through which they are expressed cannot be directly reduced to economic categories owing to the relative autonomy between the levels. In other words, we do not find wage-labour and capital necessarily confronting each other directly at the political level, but this does not mean that the groups that do confront each other there are not engaged in class struggle.

It is evident from all of this that class practices bring about system change (since they are reflected in state intervention), but that such practices are in turn determined to some extent by the development of system contradictions. Class struggle is in this sense the link in the causal chain between contradictions in the system and state intervention which attempts to resolve them. The greater the contradictions, the greater will be the intensity of political struggle, and the more the state will intervene as a result. However, both Poulantzas and Castells then go on to argue that class practices are determined by the structure only *to some extent*. Thus, not only is there a relative autonomy between the different levels of the structure (the political is relatively autonomous from the economic), but there is also a relative autonomy between the levels of the structure and the practices to which they correspond (political struggles are not merely the expression of contradictions condensed at the political level). This is because practices do not simply express contradictions but bring them together and articulate them. Contradictions in the structure exist only through practices, and (as we saw in the last chapter with reference to the notion of theoretical practice) the very concept of practice entails the production of qualitatively new effects. This is why Poulantzas insists on 'conceiving of practice as a production, i.e. a work of transformation. It is important to see that in this sense a structural instance does not as such directly constitute a practice' (1973, p. 87). Similarly, Castells argues that political practice 'is not simply a vehicle of structured effects: it produces new effects. However, these new effects proceed not from the consciousness of men, but from the specificity of the combinations of their practices, and this specificity is determined by the state of the structure' (1977a, p. 125; see also p. 244). Practices are therefore determined by the structure in the sense that structural contradictions give rise to them, but they generate new effects within the system according to how they articulate these contradictions. The state thus performs its functional task in regulating the system by responding to the particular way in which different classes mobilize around system contradictions.

But if class struggle arising out of system contradictions is the immediate cause of state intervention, how does this enable the state to fulfil its regulative function in the system? Poulantzas's answer is two-fold. First, the state organizes and unifies the divergent interests of different fractions of the capitalist class under the hegemony of the dominant fraction (monopoly capital): 'It takes charge, as it were, of the bourgeoisie's political interests and realizes the function of political hegemony which the bourgeoisie is unable to achieve. But in order to do this, the capitalist state assumes a relative autonomy with regard to the bourgeoisie' (1973, pp. 284–5). In other words, by reflecting in its policies the different interests of different fractions of capital (even if, on occasion, this necessitates the pursuit of a policy that is against the interests of the dominant fraction in the short term), the state maintains the unity of the capitalist 'power bloc' and thus acts in the long-term interests of monopoly capital which dominates the power bloc.

Second, while unifying an inherently fragmented capitalist class, the state also fragments the dominated classes. This it does in two ways. First, the legal system, the electoral system and so on produce and sustain an ideology of the individual through which members of these classes come to conceive of themselves and to live their lives as atomized individual subjects rather than as class agents (an argument that closely reflects Althusser's concept of the interpellation of individual subjects discussed in Chapter 5). Having created isolated individuals out of objective social relations, the state can then function 'to represent the unity of isolated relations founded in the body politic' (Poulantzas 1973, p. 134) – e.g. by representing the 'public interest'. Second, and more significantly from our present perspective, the state fragments the lower classes in the very process of responding to their political class practices. Precisely because the state is relatively autonomous of any one class, it is quite possible for it to cede concessions to dominated classes at the economic level provided this does not threaten the domination of capital at the political level: 'Within these limits it can effectively satisfy some of the economic interests of certain dominated classes. . . . While these economic sacrifices are real and so provide the ground for an equilibrium, they do not as such challenge the political power which sets precise limits to this equilibrium' (p. 192). This, according to Poulantzas, is the explanation for the growth of the capitalist welfare state.

This argument is fundamental to Castells's analysis, for it explains how it is that the state may come to respond to working-class pressure, increase its spending on social items that benefit this class (even though this may not be in the immediate interests of the dominant class – for instance since it raises taxation), and yet still function in the long-term interests of monopoly capital by main-taining social cohesion. As he puts it,

The state apparatus not only exercises class domination, but also strives, as far as possible, to regulate the crises of the system in order to preserve it. It is in the sense that it may, sometimes, become reformist. Although reforms are always imposed by the class struggle and, therefore, from outside the state apparatus, they are no less real for that: their aim is to preserve and extend the existing context, thus consolidating the long-term interests of the dominant classes, even if it involves infringing their privileges to some extent in a particular conjuncture. [Castells 1977a, p. 208]

In the particular case of collective consumption provisions, state intervention performs this function of system maintenance in at least four different ways. First, it is essential to the reproduction of labour-power required by the various fractions of capital. Second, it regulates the class struggle by appeasing lower-class groups with economic concessions while leaving the relations of political domination intact. Third, it stimulates demand in the economy both directly (for example through state purchases from the private sector) and indirectly (through the multiplier effect), thereby combating crises of under-consumption/over-production. And fourth, by investing in unprofitable areas, the state counters the falling rate of profit in the private sector:

Public investment, as we know, is an essential form of 'devaluation of social capital', a major recourse for counteracting the tendency toward a lowering of the profit margin. By investing 'at a loss', the general rate of profit in the private sector holds steady or increases in spite of the lowering of profit relative to social capital as a whole. In this sense, 'social' expenditures of the state not only thus favour big capital, but they are also indispensable to the survival of the system. [Castells 1978, pp. 18–19]

So it is that the growth of collective consumption, brought about by the development of working-class struggle (which itself reflects the development of the contradiction within the system between profit and need, production and consumption), functions in the long-term interests of monopoly capital and allied fractions by aiding the reproduction of labour-power, regulating class conflict, orchestrating new solvent demand and countering the tendency for the rate of profit to fall in the private sector.

Two further points should be made about this argument. First, as we noted earlier, Castells has tended to shift the emphasis of his analysis between his earlier and later writings. This is revealed most clearly in the way in which he has applied his theory of state intervention to the specific question of urban planning (the political level within the urban system). In his earlier essays, urban planning is explained almost entirely in terms of its necessary function within the structure of regulating system contradictions: 'If one accepts the idea of the political system as regulating the system (concrete social formation) as a whole, according to the structural laws on which it is based, then urban planning is its intervention on a given reality in order to counteract the dislocations expressed' (1976c, p. 166). In his later work, however, and in the light of his empirical research in Dunkerque, much greater emphasis comes to be placed on planning as the expression and mediation of class relations: 'The political role of urban planning is due essentially to its capacity to act as an instrument of mediation and negotiation between the different fractions of the dominant class and between the various requirements necessary to the realization of their overall interests, as well as *vis-à-vis* the pressures and demands of the dominated classes' (1977b, p. 77).

The point about this shift is that it represents more a modification of his earlier theoretical position than a fundamental break with it. It is true, of course, that the earlier emphasis on the functional determination of the state by its location in the structure assumes a general theory of the capitalist state whereas the later emphasis on the determinate role of class struggle recognizes that the character of state intervention will vary across different societies in different historical periods (hence Castells's call in his later writings for a 'theorized history of states' – 1978, p. 181). However, it is equally clearly the case that, just as the earlier formulation recognizes that class struggle is the means whereby structurally determined functions are achieved, so the later formulation recognizes that the state performs a regulatory role within the system as a result of its mediation between the demands of different classes and class fractions. The emphasis has changed but the components of the analysis remain the same, for both formulations necessarily include the elements of structure and function on the one hand, and practice and class struggle on the other. As we shall see in the next section, the tension between these two necessary aspects of the theory is in no way resolved by switching the primary focus of attention from one to the other.

The second point to be noted is that, although Castells argues that the growth of state intervention in the sphere of collective consumption has produced a number of positively functional effects (reproduction of labour-power, appeasement of class struggle, etc.), he then goes on to suggest that it nevertheless also generates a new set of contradictions within the system. These basically derive from the 'dislocation between the private control of labour-power and of the

means of production and the collective character of the (re)produc-
tion of these two elements' (1977a, p. 279). In other words, the state
pays the increasing cost of reproducing labour-power while private
capital retains the profits created by this labour-power. The more the
state is driven to increase its social provisions, the wider the gap
becomes between its expenditure and its revenues. The result is a
fiscal crisis of the state which, in the United States at least, has
dramatically been reflected in a fiscal crisis of the cities (the most
celebrated example being the near bankruptcy of New York City),
and which has become manifest in other countries to a greater or
lesser degree (for example through massive rate increases in British
cities). As Castells puts it, 'The fiscal crisis of the inner cities was a
particularly acute expression of the overall fiscal crisis of the state,
that is, of the increasing budgetary gap created in public finance in
advanced capitalist countries because of the historical process of
socialization of costs and privatization of profits' (1977a, p. 415).

Although taxation may be increased in response to fiscal crisis,
such a policy cannot resolve the problem, for taxation on profits
would undermine the profitability of the private sector which the
state must act to sustain, while taxation on wages (which Castells
suggests has increased – 1978, p. 21) is limited and, in the long run,
counter-productive (since it will tend to result in demands on capital
for higher wages together with a heightened level of working-class
mobilization):

State intervention in the maintenance of essential but unprofitable public
services has effectively been carried out at the cost of an inflationary and
growing public debt, for the financing of these growing and indispensable
public expenses could not be achieved through an imposition on capital
(which refused to yield part of its profits) or, completely, through increased
taxation – the eventual social struggles and political oppositions spelled out
the limits of such a strengthening of state power at the expense of wage
earners. [Castells 1978, pp. 175–6]

Faced with an inflationary spiral and encroaching recession, the state
reacts by cutting its level of expenditure and redirecting resources
from the support of labour-power to the direct support of capital.
The result is a crisis in the provision of collective consumption.

The basic problems – lack of housing, poor health care, inadequate
schooling, poor transportation facilities, shortage of cultural
amenities and so on – that led the state to intervene in the process of
consumption in the first place thus reappear. What is different,

however, is that the whole area of consumption has now become politicized; the more the state assumes responsibility for the provision of social resources, the more centrally involved it becomes in the organization of everyday life and the more everyday life is politicized as a result. If one function of this increased level of collective provision has been the appeasement of the lower classes, then it follows that a reduction in the level of such provision carries with it the possibility of a strong and politically organized lower-class reaction against the state itself (and hence against the political dominance of monopoly capital).

Castells is careful to argue that the politicization of the urban question does not necessarily result in an intensification of class struggle. This is because, as we saw earlier, system contradictions do not determine class practices but are rather articulated through such practices. Thus Castells writes:

The permanent and ever extending intervention of the state apparatus in the area of the processes and units of consumption makes it the real source of order in everyday life. This intervention of the state apparatus, which we call urban planning in the broad sense, involves an almost immediate politicization of the whole urban problematic. . . . However, the politicization thus established is not necessarily a source of conflict or change, for it may also be a mechanism of integration and participation: *everything depends on the articulation of the contradictions and practices.* [Castells 1977a, p. 463; emphasis added]

The factor that determines how these contradictions will be articulated in terms of class practices and how effective these practices will be in terms of fundamental social change is political organization. Without socialist organization, contradictions will be reflected in an unco-ordinated, fragmented and ultimately ineffective way:

The role of the organization (as a system of means specific to an objective) is fundamental for . . . it is the organization that is the locus of fusion or articulation with the other social practices. When there is no organization, urban contradictions are expressed either in a refracted way, through other practices, or in a 'wild' way, a pure contradiction devoid of any structural horizon. [Castells 1977a, pp. 271–2]

The role of political organization is to link contradictions in practice. This means not only bringing together different urban struggles (e.g. housing struggles, education campaigns and so on), but also locating urban struggles as a whole within the wider context of class struggle. A failure to achieve the first will result in the perpetuation of divisions between different groups such that concessions gained by one group will be won at the expense of another, and this can only result in the reproduction of the system rather than an effective challenge to it. A failure to achieve the second will limit any popular movement to reformism. This is because urban contradictions are secondary: 'Whatever the level and the content of the various "urban issues", they can all be characterized as secondary structural issues, that is to say, ones not directly challenging the production methods of a society nor the political domination of the ruling classes' (Castells 1977a, p. 376). It follows that urban struggles cannot themselves provoke fundamental social change, but can only effect limited changes within the confines of the urban system: 'a municipal revolution and nothing more' (p. 360).

To be effective and politically pertinent within the society as a whole, urban protest must therefore be assimilated into the working-class movement (which for Castells means the Communist Party). If such a movement does not exist in any developed form (as is presumably the case in Britain and the United States), then urban issues will remain of secondary political significance (see Castells 1977a, p. 465). If such a movement does exist, however, then urban protests may come to fulfil a crucial role within it. This is because 'the working class cannot on its own, in the 1970s, pose a socialist alternative in Western Europe' (1978, p. 172). The significance of urban protest is that it cross-cuts traditional class divisions between manual workers, professional workers and the petty bourgeoisie, for the crisis of collective consumption affects all the popular classes and mobilizes sections of the population that have traditionally remained aloof from the struggle against monopoly capital:

One finds new disparities emerging from the historical mode of dealing with collective consumption which do not correspond to the position occupied in class relationships but to the position in the consumption process itself . . . it is at the level of urban problems that one can see most easily how the logic of capital oppresses not only the working class but all the possibilities for human development. [Castells 1978, pp. 34–5]

Polluted air does not stop at the boundaries of middle-class suburbs; cuts in education do not discriminate between working-class and middle-class children; the shortage of hospital beds affects professional workers as much as it does manual workers; and so on. Urban contradictions, in short, are inherently 'pluri-class' in nature, and they therefore provide a basis on which to build new anti-monopoly capital class alliances.

To the extent that socialist organizations succeed in building alliances between the 'popular classes' around urban issues, and to the extent that such alliances are successful in bringing about fundamental changes within the urban system and in shifting the balance of class power in society as a whole, Castells speaks of the development of 'urban social movements'. It is in the potential growth of such movements, consequent upon the worsening of the urban crisis, that he locates the political significance of the urban question. Although in his earlier work he suggests that 'urban power lies in the streets' and that the new bases of urban politics 'reopen the roads to revolution' (1977a, p. 378), it is evident from his later writings that he now sees the primary role of urban social movements in terms of the development of radical consciousness through struggle and thus as a means of widening the electoral base of the socialist and communist parties:

> The articulation of new social struggles with alternative democratic politics can lead to a Left-wing electoral victory based on a programme opening the way to socialism. For such a victory to be possible and to not get bogged down in the administrative underground of the bourgeois state, it must not support itself on a coalition of dissatisfactions, but on the political and ideological hegemony of the socialist forces at the mass level. We know that this hegemony must necessarily depend on a transformation of mass consciousness, and that this transformation will not be brought about by televised electoral speeches but by and in struggle. In our historical conditions, the revolutionary's essential task consists above all in winning the masses. The battle for the masses replaces the battle of the Winter Palace. [Castells 1978, p. 60]

In arguing thus, it is apparent not only that the influence of the May 1968 events in Paris on his earlier work has given way to the influence of the 'Eurocommunist' strategy of the 1970s in his later writings, but also that his theoretical emphasis has shifted markedly from a concern with structures to a concern with practices. The Castells of the early essays could only endorse an insurrectionary socialist strategy given his commitment to a structural-functionalist analysis of the state, while the Castells of the later essays was able to support a democratic strategy by emphasizing instead the determinate role of class struggle. The democratic road to socialism becomes a viable strategy only when the state's functions are seen as historically contingent rather than structurally determined.

Relative autonomy, space and collective consumption

Of the many criticisms that have been made of Castells's approach to the analysis of the urban question, two appear crucial as regards the central concerns of this book. The first concerns the theoretical problems to which the concept of relative autonomy refers, namely, the question of the relationship between structure and practice (which in Castells's work relates to the question of urban social movements), and that of the relationship between the economy and political intervention (which in Castells's work relates to the question of the capitalist state). The second significant area of criticism concerns the conceptual problem of collective consumption, and in particular the attempt by Castells to specify urban processes in terms of this concept. Much of the recent debate within Marxist theory and between Marxist theorists and their critics has revolved around these two issues, and although we shall consider them mainly in the context of Castells's work, they are clearly problems that have inevitably been confronted by other writers (e.g. Lojkine) who have attempted to apply Marxist theory to urban analysis. In other words, the question of class struggle and state intervention in the urban system, and of the relationship between urbanism and the capitalist mode of production, are both central to any Marxist theory of urbanism and are by no means specific to Castells's work. Although they differ in their approaches to these questions, therefore, most contemporary Marxist writers agree on the main issues to be addressed.

The concept of relative autonomy is in many ways the lynchpin of Castells's theory, for it is the means by which he attempts to avoid the two traditional problems of voluntarism/determinism and political autonomy/economism. Thus, on the one hand stands Weberian sociology with its emphasis on the effectivity of individual actors and on the analytical separation of economic power (classes) and political power (parties), while on the other stands traditional Marxist theory with its emphasis on objective class relations (individuals as 'bearers' or personifications of determinate structural relations) and on the subordination of the state to the interests of dominant economic class interests. Relative autonomy is the concept whereby Castells seeks to retain an analysis of structural determination while at the same time recognizing that men (to some extent) make their own history, and to retain an emphasis on the primacy of the economy while recognizing that the state (again to some extent) may act in the short run against the immediate economic interests of the capitalist class and its dominant fraction (monopoly capital).

In both of its areas of application (structures/practices and economics/politics), however, the concept of relative autonomy has proved inadequate to the tasks it has been set to perform, and it is apparent that it has not so much resolved the problems to which it has been addressed as obfuscated them. The main reason for this is that the concept is logically incoherent in that the tension it is designed to resolve is merely reproduced within the concept itself. This argument, which owes much to recent work by Hirst (1977) and Hindess (1978), is best illustrated with reference to the fundamental problems that arise out of Castells's discussion of urban social movements and state intervention in the urban system.

We have seen that, for Castells, urban social movements are a response to the development of structural contradictions (urban crisis), but whether and how they develop and with what effects for system change is contingent on external factors (namely coherent political organizations): 'Since the structures exist only in practices, the specific organization of these practices produces autonomous (though determined) effects that are not all contained simply in the deployment of structural laws' (1977a, p. 244). Castells evidently wishes to argue, therefore, that the source of significant system change lies in the structure (contradictions) as mediated by specific class practices. Political struggles will not be effective unless they express a fusion of contradictions, but contradictions will not generate pertinent political effects unless they are expressed through organized political struggles.

The problem, however, is that if structural contradictions do not in themselves determine class practices, then there must be some other causal agency at work. If the same structural contradictions manifested in the same sorts of crises can result in different modes of political struggle (participation in one case, 'wild' reactions in another, organized social movements in a third, fatalistic resignation in a fourth), and if these different types of reaction result in different political effects within the system as a whole, then practices clearly cannot be explained within a theory of structures. Put another way, structural contradictions may be seen as the conditions of existence, but not the causes, of class practices. Or in everyday language, significant political struggles will not arise without an issue, but the issue will not determine the form that such struggles may take.

This conclusion creates a problem for Castells since his commitment to a structural theory cannot enable the development of an explanation of class practices except through a totally deterministic argument such as he wishes to avoid. The problem was built into his approach from the outset, but as he came to place increasing emphasis on class struggle in his later writings, so it became increasingly manifest since the crucial (indeed, only) mechanism of social change identified in his approach (class struggle, urban social movements) could not be explained by his theory. He thus ends up by arguing that class struggles arise as a result of system contradictions, but while he can theorize the latter, he has no way of linking them to the former. As Lojkine suggests, practices lie outside the scope of Castells's theory and are merely tacked on to the end of his analysis as the way of explaining change within an otherwise self-regulating system:

There is an epistemological hiatus between the 'abstract' analysis of the structural laws and the 'concrete' analysis of the system of actors and social practices which alone change the system.... If we have understood Castells properly, the contradiction and the transformation are therefore not 'in' the system, 'in' the structure, but in the practice which leads us to fall back on classical idealist distinctions found in history as well as sociology between the 'intelligence' of social determinations and the 'understanding' of 'concrete situations' in which the 'freedom' and the 'will' of actors can become manifest. [Lojkine 1977a, p. 56]

The theory, in other words, necessarily entails a notion of conscious human subjects who act, for while the system is apparently riven with contradictions, these count for nothing unless people *act* upon them. Castells, however, remains implacably opposed to the 'ideological' analysis of 'actors', and as a result his theory stops at the crucial point regarding the explanation of class 'practices'.

By attempting to avoid both structural determinism and an action frame of reference, Castells's theory therefore falls between the two. To save it, it would be necessary (as Pickvance (1977a) has argued) to introduce the concept of human actors with particular values, goals, beliefs and so on, for only in this way would it be possible to explain why certain types of issues (or 'stakes', in Castells's terminology) affecting certain types of groups ('classes' and 'class fractions') result in different types of political strategies ('practices'). In order to explain how class practices mediate structural contradictions, it seems necessary to understand how the members of different classes come to interpret their objective situations.

Now it is often argued at this point that Marxist analysis is inherently incompatible with an emphasis on the Weberian problem of the subjective meaningfulness of human action (e.g. see Harloe (1977), p. 36) and that attempts such as that by Pickvance to relate the two are therefore misconceived. Yet as Andrew Sayer (1979) has noted in his 'sympathetic critique' of recent Marxist urban theory, any theory must take account of the problem of meaning if it is to relate an explanation in terms of structural necessity to the question of how such 'necessities' become manifest in historically contingent conditions. A consideration of actors' definitions of their situation need not preclude attempts at sociological explanation that go beyond the level of actors' consciousness; indeed, this was precisely the point of Weber's insistence on theoretical adequacy *both* at the level of meaning *and* at the level of causality. A theory such as that of Castells which resolutely refuses to entertain the question of subjective meaning is inevitably and inherently inadequate.

The result of this inadequacy is demonstrated in the highly implausible results of Castells's analysis of urban social movements – a consequence that could have been avoided had he been prepared to consider the question of how those who suffer the effects of urban crisis may come to understand their objective situation. Of particular significance here is what Pickvance (1977b) has identified as the 'urban fallacy' in much of the current Marxist work (including that of Castells and Lojkine). This fallacy relates to the argument that urban crisis is the crucial condition for a broadening of the class struggle against monopoly capital since it affects all the 'popular' classes and thus enables new class alliances (for example between manual workers, professional workers and – for Lojkine at least – sections of the bourgeoisie such as small shopkeepers who suffer from policies designed to support the profitability of large companies) under the socialist leadership of the proletariat. Such an argument can seriously be put forward only if we ignore the question of how actors understand their situation and assume a deterministic analysis in which contradictions automatically provoke radical class practices provided there is an organization that can impose the 'correct' strategy. Human consciousness, in other words, has to be taken as infinitely malleable so that individuals whose economic situations (wages, conditions of work, area of residence, etc.) are in all other respects totally divergent from each other nevertheless in some way forget their differences and join together in the fight for socialism.

Once we conceptualize practices in terms of subjectively meaningful actions (as we must once we recognize that practices cannot be explained through the determinism of structure), then it becomes clear that, *from the point of view of the actor* — say, the shopkeeper threatened by a loss of trade as a result of urban renewal, the professional employee waiting for a year or more for a hospital bed as a result of health cuts, and so on – urban crisis may well result in a willingness to engage in limited protests against specific issues but equally may be far from sufficient grounds for joining a workers' socialist movement whose objectives go far beyond the question of patterns of urban planning and provision of health care facilities (see Saunders 1980). To assume that the consciousness of such groups can be moulded by political organization in order to build a broad Left coalition against monopoly capital is to betray either a frightening ignorance or a blinkered optimism.

Castells's theory of urban social movements is weak and unconvincing (and arguably politically counter-productive) precisely because the concept of relative autonomy between structures and practices is incoherent. If we are to take Castells's critique of structural determinism seriously, then this means reintroducing the notion of actors engaging in purposeful strategies in response to their definitions of an (increasingly worsening) objective situation. Because Castells refuses to adopt such a mode of analysis, his notion of relative autonomy serves only to obscure a deterministic theory which gives rise to implausible political conclusions.

Much the same problem arises out of the second way in which the concept of relative autonomy is pressed into service in his theory; namely, to 'explain' the relation between the state and the economy. Whereas the theory of urban social movements rests on the relative autonomy of structures and practices, the theory of the state rests on the relative autonomy of different levels within the structure. This is because, according to Castells's theory, urban social movements are the source of change in the system while the state is limited in its role to system regulation. In other words, the distinction between structure and practice becomes equated with that between function and transformation and, derivatively, with that between the state and urban social movements (see Harloe 1979). Thus, while the theoretical problem in the study of urban social movements concerns how system contradictions (structure) become represented in effective struggle (practice), the theoretical problem in the study of the state concerns how the interests of the dominant class at one level (the economic) become represented in the regulation of the system at another (the political).

As we saw in the previous section, the state is defined in terms of its role or function within the structure of the capitalist mode of production. This role is regulative and involves the fragmentation of the working class and the unification of the different fractions of capital within a power bloc under the hegemony of the monopoly fraction. While the long-term political domination by monopoly capital is maintained by short-term economic concessions to other classes (including the working class), the state cannot pursue policies that undermine the long-term hegemony of monopoly capital: 'Not every conceivable intervention by M [political management; the state] is possible, because it must take place within the *limits* of the capitalist mode of production, otherwise the system would be *shaken* rather than regulated' (Castells 1976c, p. 166).

The causal mechanism through which the state performs its regulative function is class struggle. In other words, the balance of class forces at any one time becomes reflected in state intervention (for example social reform at periods of relative working-class strength) which has the effect of damping down the class struggle and maintaining the system intact. This argument, however, raises two problems.

First, if class struggle is the motor of state regulation, then the possibility of effective struggle resulting in fundamental system change appears remote. As Harloe (1979) has pointed out, the essentially functionalist theory of the state developed by Castells (and, indeed, by one of his main critics, Lojkine) seems incompatible with the emphasis on urban social movements as agencies of transformation. It is hardly surprising, then, that in his work in Dunkerque, Castells should have found so little evidence for the existence of urban social movements, for his theory of the state leads him to dismiss as ineffective virtually all examples of political protest. This problem becomes all the more evident in Castells's later writings where he endorses a democratic socialist strategy. As we saw earlier (page 199), he argues that socialist electoral struggles must be grounded in mass mobilization in order to avoid the bureaucratic stranglehold of the 'administrative underground of the bourgeois state', but it is evident that, according to his own theory of the state, the problem is not so much circumventing the bureaucracy (the classic political problem posed by Weber) as breaking the structurally imposed limits on state intervention. If the role of the state is inherently limited to regulation rather than transformation, then it is difficult to see how an electoral victory by the Left could lead to any fundamental political change. This problem, which is by no means unique to Castells's approach (see my discussion of a similar problem in Lojkine's work in Saunders (1979), pp. 163–6) can be resolved only by rejecting Castells's earlier structural theory of the relative autonomy of the state in favour of an approach that recognizes the historically contingent character of state intervention. While there are signs in his later work of his willingness to move in this direction (for instance, the call for a theorized history of states), it is clear that he has yet to develop a theoretical perspective consistent with his new political strategy.

The second problem is that it is by no means clear how the cause of state intervention (class struggle) necessarily produces its functional effects (system regulation). Is it not possible, as Szelenyi (1979) has argued, that the state may be driven by the power of the working class to pursue policies that have a directly deleterious effect on the long-term profitability of monopoly capital? According to Castells's structural theory, the answer has to be 'no'. But this raises the two crucial questions of, first, what prevents this from happening and, second, how would we recognize a situation where it did happen?

In their discussion of Poulantzas's work, Gold, Lo and Wright suggest that 'Although there is a fairly rich discussion of *how* the relative autonomy of the state protects the class interests of the dominant class, and of the functional *necessity* for such a state structure, there is no explanation of the social mechanisms which guarantee that the state will in fact function in this way' (1975, p. 38). The same criticism can be made against Castells, for his functional theory of the state rests wholly on the assumption that reform is always ameliorative as regards the working class and non-threatening as regards the long-term interests of monopoly capital. This argument appears dubious both theoretically (for it can be argued that the fact of change is likely to increase rather than reduce working-class aspirations – for instance see Runciman 1966) and historically (for radicalism is often higher during periods of reform than during periods of stability). Again, therefore, we see here the need for an appreciation of how actors understand and interpret their situation, for Castells's assumption that political zeal varies inversely with political concessions wantonly disregards a long tradition of sociological inquiry which if anything points to the opposite conclusion.

Castells seems implicitly to recognize this problem, and in attempting to demonstrate why class struggle cannot lead the state to adopt policies that undermine the hegemony of monopoly capital he is driven, just as functionalist theories before him have been driven, into what amounts to a teleological explanation (that is, one that accounts for given effects in terms of some prior and ultimate purpose). This becomes clear in his definition of urban planning as 'the intervention of the political in the specific articulation of the different instances of a social formation within a collective unit of reproduction of labour power *with the aim of* assuring its extended reproduction. . . .' (Castells 1977a, p. 263; emphasis added). The state, that is, performs a regulative function because this is the aim or intention of its interventions. But if the state is merely the condensation of the political relations between different classes, how can it have aims and intentions? Where, apart from human agency, is the source of such aims and intentions? Clearly, just as conscious human subjects are entailed by Castells's discussion of the development of urban social movements, so too they are entailed by his explanation of the regulative role of the capitalist state, for unless we argue that those who control the state apparatus consciously pursue policies that are designed to maintain the system in the long-run (which is not an implausible suggestion), then there are no grounds, for arguing that this is the necessary result (still less the fundamental aim) of state intervention. Without human subjects the state cannot have aims, and without aims there is no mechanism to explain its necessary function.

If there is nothing in Castells's theory to preclude the possibility of state intervention bringing about transformation rather than regulation, then Pickvance is surely justified in arguing that 'Governmental institutions cannot be dismissed as sources of minor changes . . . the role of authorities in initiating change is an empirical question' (1976b, p. 204). The problem, however, is that Castells's functional theory of the state effectively precludes any attempt at empirical evaluation.

The reason for this is that the argument that the state is relatively autonomous enables its adherents to 'explain' both those situations where capital benefits as a result of state policies and those where interests opposed to capital prevail. As Pahl (1977b) has noted, such a theory is immune to empirical criticism since, no matter how far the capitalist state goes in responding to working-class pressure, the theory always ensures in advance that such 'concessions' must operate in the long-term interests of monopoly capital. As Lefebvre suggests, 'This structural (non-dialectical) analysis is not false. It is not true either. It is trivial. It bears no date. It can be true or false anywhere and everywhere' (1976, p. 66). It is, in short, a tautology.

For as long as the theory purports to explain everything, it actually explains nothing. What is necessary yet lacking is a counterfactual statement to the effect that, *if* the state necessarily acts in the long-term interests of monopoly capital (even when it appears to be acting in the interests of other classes), then certain types of interventions *cannot* occur. Only in this way is it possible to assess the plausibility of the theory in the light of historical evidence. Three points can be made about this requirement.

The first is that there is a spurious counterfactuality in Castells's theory, for he argues that the state cannot intervene to change the capitalist ownership relationship, nor can it intervene directly in the process of production (1976c, p. 166). However, he nowhere discusses how a change in the ownership relation could be identified or what type of policy would constitute a direct intervention in production. In other words, his counterfactual amounts merely to the argument that the state cannot legislate capitalism out of existence while he provides no criteria by which even this broad claim could be examined. Furthermore, for as long as capitalism continues, the theory contains no counterfactual at all; the only thing that the state could do that would be against the long-term interests of monopoly capital is to abolish monopoly capitalism! Thus, if monopoly capitalism continues (in one form or another), it follows that the state must still be acting in the long-term interests of the dominant class. We then find ourselves back into tautology again.

The second point is that this tautology is underpinned and safe-guarded by another which derives from Marx's theory of value. When Castells argues that an increase in the provision of collective consumption functions in the interests of capital because it ensures the continued reproduction of labour-power, his argument rests on Marx's theory of the value of labour-power. According to this theory, 'The value of labour-power is the value of the means of subsistence necessary for the maintenance of its owner' (Marx 1976, p. 274). However, Marx also argues that the necessary level of such subsistence is determined socially (by what is normal in any given society at any given time) rather than biologically, and that, unlike other commodities, the value of labour-power therefore 'contains a historical and moral element' (p. 275). For Marx, in other words, what is socially necessary if labour-power is to be reproduced effectively and fully is determined by what is socially normal as regards working-class living standards.

The problem with this argument is that it rules out even the possibility that there may develop a gap between the level of subsistence necessary for the efficient reproduction of labour-power and current levels of provision (that is, between what is necessary, from the point of view of capital, and what is normal). Whatever the working class achieves through political struggle becomes the norm, and whatever is the norm is socially necessary. Given that it is in the long-term interests of capital as a whole that labour-power should adequately be reproduced (for the provision of socially necessary levels of subsistence is as vital to the reproduction of labour-power as necessary amounts of fertilizer are to the reproduction of the fertility of the soil – see Marx 1976, p. 348), and given that adequate reproduction is determined by normal living standards pertaining in a given society, it follows from Marx's theory that when the state assumes part of the responsibility for providing 'subsistence', it must be operating in the general interests of capital. This, then, is the basis for the logically impeccable yet politically absurd thesis that, say, council houses with garages, language teaching in schools, free meals in hospitals, a rising level of pensions and a multitude of other social provisions made by the state in Britain during this century are all 'in fact' in the interests of the capitalist class. The inherent tautology in Castells's theory of the state is therefore underpinned by the inherent tautology in Marx's theory of the value of labour-power; and although both emphasize the importance of class struggle in determining socially necessary levels of subsistence, both end up in the argument that every working-class gain short of a fundamental transformation of the system is in addition a consolidation of the economic interests of capital (although each gain may hasten the development of contradictions that threaten the system).

The third point is that, in arguing for the necessity of counter-factuality, I am not suggesting that any theory should be capable of empirical test and falsification, but only that any theory should stipulate its own criteria of empirical adequacy. To insist on such 'internal' criteria of adequacy is not, therefore, to assume that empirical evidence can necessarily be employed to evaluate different theories against each other (although this is not necessarily impossible either), nor is it to reject any theory of underlying essences as empirically untestable (since, as we saw in Chapter 1, such a theory can still support empirical statements and can be evaluated on its own terms according to whether the essential relations which it posits could account for the development of phenomenal forms). This argument is developed more fully in the Appendix. Suffice it to say here that to criticize Castells's theory on the grounds that it is inherently self-confirming and immune from empirical evaluation is not necessarily to adopt an empiricist epistemology or a naive falsificationist methodology. There is a middle way between faith in 'facts' and faith in dogma.

Castells's theory of the relative autonomy of the state is teleological (yet lacks any theory of purposive agency) and tautological (and therefore lacks any criteria of empirical adequacy). It encompasses every eventuality and explains none. It does, however, point to a very real problem, for it is apparent that the capitalist state does respond to working-class interests, and does at the same time attempt to safeguard the fundamental economic interests of key sectors of capital. In this sense, crude instrumentalist theories (which conceptualize the state as an apparatus controlled by dominant class interests) and crude pluralist theories (which conceptualize the state as a neutral body responding to the relative pressures of different coalitions of interests in different issues) both appear incapable of explaining this essential dualism. The theory of relative autonomy does at least provide a reasonable description of what the state does; its problem is that it fails to explain how it does it.

I shall argue in Chapter 8 that this dual role of the state cannot be subsumed under a single explanatory theory, and that the state operates in a different way according to the type of policy in which it is engaged. In order to develop this argument, it is necessary first to distinguish conceptually between different types of state policy, and it is here that Castells's work may still prove useful as a first step. In other words, while rejecting his theory of state, it is worth retaining (in considerably modified form) his major conceptual innovation, namely the concept of collective consumption.

The concept of collective consumption has been subject to intense criticism and has in any case gone through a number of modifications as Castells's work has developed. Three problems in particular need to be considered. First, can collective consumption be equated with spatial units as Castells suggests? Second, can collective consumption be defined in terms of its function in reproducing labour-power as Castells argues? And third, what sort of provisions does the term 'collective consumption' actually refer to?

The first problem is that Castells's assertion that spatial units of everyday life can be conceptualized as units of collective consumption provides an unnecessarily limited scope for analysis. If we assume for the moment that collective consumption refers to social provisions made and managed by the state, then it is apparent that, while some such provisions have a spatial reference (public housing, hospitals, schools), others do not (social security payments, family allowances, pension schemes). Just as Pahl's concept of a socio-spatial system seems unnecessarily exclusive (see page 136), so too does Castells's emphasis on the spatial aspect of collective consumption, for there appears little theoretical rationale in the work of either of these two writers for ignoring the a-spatial aspects of state social expenditure. It is not space that is essential to Castells's theory but collective consumption, for space is simply the medium through which certain social processes are expressed: 'A "sociology of space" can only be an analysis of social practices given in a certain space. . . . Of course, there is the "site", the "geographical" conditions, but they concern analysis only as the support of a certain web of social relations' (Castells 1977a, p. 442). Castells develops not a theory of space, but a theory of processes that occur within a spatial context, and his key theoretical problem is that of collective consumption which is prior to and more extensive than any specific concern with spatially delimited units. The point, in other words, is that a theoretical concern with collective consumption need have no necessary reference to a theoretical concern with space, and the ellision of the two is unnecessary.

The second problem is that the reproduction of labour-power, which Castells equates with collective consumption and hence with the concept of the urban, is only one aspect of urban processes. This argument is put forcefully by Lojkine (1976, 1977b) who suggests that socialized provisions may function not only in aiding the reproduction of labour-power (social infrastructure), but also in securing the general conditions of capitalist production through investment in necessary but non-profitable economic infrastructure such as roads, telecommunications, ports and so on. Lojkine argues that capitalist urbanization cannot be understood in terms of consumption processes alone since the city simultaneously reproduces labour-power and supports capital accumulation (for example by speeding the circulation of capital through improved communications):

The concentration of population, instruments of production, capital, of pleasures and needs – in other words, the city – is thus in no sense an autonomous phenomenon governed by laws of development totally separate from the laws of capitalist accumulation: it cannot be dissociated from the tendency for capital to increase the productivity of labour by socializing the general conditions of production. [Lojkine 1976, pp. 123–4]

For Lojkine, therefore, urban space is subordinated to the process of accumulation in the monopoly capital sector. Through its interventions (urban planning, provision of infrastructure, etc.), the state facilitates and supports the profitability of monopoly capital, although it may at times take account of the interests of other classes in order to maintain political stability. In general, however, the effects of state support for large companies prove deleterious not only for the working class, but also for groups such as small shopkeepers (for example, Lojkine shows how local commercial capital is often excluded from urban redevelopment schemes that serve the interests of large national firms). It therefore follows that urban social movements may encompass a wide range of anti-monopoly capital interests, and that such movements involve a direct class confrontation involving issues of consumption *and* production. Like Lefebvre, then, Lojkine sees the urban question as crucial in maintaining capital accumulation (as well as in reproducing labour-power), and he is highly critical of theories, such as that of Castells, that 'reduce policy simply to the "management of the reproduction of labour-power" (housing and social infrastructure) and exclude its economic dimension' (Lojkine 1977b, p. 142). Indeed, in a scarcely veiled reference to Castells he attacks 'the ideological boundaries within which some have attempted to confine the urban' (p. 142), suggesting that the separation of the questions of production and consumption, capital accumulation and reproduction of labour-power tends to reproduce traditional 'bourgeois' conceptions that attempt to analyse urban problems (inner-city decline, housing shortages, etc.) apart from an analysis of the political economy of capitalism.

Lojkine is not alone in developing a criticism of the production/consumption division found in Castells. Harloe, for example, suggests that 'It seems quite unhelpful to place a special emphasis on consumption considered in isolation from production, for they are inseparable in the Marxist analysis of capitalism' (1979, p. 136), and he shows how urban planning necessarily affects private sector profitability as well as the reproduction of labour-power. Similarly, Harvey argues that the division between work and community is an artificial separation imposed by capitalism itself, that the class struggle between capital and labour occurs in both spheres, and that analysis must therefore go beyond ideological appearances and penetrate to the essential contradiction within capitalism which gives rise to particular conflicts: 'The separation between working and living is at best a surficial estrangement, an apparent tearing asunder of what can never be kept apart. And it is at this deeper level too that we can more clearly see the underlying unity between work-based and community-based conflicts' (Harvey 1978b, p. 35).

There can, of course, be no argument with the view that an analysis of consumption must be situated in a theoretical understanding of the relationship between it and other key processes (within the economy and within politics). In this sense, however, it is clear that Castells does not ignore questions of production as they relate to the urban question. We have seen in this chapter that his concept of the urban system identifies three economic elements (production, consumption and exchange) as well as political and ideological levels, and that his analysis of the functions of collective consumption provisions includes not only the reproduction of labour-power, but also the stimulation of demand for the products of the private sector and the devalorization of capital as a means of countering the falling rate of profit. Furthermore, in his study of Dunkerque, he and Godard approach the analysis of collective consumption precisely in terms of the contradiction that developed between economic and social priorities as a result of the development of two large industrial complexes in the region.

Castells's emphasis on collective consumption does not therefore imply that this can be understood apart from an analysis of production, nor that the only processes that occur in cities are processes of consumption. He makes this clear in the afterword to *The Urban Question* where he writes,

A concrete city (or an urban area, or a given spatial unit) is not only a unit of consumption. It is, of course, made up of a very great diversity of practices and functions. It expresses, in fact, society as a whole, though through the specific historical forms it represents. Therefore, whoever wishes to study a city (or series of cities) must also study capital, production, distribution, politics, ideology, etc. [Castells 1977a, p. 440]

But it is precisely because any given city includes 'a very great diversity' of processes that Castells finds it necessary to identify what from his perspective is the most significant process, for it is only in this way that the theoretical problem posed in the analysis of cities can be specified. In the absence of such a specification, urban theory becomes chaotic as it attempts to analyse and explain everything that happens in cities.

What Castells has done, therefore, is to simplify and 'purify' a complex reality in order to make it amenable to analysis. Like Weber, faced with an infinite variety of empirical cases, he has attempted to identify what for him constitutes a key factor which can distinguish 'urban' and 'non-urban' questions and which can facilitate the development of generalizable hypotheses. This key factor is collective consumption, and other processes that can be identified in particular cities (for instance production, circulation, administration, etc.) are therefore theoretically significant only to the extent that they affect or are affected by collective consumption processes. The question that is specific to urban analysis is thus the question of collective consumption and the reproduction of labour-power:

What is an 'urban area'? A production unit? Not at all, insofar as the production units are placed on another scale (on a regional one at least). An institutional unit? Certainly not, since we are aware of the almost total lack of overlap between the 'real' urban units and the administrative segmentation of space. An ideological unit, in terms of a way of life proper to a city or to a spatial form? This is meaningless as soon as one rejects the culturalist hypothesis of the production of ideology by the spatial context.... What is, then, what is called an urban unit? ... It is, in short, the everyday space of a delimited fraction of the labour-force ... it is a question of the process of reproduction of labour-power [Castells 1977a, pp. 444–5]

Now we have already seen that the equation of collective consumption with spatial organization appears unnecessarily restrictive and that an explanation of the development of collective consumption in terms of reproduction of labour-power is founded on the tautological theory of the value of labour-power. The way in which Castells employs the concept of collective consumption in his theory therefore invites criticism. The concept itself, however, may remain useful as an ideal type, for some such specification of what the urban question is is an essential prerequisite for any theoretical and empirical research. Obviously cities do not involve only processes of consumption, any more than they involve (following Lojkine's formulation) only material supports for the general conditions of capital accumulation. The point is that Castells and Lojkine are basically interested in different, but equally valid, theoretical questions about the role of cities in modern capitalist societies; while Lojkine is interested mainly in the economic significance of physical infrastructure for capitalist profitability, Castells is interested mainly in the significance of social provisions for the working population. Given these different interests (or, in Weber's terms, different value-relevances), they are led to construct different ideal type conceptualizations of the urban, and which (if either) we accept will depend entirely on the theoretical questions we wish to pursue. As Castells himself recognizes, 'The urban system is only a concept and, as such, has no other use than that of elucidating social practices and concrete historical situations in order both to understand them and to discover their laws' (1977a, p. 241).

Once we recognize that the conceptualization of the urban in terms of the concept of collective consumption is simply an ideal typical construct, and, indeed, that 'All specifically Marxian "laws" and developmental constructs – insofar as they are theoretically sound – are ideal types' (Weber 1949, p. 103), then we can pass over the tedious disputes between different Marxist theorists in which different one-sided conceptualizations are pitted against each other, and turn instead to an examination of Castells's concept of collective consumption in terms of its relevance and usefulness.

The relevance of the concept is that it defines an area of analysis – state social consumption provisions – that appears crucial to an understanding of processes within contemporary capitalism. Since the war, the scope of such provisions has expanded dramatically (though in different ways and at different rates) throughout the Western world. In recent years, however, a developing economic crisis, manifest in rising unemployment, inflation, falling rates of profit and so on, has resulted in a reduction in the scale of such provisions, and this in turn has led (again, to a different extent in different countries) to the development of new areas of political conflict, often expressed through new types of organizations (community action groups, claimants' unions, tenants' associations and so on). There is an obvious need both for comparative empirical research to document these processes in different countries, and for theoretical work which can help to explain the different causes and consequences of these developments. While Castells's theories are certainly inadequate, it is clear that he has posed some crucial questions and that the concept of collective consumption is the framework within which these questions may still be addressed.

The problem, however, is that Castells's concept of collective consumption has been subject to considerable confusion and criticism. For a start, his definition of the term has varied between his earlier essays (where he refers to 'consumption processes whose organization and management cannot be other than collective given the nature and size of the problems' – 1976b, p. 75) and his later work (where he refers to 'socialized consumption processes which are largely determined by state activity' – 1978, p. 179). It is not always clear, therefore, whether consumption is 'collective' because it is communal or because it is socialized through state provision (the point being that communal resources can be and often are supplied by private capital), and whether it is inherently collective (owing to factors like size) or historically variable. These questions have been considered at some length in the literature (see Pahl 1977a, 1978 and Saunders 1979, ch. 3), although, as Harloe (1979) suggests, Castells does now seem to have settled on a definition that limits the concept to social provisions provided and managed by the state. Even so, problems remain, for some provisions may be provided by capital and managed by the state (e.g. much British council housing), and such distinctions appear crucial in terms of the theoretical and political implications that may be drawn from them. It is clearly important, for example, to distinguish between the private and public sectors in housing since, as I have shown elsewhere, Castells's tendency to elide the two in his discussions of collective consumption crises leads him to assume a communality of interests between council tenants and owner-occupiers which may be far from the case.

Clearly, the concept of collective consumption needs to be specified more coherently by breaking it down into various sub-types and categories, and this is what Dunleavy (1979b) has recently attempted to do. Dunleavy identifies four dimensions along which consumption provisions may vary. Thus consumption may take the form of commodities or services; it may be managed publicly or privately; access may be on market or non-market criteria; and provisions may be subsidized or unsubsidized by the state. On the basis of these distinctions, he constructs four ideal types of consumption processes, each of which can be further sub-divided, and each of which will tend to be associated with different attitudes on the part of consuming groups and with different degrees of politicization. Individualized consumption includes both commodities and services which may be privately or publicly organized (examples include consumer durables, privately rented housing and public utilities such as gas and electricity supplies), and this type of consumption tends to be associated with individualized attitudes and a low level of politicization. The second type is quasi-individualized consumption which involves consumption of commodities that may or may not be publicly administered but are all characterized by some degree of state subsidization. The obvious example here is owner-occupied housing in Britain, and although attitudes of consumers of such commodities will usually be individualized, the level of politicization is potentially high owing to the involvement of the state in providing subsidies (such as tax relief on mortgages).

The third type is quasi-collective consumption, which includes three main sub-categories: privately organized services with non-market access (such as National Trust land), privately organized services with market access but supported by state subsidy (for example the arts), and privately organized state-subsidized services with non-market access (such as voluntary welfare agencies). In all three cases, attitudes among consumers may well be collectivistic although the level of politicization normally remains low. Finally, Dunleavy defines the scope of collective consumption proper, and again he identifies three sub-categories: publicly organized but unsubsidized services with non-market access (the closest approximation to this category being public housing), publicly organized and subsidized services with market access (such as public transport), and – at the core of collective consumption – publicly organized and subsidized services with non-market provision (for instance health and education). In all three cases, social attitudes among consumers are likely to be collectivistic while the level of politicization may well be high.

While there are certainly problems with Dunleavy's paper (not least of which is his attempt to justify his approach with reference to a commonsense notion of the 'urban'), and while we may well seek to add additional dimensions to his analysis (most importantly the distinction between facilities that represent a subsidy to capital – for example roads – and those from which capital derives no direct benefit in terms of their use), it does serve a fruitful purpose in clarifying the specific problems to which analysis may be directed. As he himself concludes,

The expanded typology of modes of consumption given here would allow a genuinely comparative urban sociology to map out the variable handling of the same consumption crises in different economic, political and ideological contexts. I would tentatively suggest that if Castells's suggested focus for urban sociology is expanded to include quasi-collective and quasi-individualized consumption, then it does provide a definition of urban issues and conflicts which is applicable in a cross-national way, and yet relates to distinctively important aspects of consumption-based politics in advanced capitalist societies. [Dunleavy 1979b, pp. 21–2]

Thus, as we shall see in Chapter 8, such a mode of conceptualization may at last succeed in specifying a distinctive problem or question for an 'urban' sociology to answer.

Unlike the previous approaches we have discussed in earlier chapters, Castells's attempt to specify the urban question does not, therefore, appear to end up in a total impasse. Nevertheless, the fruitful residue from his writings represents only a small part (and a considerably amended part at that) of his overall perspective. Three points in particular should be emphasized in conclusion. First, Castells's theory may be rejected on grounds 'internal' to its own discourse (namely that it is premised on a theory of action, which it denies, and that it requires counterfactual conditions, which it cannot identify). Second, his concept of collective consumption may be retained as the initial basis for an ideal-typical conceptualization of 'urban' problems (the implication of this being that it should be assessed according to its heuristic value and not criticized for failing to include aspects of 'urbanism' that it was never intended to encompass), although it needs to be modified and qualified along the lines suggested by Dunleavy in order to avoid subsequent theoretical confusions. Third, the use of such a concept as the organizing principle of research has no necessary foundation in the question of space since the process of consumption is not confined to spatially delimited units, nor are all consumption provisions organized in and through a spatial context.

The implication of this third conclusion is that the 'urban question' should be specified in terms of a theoretically significant process (consumption) and cannot be equated with any particular 'concrete' object (the city). To label such analysis as 'urban' therefore becomes merely a question of convention, for space has dropped out of the analysis except in the sense that the study of any social process must take account of spatial and temporal dimensions. This, of course, raises the question of whether space *can* be an object of specific study, and this necessarily leads us back to the work of writers such as Lefebvre and his concept of the 'urban revolution'. Before developing a framework for an 'urban' sociology of consumption in Chapter 8, therefore, we must pause to consider the possibility of an urban sociology based specifically on an analysis of the social significance of space. This is the concern of the chapter that follows.

7 Political economy and the urban question

(with John Lloyd)

We have seen that, for Castells, space is not itself a theoretically significant problem. Consistently with the urban sociology tradition of which he is so critical, his concern is to identify social phenomena that are spatially specific, but having done so, his interest is focused on the social processes that go on within a spatial context rather than on that context itself. He is interested in collective consumption because it is, in his view, contained in some way within spatial boundaries, but his theoretical concern with the question of space extends no further than this. As Andrew Sayer notes,

Castells . . . repeatedly refers to space and 'urban space', but these turn out to be references to objects whose spatial structure and setting is then ignored. Certainly, when we talk about housing and factories we are referring to things which could not possibly be aspatial, but this hardly justifies the claim that space is being discussed properly, for we are told nothing about the internal spatial organisation of these objects or their spatial relations with other objects. . . . What Castells offers is more in the nature of classification of objects, activities and social relations in 'urban space' rather than an analysis of their spatial form. [A. Sayers 1979, pp.65–6]

The literature to be discussed in this chapter represents in some ways the reverse of Castells's approach, for it attempts not to locate specific social phenomena (such as processes of collective consumption) within a spatial context, but rather to locate the question of space itself within the context of the political economy of advanced capitalism. Space, in other words, is seen as important not simply with reference to the reproduction of labour-power, but in respect of the role it plays in the continuing and expanding process of capital accumulation. Seen in this way, this literature has more in common with Lojkine than Castells, although its strongest affinity is undoubtedly with Lefebvre. Thus, while he treats Lefebvre's notion of an 'urban revolution' with some caution, David Harvey (who is arguably the key figure in this tradition) addresses himself to the same problem of developing a theory of the production of space in relation to a Marxist analysis of the accumulation and circulation of capital.

This immediately raises the question of whether such an approach falls within the framework of an urban sociology; that is, of whether the problems it poses can be understood as sociological ones. Two points may be made about this. The first is that most Marxist theorists would undoubtedly reject this question as spurious, for, as we noted in Chapter 1, the dialectical method rejects the one-sidedness of disciplinary approaches in favour of a theory that encompasses all aspects of social relations – economic, political and ideological – by developing a conception of totality within which each is related to each other. Nevertheless, it is apparent that Marxist urban analysis has tended to develop along two different paths, one of which has been pursued by, and has attracted the attention of, those with a background in geography or economics, while the other is articulated more closely with the traditional concerns of urban sociology and political science. Furthermore, these two approaches have remained relatively distinct and have not generally engaged with one another, and attempts to represent them both under the same label (for example as 'the political economy of space': Anderson 1975) appear somewhat misleading. As we shall see in Chapter 8, the division between them is in fact fundamental in that it expresses the recurrent tension noted in earlier chapters between the (geographical) problem of space and the (sociological) problem of the social processes that take place within it. The division between these two approaches is thus a reflection of the same tension that has been noted in relation to ecological, cultural and socio-spatial perspectives.

The second point is that, although its primary concern is with the economic question of the significance of space for the production and realization of surplus value, the literature to be discussed here obviously does address itself to broader 'sociological' questions regarding the social and political implications of this process; for, given the dialectical principle of totality, a 'one-sided' concern with the economy would clearly be inadequate. It is at this point in its analysis that this literature leads us on to more familiar territory by posing the familiar questions (which are also addressed in the work of Castells and Rex and Pahl) of the relation between urban processes, the capitalist state and the development of class struggle. As we shall see, however, given its starting-point (the problem of capital accumulation), these questions are tackled in a rather different way than in the work of writers such as Castells, and they result in a tendency to reduce analysis of both the state and political struggle to the economic class categories of capital and labour and the various 'fractions' within them.

David Harvey: space and the problem of over-accumulation

We saw in Chapter 5 (page 153) that, like Lefebvre, Harvey regards the scientific method as normative and rejects the epistemological distinction between science and ideology. Hence in his major work, *Social Justice and the City* (1973), he suggests that the reader must determine for himself or herself the relative fruitfulness of the 'liberal formulations' and 'socialist formulations' that he discusses in the two parts of the book. There is, in other words, no claim that the latter are in some way privileged, but only that they are critical and hence consistent with a radical political position:

Marx gives a specific meaning to ideology – he regards it as an unaware expression of the underlying ideas and beliefs which attach to a particular social situation, in contrast to the aware and critical exposition of ideas in their social context which is frequently called ideology in the west. The essays in Part 2 are ideological in the western sense whereas the essays in Part 1 are ideological in the Marxist sense. [Harvey 1973, p. 18]

Liberal approaches therefore take existing ideas as given while Marxist approaches examine them critically.

The similarity between Harvey's and Lefebvre's approaches are not confined to questions of epistemology, however, for their theoretical concerns are also broadly consistent. Both see space as crucial in maintaining an expansive capitalism, although the emphases of their analyses are rather different. As we saw in Chapter 5, Lefebvre argues that space has become a – even *the* – key commodity by means of which capitalist production has been extended into new areas, and the production of space thus reflects and sustains the process of surplus value creation. The concept of an 'urban revolution' expresses this argument that the capitalist colonization of space is increasingly becoming the dominant sphere of capital accumulation. Harvey, however, rejects this assertion:

Urbanism possesses a separate structure – it can be conceived as a separate entity – with a dynamic of its own. But this dynamic is moderated through interaction and contradiction with other structures. To say that urbanism now dominates industrial society is to say that contradictions between urbanism as a structure in the process of transformation and the internal dynamic of the older industrial society are usually resolved in favour of the former. I do not believe this claim is realistic. In certain important and crucial respects industrial society and the structures which comprise it continue to dominate urbanism. [Harvey 1973, p. 311]

Harvey justifies this argument by suggesting that the creation of space is still largely dependent upon the investment decisions of industrial capital (decisions regarding the location of factories, offices and so on), that the key function of urbanization is that it stimulates new effective demand for the products of industrial capital (for instance, the spread of the suburbs increases the demand for cars), and that investment in the built environment, although increasingly significant in recent years, is largely a function of problems encountered by industrial capital in respect of the creation and realization of surplus value. While these arguments are certainly present in *Social Justice and the City*, they have been more fully developed in Harvey's later work, and particularly in his essay on the urban process under capitalism (1978a).

In this essay, Harvey begins by identifying the two basic contradictions within capitalism. These are, first, that competition between individual capitalists results in aggregate effects which are detrimental to their own individual and class interests (such as impairment of the quality of the work-force by intensification of the labour process) and, second, that the exploitation of labour-power creates a class that increasingly confronts capital. The first of these contradictions is particularly significant for Harvey's analysis since it creates a tendency towards the over-accumulation of capital. In other words, the pursuit of accumulation by individual capitalists in competition with one another tends to result in too much capital being created in the system as a whole relative to the opportunities for employing it profitably. This reflects the distinction drawn in Marxist theory between the creation of surplus value (which is a function of the production process in which labour-power is used to create additional value) and its realization in the money form (which is a function of the circulation process in which commodity capital is transformed into money capital at the point of sale). Harvey's argument is that the unregulated character of capitalist production tends to lead to crises in the realization of surplus value within what he terms the 'primary circuit' of capital (namely, the industrial sector): 'Here we can clearly see the contradictions which arise out of the tendency for individual capitalists to act in a way which, when aggregated, runs counter to their own class interest. This contradiction produces a tendency towards over-accumulation – too much capital is produced in aggregate relative to the opportunities to employ that capital' (1978a, pp. 104–6). This tendency becomes manifest in gluts on the market, falling prices, excess productive capacity and rising unemployment.

One way in which such over-accumulation problems may temporarily be resolved is through a switch of investment into the secondary and tertiary circuits of capital. The secondary circuit is here taken to refer to investment in fixed capital assets which aid production but do not themselves constitute direct raw material inputs, and to investment in what Harvey terms the 'consumption fund', which similarly takes the form of commodities that aid the process of consumption rather than being the immediate objects of this process. The built environment is an important aspect both of fixed capital (factories, offices and so on) and of the consumption fund (housing being the prime example), for in both cases it represents a physical framework within which production or consumption (or in some cases – such as transport facilities – both) take place. Investment of capital in physical infrastructure thus represents a significant aspect of the secondary circuit of capital. Investment in the tertiary circuit (which is not immediately relevant to Harvey's analysis), by contrast, may take the form either of investment in science and technology (which aids capital by revolutionizing the productive forces) or of investment in social expenditures (which aid capital by improving the quality of labour-power, as in educational expenditures, or by controlling the work-force through ideology or coercion).

The diversion of capital into the secondary and tertiary circuits will represent productive investment to the extent that it contributes directly or indirectly to the expansion of surplus value. Such a switch at times of over-accumulation in the primary circuit may therefore go some way to resolving the problem. However, Harvey suggests that such a switch is itself problematic. For a start, it poses what Offe (1975) has termed a 'rationality problem'. In other words, it is by no means clear to individual capitalists how far and under which conditions investment in these circuits will prove productive, and this has given rise to attempts at long-term planning, both by large companies and by the state (which has assumed much of the responsibility for such investments), but these remain hazardous given the lack of unequivocal profit signals. Furthermore, such a switch cannot easily be effected since investment in physical infrastructure involves long-term commitments to immobile assets and may not appear attractive to individual capitalists. As Harvey puts it, 'Individual capitalists left to themselves will tend to under-supply their own collective needs for production precisely because of such barriers. Individual capitalists tend to over-accumulate in the primary circuit and under-invest in the secondary circuit' (1978a, p. 107). Here again, therefore, the state may need to assume some responsibility as the representative of the interests of capital in general, although finance capital will also play a crucial role in making loans available for such switches. The capital market, in other words, is significant in mediating between the primary and secondary circuits, and this is why Harvey has suggested in another paper that 'The financial superstructure provides the mediating link between the urbanization process . . . and the necessities dictated by the underlying dynamic of capitalism' (1977, p. 138).

The main problem with switching circuits from primary (industrial) to secondary (urban), however, is that it must eventually lead to a replication in the secondary circuit of the same crisis of over-accumulation that originally developed in the primary one:

As the pressure builds, either the accumulation process grinds to a halt or new investment opportunities are found as capital flows down various channels into the secondary and tertiary circuits. This movement may start as a trickle and become a flood as the potential for expanding the production of surplus value by such means becomes apparent. But the tendency towards over-accumulation is not eliminated. It is transformed rather into a pervasive tendency towards over-investment in the secondary and tertiary circuits. [Harvey 1978a, pp. 111–12]

Investment in the secondary circuit thus results finally in the exhaustion of its potential for productive purposes, and hence in the devaluation of fixed assets and the consumption fund prior to a later renewed burst of accumulation. This becomes manifest in empty office blocks, demolition of buildings long before their useful life has ended, and so on. The main difference between Harvey and Lefebvre, therefore, is that the latter sees the secondary circuit as increasingly the dominant form of investment and as the means whereby capital may overcome the problems of creating surplus value, whereas the former sees it as subsidiary to industrial investment and as a temporary expedient which soon reveals the same problems of over-accumulation that necessitated its expansion in the first place. Thus Harvey shows how, at the onset of industrial crises, investment funds have tended to flow into the built environment (as in the case of the property boom in the early 1970s), only to find that the productive possibilities here very soon become saturated:

Each of the global crises of capitalism was in fact preceded by the massive movement of capital into long-term investment in the built environment as a kind of last-ditch hope for finding productive uses for rapidly over-accumulating capital. The extraordinary property boom in many advanced capitalist countries from 1969–73, the collapse of which at the end of 1973 triggered (but did not cause) the onset of the current crisis, is a splendid example. [Harvey 1978a, p. 120]

Harvey therefore approaches the question of urban processes through an analysis of capital accumulation in which the switching from primary to secondary circuits is seen as crucial in determining patterns of investment in the built environment. Urban processes, by which he means 'the creation of a material physical infrastructure for production, circulation, exchange and consumption' (1978a, p. 113), are thus seen as dependent upon the possibilities for productive investment in the primary circuit. However, as his commitment to the dialectical method implies, he does not see this simply in terms of a one-way relationship, for he recognizes that urban processes will themselves have effects on the primary circuit and, indeed, on other areas of economic and political activity. This point is well illustrated by his discussion of suburbanization in the United States.

In 1945, he suggests, the United States was faced with the problem of how to employ a vast productive capacity which had been developed during the war. A number of solutions were found including the export of surplus product to Europe through Marshall aid and continuing investment in armaments, but a crucial strategy was the stimulation of suburbanization: 'A variety of strategies emerged for stimulating consumption, not least of which were a set of fiscal and monetary policies designed to accelerate and enhance the suburbanization process' (1977, p. 124). In terms of the argument set out above, the state (through, say, tax concessions to home-owners and the construction industry) and finance capital (for example through special credit arrangements) facilitated a massive switch of investment into the secondary circuit. The effect of this was not only that capital found a new area of productive investment as the means for avoiding a potential crisis of over-accumulation in the primary circuit, but also that this new investment itself stimulated fresh demand for the products of industrial capital. The boom in the construction industry thus itself helped to stimulate a boom in the car industry, the energy supply industry and so on. Furthermore, the spread of home ownership also helped to maintain political stability by creating 'a large wedge of debt-encumbered home owners who are unlikely to rock the boat because they are both debt-encumbered and reasonably well-satisfied owner occupiers. Home ownership . . . as a device for achieving social stability went hand-in-hand in the post-war period with the drive to stimulate consumption through sub-urbanization' (1977, p. 125; we shall return to the question of the political significance of home ownership later in this chapter).

Harvey goes on to suggest, however, that this process is itself con-tradictory. This is because investment in the built environment overcomes problems of over-accumulation at one point in time only to block the resolution of these problems at a later period:

Spatial structures are created which themselves act as barriers to further accumulation. . . . Capitalist development has therefore to negotiate a knife-edge path between preserving the exchange values of past capital investments in the built environment and destroying the value of these investments in order to open up fresh room for accumulation. Under capitalism there is, then, a perpetual struggle in which capital builds a physical landscape appropriate to its own condition at a particular moment in time, only to have to destroy it, usually in the course of a crisis, at a subsequent point in time. [Harvey 1978a, pp. 123–4]

Moreover, attempts to overcome the barrier to accumulation which is represented by the immobile physical investments of an earlier period may well undermine political cohesion and stimulate a challenge on the part of those most affected, for 'people who live in the communities being "obsolesced" resist and resent the process for the most part. Community activism arises as a response to the pressures for change' (1977, p. 137).

This last point leads us into an examination of how the second con-tradiction identified by Harvey at the start of his paper – namely that between capital and labour – relates to his analysis of urban processes. The question at issue here is, of course, the same as that addressed by Rex in his concept of housing classes and by Castells in his concept of urban social movements, namely the relationship between urban struggles and class struggles. But whereas Rex sees urban struggles as involving a different basis of class alignments than that found in the world of work, and Castells sees them as involving different and cross-cutting alliances of classes, Harvey's basic position is that urban struggles are simply one form of expression of class struggles.

Harvey does, of course, recognize that 'Internecine conflict within a class and faction is . . . just as common as conflict between classes and factions' (1978b, p. 12). In particular, he notes that certain sections of the capitalist class may often ally themselves with working-class struggles over the consumption fund, and that the working class itself may be split internally in respect of urban questions.

Alliances between capital and labour are made possible because the consumption demands of the working class may often be consistent with the economic or political interests of the capitalist class as a whole, or of certain sections of it. For example, workers may seek to own their homes (say, because of the potential for accumulation that home ownership affords), and this will tend to be in the interests of finance capital (which can lend on house purchase) and of industrial capital (since it performs an ideological function and underpins worker commitment). The result may therefore be an alliance between these various groups against landed interests (such as private landlords). Similarly, industrial capital will support working-class demands for cheap housing since lower rents or mortgage charges will facilitate a reduction in wages (because a reduction in the costs of reproducing labour-power reduces the value of labour-power and hence enables a lowering of wages if other factors remain constant). Working class demands for a variety of consumption provisions may also be consistent with the interest of capital so long as the resources in question (schooling or health care for example) can be made available in the commodity form, and even struggles over questions concerning 'community' and the 'quality of life' may reinforce capitalist domination by attempting to re-establish in the sphere of consumption some spurious relation to nature (as in municipal parks) that the very process of capitalist production has torn asunder: 'Capital . . . seeks to draw labor into a Faustian bargain: Accept a packaged relation to nature in the living place as just and adequate compensation for an alienating and degrading relation to nature in the work place' (1978b, p. 29; the parallel with the argument of Raymond Williams, discussed in Chapter 3, is here clearly apparent).

Splits within the working class, on the other hand, become possible because of the artificial division, which capitalism has itself created, between work and home, the factory and the community, productive activity and consumption activity. The result is that the working class finds itself involved in what appear to be two distinct areas of struggle: 'The split between the place of work and the place of residence means that the struggle of labor to control the social conditions of its own existence splits into two seemingly independent struggles . . . [yet] the dichotomy between living and working is itself an artificial division which the capitalist system imposes' (1978b, p. 11). It follows from this that the solidarism that may develop at the work-place becomes fragmented outside the factory gate as different groups of workers pursue their own immediate interests as consumers. Thus Harvey distinguishes three types of working-class response to questions of consumption – market-based individualism, self-interested collectivism and class-conscious collectivism – suggesting that community politics in the USA generally fall nearer the first while those in Europe tend to get closer to the third.

Irrespective of how different sections of the working class respond to urban questions, however, Harvey insists that urban struggles must be seen as an expression or extension of the fundamental class struggle in society between capital and labour:

The overt struggles . . . between landlord-appropriators, builders and labor are to be seen as mediated manifestations of the deeply underlying conflict between capital and labor. . . . From this standpoint it must surely be plain that the separation between working and living is at best a surficial estrangement, an apparent tearing asunder of what can never be kept apart. And it is at this deeper level too that we can more clearly see the underlying unity between work-based and community-based conflicts. [Harvey 1978b, pp. 34–5]

This underlying unity therefore denies any specificity to urban struggles in that they are seen simply as 'displaced' class struggles; that is, the fundamental class antagonisms that derive out of the process of production reverberate 'to every corner of the social totality' and throughout all aspects of life that have been subordinated to the requirements of capital accumulation (see 1978a, p. 125).

As we shall see in the next section, this argument has been echoed by a number of writers in the urban political economy tradition, but before we turn to this literature it is necessary to make two final points about Harvey's work. The first relates to his analysis of the problem of over-accumulation; the second to his analysis of class struggle.

As we noted earlier (page 222), Marxist theory distinguishes between the production process, within which surplus value is created, and the circulation process, within which it is realized. Competition between capitals is held to result not simply in periodic crises of over-production/under-consumption (which are resolved by means of a restructuring of capital through the collapse of smaller and less efficient producers and the growing concentration and centralization of capital into smaller numbers of larger firms employing the most advanced technology), but, more importantly, in a tendency for the organic composition of capital as a whole to rise (that is, an increase in value terms in the proportion of constant to variable capital employed in the production process), and thus for the rate of profit in the economy as a whole to fall. Periodic crises in which capital tends to over-produce are therefore underpinned by a long-term tendency towards a crisis in the very creation of surplus value.

In his discussion of the 'urban revolution', Lefebvre explicitly addresses this problem as it relates to the question of space, and he shows how the capitalist colonization of space may not only provide new markets (and therefore go some way towards overcoming the problem of over-production), but may also help to counter the tendency for the rate of profit to fall owing to the relatively low organic composition of capital employed in the construction and leisure industries. Harvey, however, concentrates his analysis on the first of these two aspects and tends to neglect the second. This is seen most clearly in his work on American suburbanization, for as Harloe (1977) suggests, his analysis here has much in common with the under-consumption theory of monopoly capitalism proposed by Baran and Sweezy (1966), according to which the transcendence of price competition in monopolistic market conditions has overcome the tendency for the rate of profit to fall (because large companies can now agree to fix prices at a level that will ensure required rates of return) but has exacerbated the problem of disposing of an ever-increasing mass of surplus generated by production at full capacity.

Such arguments have, however, attracted considerable criticism in the Marxist literature, mainly on the grounds that the problem of creating surplus value (and thus the question of the falling rate of profit) exists irrespective of the ability of companies to fix prices since it is a function of changes in the value composition of capital at the point of production rather than of price determination at the point of sale of commodities produced. From a Marxist viewpoint, therefore, Harvey's analysis appears one-sided and incomplete in that it fails to address the central question of how investment in urban infrastructure may affect the rate of profit in the economy as a whole.

It is perhaps in response to such criticisms that Harvey has, in his later work, developed his analysis of investment switches between the three circuits of capital, but this does not resolve the problem. The crucial concept developed in this later work is that of 'productive investment' by which he means investment 'which directly or indirectly expands the basis for the production of surplus value' (1978a, p. 110). According to this definition, investment in the built environment will be productive to the extent that it aids the creation of surplus value by providing resources such as housing, roads or whatever that benefit industrial capital (by reproducing labour-power more cheaply or efficiently, by overcoming blockages in the circulation of industrial capital, and so on). But not only does this concept of 'productive investment' beg the question raised by Lefebvre of whether production of the built environment is itself a way in which the falling rate of profit may be countered (because of a lower organic composition in the industries involved), but it also still depends on crises of realization as the cause of investment switches out of the primary circuit. An analysis that took as its starting point the problem of generating surplus value would explain such switches, not in terms of over-accumulation, but rather as the result of the tendency within capitalism for the profit rate to be equalized across different sectors (that is to say, capital will move from sectors of higher to sectors of lower organic composition in order to secure a higher rate of surplus value, and this will result in an equalization of profit rates between different capitals in different sectors of production). Harvey rejects such explanations on the grounds that analysis of value (as opposed to prices) appears inappropriate to the study of investment in the secondary and tertiary circuits, but his argument here is, to say the least, underdeveloped. The first major problem with his approach, therefore, is that the emphasis on the problem of over-accumulation is nowhere justified in theoretical terms (which is not, of course, to suggest that it could not be justified, but rather that in Harvey's work it is simply asserted as the starting point of analysis).

The second problem with his work, which follows directly from his central concern with over-accumulation as the fundamental contradiction within advanced capitalism, is that the significance of class struggle appears only as a secondary factor in his analysis. In part this reflects his argument regarding the 'displacement' of class struggles into the urban context, for as we have seen Harvey recognizes that this context may have important effects for the struggle between wage-labour and capital (by fragmenting working class consciousness, for example) but is not central to it. In this sense, an analysis of urbanism will necessarily focus primarily on capital (for which the urban may be crucial in temporarily resolving problems of over-accumulation) rather than on the working class (for which the urban is but a reflection of capitalist domination in the sphere of production).

The problem, however, goes deeper than this, for an emphasis on the question of over-accumulation necessarily disregards the role of working-class struggle in determining the limits of capital accumulation. This point has been made by Gamble and Walton in their criticism of Baran and Sweezy's work: 'Their starting point for analyzing capitalism is class ownership and control of the means of production. Yet they do not, as Marx himself did, concentrate on how the classes are established in the process of production itself and how the class relationships of production both determine and set limits to the accumulation of capital' (Gamble and Walton 1976, p. 107). While the role of class struggle is central to a Marxist analysis of the generation of surplus value (since the strength of the workers' movement will be reflected in the extent to which wages can be forced up above the value of labour-power), it appears only as a secondary factor in an approach such as Harvey's which identifies the fundamental problem for capital as that of disposing of surplus rather than creating it. Class struggle is tacked on to the end of Harvey's analysis – crises of over-accumulation may provoke some sort of working-class response – but is in no way central to it since the major contradiction of over-accumulation is not brought about by the working class at all, but is simply the result of competition between individual capitalists which produces an aggregate effect detrimental to the interests of that class. From such a perspective, the crisis of capitalism is largely self-engendered; the working class stands by on the sidelines of history and at most plays a reactive role, while capital inflicts its own wounds as a result of the incessant drive to accumulate.

The basic weakness in Harvey's approach is his failure to relate the questions of production and reproduction, capital accumulation and class struggle. This is a problem that recurs through much of the literature on urban political economy and which becomes particularly acute in respect of its analysis of the two related issues identified at the start of this chapter, namely the relation between urbanism and class struggle and between urbanism and state intervention. It is to these two questions that we now turn.

The political economy of housing

✓ As we have seen in previous chapters, housing has always been a central concern of urban sociology, largely because it has posed important questions for both Weberian and Marxist analyses of class struggle in capitalist societies. Thus we have seen that writers as diverse as Rex and Castells have been concerned to trace the significance of housing as a crucial aspect of consumption for the development of class struggles that derive out of relations of production. This theme is also taken up in the political economy literature, but, given its primary concern with the significance of the urban for capital accumulation, this literature has also posed new questions regarding the role of housing as a commodity. In other ✓ words, it has addressed itself not only to housing as an aspect of consumption and reproduction of labour-power, but also to the significance of housing in the creation and distribution of surplus value. In this way it has come to pose three questions relating to the production of housing (creation of surplus value), the ownership of housing (distribution of surplus value in rent) and the consumption of housing (reproduction of labour-power).

From a Marxist standpoint, the production of housing in a capitalist society takes the form of commodity production to the extent that it is produced for its exchange value, and in this sense it can be analysed in the same way as the production of any other commodity. It is, however, somewhat unique in that housing constitutes a key element in the reproduction of labour-power (that is, in the productive consumption of the work-force), and as such is an important condition of continued industrial production – and is, furthermore, an unusually expensive commodity to produce and thus to purchase. Housing, unlike most consumer goods, cannot be sold to workers in a single transaction but must rather be paid for over an extended time period. If sufficient housing is to be produced in order to reproduce labour-power at an adequate level, it is necessary for a variety of financial institutions to mediate between producers and consumers by advancing credit for house purchase, or for some means to be found whereby housing is purchased by a third party (either private landlords or the state) and then rented to consumers over a long period. Groups and institutions such as building societies on the one hand and private landlords on the other thus play a crucial role, not only for that section of industrial capital that is directly engaged in the production of housing (since they can convert their commodity capital back into money capital without long delays and can therefore recommence the production cycle), but also for industrial capital as a whole (since the means for reproducing labour-power are thereby ensured). From this perspective, therefore, the principal significance of building societies, landlords, local housing authorities and so on lies not so much in the question of how housing as a consumption resource is allocated (the issue addressed by Rex and Pahl) as in how housing as a commodity is exchanged and how the surplus value embodied in it is realized.

According to Ball, however, this problem of realization must itself be situated within an analysis of production in the house-building industry. This is because the realization problem only reflects the fact that housing is a high-value, and hence high-price, commodity, a fact that has itself to be explained in terms of the archaic organization of the industry: 'The statement that housing requires forms of finance over and above that derived from wages because housing is expensive to build is obviously a truism. But it is a truism which sites the reason for the necessity in the sphere of production and not in the sphere of circulation' (Ball 1978, p. 86). The starting point for a political economy of housing must therefore lie in an analysis of its production as a commodity.

Ball argues that the central problem that house production poses for capital in Britain concerns the low productivity of the industry, and he cites figures to show that the annual average rate of increase in productivity between 1907 and 1955 amounted to only 0.2 per cent in building and contracting compared with over 2 per cent in manufacturing industry. Whatever the reasons for this (and Ball admits that no adequate explanation has been put forward), the result is that housing costs have risen nearly twice as fast as the retail price index over this period. Housing, in other words, has been getting more expensive in real terms as the replacement of variable by constant capital has lagged behind other sections of industry, and this has caused problems for industrial capital as a whole in that it has worked against any substantial reduction in the necessary costs of reproducing labour-power:

There is considerable evidence that productivity in the house-building industry has increased at a much slower rate than in other sectors of industry. This means that the fall in the labour time necessary to produce housing has lagged behind that for other commodities. As a result the value of housing will not have fallen to the same extent as many of the commodities contributing to the reproduction of labour-power. Now any such commodity, whose value does not fall, limits the ability to lower the value of labour-power and will therefore act as a restriction on increases in the rate of surplus value. The rate of accumulation will be slowed and counteracting tendencies to the falling rate of profit weakened. The extent to which this occurs depends, of course, on the importance of the commodity in the value of labour-power, and housing is a significant element in that value. So the low growth of productivity in the house-building industry becomes a crucial problem for capitalism. [Ball 1978, p. 79]

It is in this context that Ball analyses the role of state intervention in the provision and distribution of housing. His argument is that such intervention was necessitated by the contradiction between industrial capital's need for cheap and reliable labour-power and the inability of the building industry to reduce the cost of housing in line with that of other basic commodities. The dynamic behind state intervention, whether in the form of rent controls, subsidies or direct provision, therefore lies in the requirements of capital rather than in the demands of actual or potential consumers of housing. Although his analysis differs from Harvey's in that it focuses on the problems encountered by industrial capital in generating surplus value rather than on the problem of disposing of surpluses, it is nevertheless similar to Harvey's in so far as both writers identify the key explanatory factor for their analyses as relating to the process of capital accumulation rather than class struggle.

It is, in fact, a characteristic feature of the political economy literature that it tends to regard the effects of class struggle as secondary to the effects and requirements of capital accumulation. The debates and disagreements within this literature tend to revolve around questions such as whether the central problem for capital is that of generating or realizing surplus value, or whether state intervention reflects the needs of industrial or finance capital, rather than questions concerning the basic assumption that most writers share, that the demands and interests of the working class are necessarily subordinate to those of some 'fraction' of capital. This point is clearly illustrated by recent work by Ball and others on the reasons for state intervention in housing, and in particular on the explanations offered for the introduction of rent controls in the private sector, the growth of state housing provisions after the First World War and the financial support of owner-occupation.

The explanation for the introduction of rent controls in 1915 generally hinges on Marx's theory of rent. This was developed primarily in relation to an analysis of capitalist agriculture, and it is by no means clear how far Marx's arguments, particularly in respect of 'differential rent', can be applied to urban land (for example see Ball 1977, who points out the difference between agriculture, where land directly affects productivity according to variations in its fertility, and urban land use, where location is important in terms of access to markets). The basic principle in Marx's theory is, however, equally applicable to both agricultural and urban rents, and this is that rent represents a deduction from the surplus value which accrues to industrial capital.

In the agricultural case this is obvious, for the capitalist farmer who employs wage-labour to produce a commodity (food) is obliged to pay part of the surplus value he extracts at the point of production to a landlord who is not himself productive. One component of this rent payment will consist of 'absolute rent' which reflects the ability of landlords as a class to exact a payment for access to even the worst-quality land. Absolute rent is significant in that it represents a barrier to investment in agriculture and thus prevents the equalization of profit rates between agriculture and other sectors of industry since a higher rate of profit in agriculture (consequent upon a lower organic composition of capital) will be creamed off as absolute rent by private landlords. A second component will consist of 'differential rent', and this basically expresses the differences in productivity between different pieces of land. Here, therefore, the owners of high fertility, improved or otherwise advantageously endowed land extract the surplus profits that can be made on such land relative to land on the economic margin of cultivation, and differential rent thus has the function of reducing surplus profits to average profits in the agricultural industry as a whole. Finally, rent may also include a 'monopoly' component which reflects the ability of some farmers to monopolize part of the market as a result of peculiarities in the land they farm. A particular plot of land, for example, may produce a unique wine, in which case the landlord will extract from the farmer in monopoly rent the increased price he is able to charge for his unique product. The important point about all three types of rent, therefore, is that land does not itself create value, and the return to landowners represents a redistribution of surplus value from industrial capital (in this case farmers) to a non-productive landlord class.

The same is true of urban rents. Again, this is obvious in the case of industrial capital paying rent directly to owners of land; for the situation of the factory owner who must pay (either in annual rent or in outright purchase) for access to a site is broadly analogous to that of the farmer who must pay rent for access to the soil. The argument also applies, however, to the rents paid by workers for their housing. This is because the cost of reproduction of labour-power will in part reflect the cost of workers' housing, and, other things remaining the same, the cost of rent will therefore be reflected in the level of wages. Although private landlords extract rent directly from their proletarian tenants, it follows that the source of this rent is actually the surplus value of the industrial capitalist since an increasing in housing rents will result in an increase in the value of labour-power, a corresponding increase in wages, and a reduction in surplus value. As Engels explains,

> The tenant, even if he is a worker, appears as a man with money; he must have already sold his commodity, a commodity peculiarly his own, his labour-power, to be able to appear with the proceeds as the buyer of the use of a dwelling. . . . No matter how much the landlord may overreach the tenant it is still only a transfer of already existing, previously produced value and the total sum of values possessed by the landlord and tenant together remains the same after as it was before. [Engels 1969b, pp. 307–8]

It follows logically from all this that the question of rent control does not directly affect the working class at all, for although (as Harvey suggests) the extraction of rent may displace class conflict from the workplace to the community, it is clear that, in so far as rent represents a deduction from surplus value, the 'real' contradiction is expressed not in the relation between landlords and tenants but in that between industrial capital and *petit bourgeois* rentiers. This is an argument on which there is broad agreement in the literature. Dickens (1977), for example, argues that the rent strike that occurred in Glasgow in 1915 and which precipitated the introduction of rent control legislation had the broad support of industrial capital in that city since a rent freeze would both ensure continued production (since it was 'a sop to industrial militancy' – p. 343) and maintain low levels of wages. Similarly, Massey and Catalano (1978, p. 150) suggest that the decline of the private rented sector (which was hastened by the introduction of rent controls) represents a victory of industrial capital over landed property interests, while Ball argues that the decline of private landlordism was the product of the contradiction between capitalist profitability (which depended upon the existence of a healthy, cheap labour force) and the viability of the private rented sector (which depended upon increased rents and poor quality housing): 'A rise in rent levels could have sufficed to increase landlord profitability but this would have necessitated increased wages, thus bringing housing landlords into direct conflict with the interests of the bourgeoisie' (1978, p. 91). For all of these writers, therefore, *petit bourgeois* landlords were sacrificed on the altar of capitalist profitability, and the explanation for state regulation of rents is to be found, not in the struggles of the Glasgow working class, but in the requirements of capitalist profitability for a cheap and appeased labour force.

Much the same arguments have been advanced to explain the growth of the public rented sector. Dickens, for example, points out that, like the introduction of rent controls, state provision of housing was supported by both the working class and industrial capital, and that it was important not only in ensuring the continued reproduction of labour-power, but also as a concession to the working class that could be made without fundamentally challenging dominant economic interests. Similarly Ball suggests that the prime function of public housing 'is to house the working class adequately as cheaply as possible' (1978, p. 92). Both writers also point out that finance capital appears as a principal beneficiary of the extension of state housing since local authorities have to borrow in order to finance house construction. Just as rent paid to private landlords represents a redistribution of surplus value away from industrial capital, so too does interest paid to loan capital, since debt charges incurred by local authorities have to be paid for out of rents and taxation and this in turn increases the necessary average level of wages. This, together with the fact that tax subsidies to owner-occupiers through mortgage relief similarly operate in the interests of loan capital (since they enable house buyers to pay high interest charges), leads Ball to conclude that 'Both local authority housing and owner-occupation enable the appropriation of surplus value by loan capital' (1978, p. 94). The conflict between industrial capital and private landlords in the early part of this century has therefore given way to that between industrial capital and finance capital today, but the source of this conflict – the distribution of surplus value among different 'fractions' of the capitalist class – is the same in both cases.

The role of the working class in such conflicts is, as we have seen, represented as somewhat peripheral. While working-class demands may influence the timing and the form of housing policies, it is the various requirements and interests of different sections of the capitalist class that determines them. As Berry observes, 'State intervention in housing is presented as a perpetual (zero sum) game between the principal fractions, deflecting attention from other causal factors, in particular the state of class struggle' (1979, p. 23). Furthermore, this literature tends to assume that, having identified the source of state intervention in the relative power at any one time of different 'fractions' of capital, it has also identified its function. In other words, not only is rent control, state housing provision, support of owner-occupation and so on explained in terms of the balance of power between private landlords, finance capital and industrial capital, but it is also argued that such policies are positively functional for capitalist interests and (therefore) dysfunctional to the long-term interests of the working class. The main reason for this is that the working class is divided among and within different housing tenure categories which serve to fragment class solidarity.

This argument has been developed both in relation to the growth of public housing and in respect of the support of owner-occupation. In the case of the former, it is argued that local authority allocation strategies systematically fragment the working class by creating divisions between 'respectable' and 'unrespectable' estates (cf. Damer 1974, Byrne 1977), by individualizing the housing question through the mechanism of the housing waiting list (cf. Paris *et al.*, 1977), and so on. In the case of the latter, it is argued by a wide range of writers that owner-occupation undermines the cohesion of the working class by fostering an ideology of possessive individualism and by sustaining worker compliance through the imposition of a long-term debt burden (see, for example, Clarke and Ginsburg 1975, Boddy 1976, Community Development Project 1976, Gray 1976, Cockburn 1977, all of which are discussed in Saunders 1979, ch. 2). The working class therefore enters into analyses of the political economy of housing not as a significant causal agent of change but as a passive and fragmented recipient of outcomes.

All this raises two fundamental questions. First, is the working class really as politically insignificant, and are capitalist interests as politically dominant, in the determination of social policies, as these writers suggest? Second, are the effects of state intervention in an area like housing really as functional to the long-term interests of capital, and as dysfunctional to those of the working class, as these arguments imply?

The claim that state intervention in the housing problem is the product of the relative power of different 'fractions' of capital at different points in time rests on what is basically an 'instrumentalist' theory of the state in which political outcomes are explained as the reflection of the power exerted by dominant economic interests in society. For such an analysis, the economic interests of capital are taken as the independent variable and state policy outcomes as the dependent variable. In his discussion of interwar housing legislation, for example, Dickens argues that 'Government housing policy was in effect capital's housing policy' (1977, p. 393). Working-class struggle may be significant in affecting when and how the state responds to the interests of capital (that is to say, it represents an intervening variable), but it cannot change the functional relation between the two. Thus Dickens argues that the Glasgow rent strike 'accelerated' rent control legislation but did not cause it, while Ball similarly suggests that, although the 'timing and form' of this legislation reflected the unrest on Clydeside, the 'fundamental explanation' for it has to be located in the economic contradictions relating to the cost of reproducing labour-power of the required quality. Furthermore, both writers stress the ideological function of this intervention in appeasing industrial militancy and fragmenting the working class.

Where these arguments differ from cruder versions of instru-mentalist theories is in their recognition that the state is not equally responsive to the interests of all sections of the capitalist class; landlords lose out to industrialists, industrialists lose out to financiers, and so on. The term 'fractions' is employed in an attempt to explain the economic diversity and political inequality between different capitalist groupings, but this term is only loosely theorized and appears to represent little more than a pragmatic response to the problems that attach to any instrumentalist theory in accounting for the variety and complexity of state policy outcomes. As Forrest and Lloyd suggest, 'In short, "fractions" as generally used we would argue are representative of nothing more than "interest groups". In this sense it is a concept that gives a bogus theoretical weight to various groups whose activities and apparent relative autonomy remain largely untheorized in Marxist terms' (1978, p. 31). The greater the difficulties encountered in trying to reduce all policy outcomes to economic class categories, the more reliance comes to be placed on *ad hoc* taxonomies of class fractions. Starting out from the assumption that a capitalist state cannot respond in any significant way to the demands of non-capitalist classes, it is incumbent on the analyst to identify one group of capitalists who, in any issue, may have exerted some power and who can then be designated the key fraction.

This systematic undervaluing of the causal significance of working-class demands in the development of state housing policies stems from the basic assumption that the dominance of capital in the sphere of production must in some way be reflected in all other areas of life in capitalist societies. The starting point for any analysis is the article of faith that, relative to capital, the working class can never win. In his analysis of the high cost of housing, for example, Ball overlooks the fact that working-class housing standards have improved dramatically in the course of this century and that these costs may therefore be explained 'not in terms of stagnant productivity, but as a consequence of rising housing standards which would have cost even more in the absence of productivity gains' (Berry 1979, p. 39). Similarly, in their haste to identify the beneficial effects for capital of an extension of public housing that aids the reproduction of labour-power, lines the pockets of finance capital and reduces the working class to an incoherent mass of competing individuals, most of the writers discussed in this section fail to consider the challenge that this form of housing provision represents to the commodity form on which capitalism depends. Something like 30 per cent of the British population is today housed on the criterion of need rather than ability to pay: 'In this wider structural sense, basic capitalist social relations are undermined, the market is only preserved by removing its most unacceptable face' (Forrest and Lloyd 1978, p. 39).

The problem, it seems, is that much of this literature too readily deduces the causes of state intervention from an analysis of its subsequent effects. Rent controls are found to have aided industrialists, council housing has increased the profits of the financial institutions, owner-occupation has provided a spurious legitimacy for private property ownership, and it is therefore assumed that these functional aspects of state intervention can be taken as indicative of the reasons for it. Yet as Gough (1975) has pointed out, it is fallacious to argue that those who benefit from a given policy are necessarily those who brought it about, and the history of twentieth-century social legislation in Britain would seem to suggest that for much of the time it has been working-class struggle that has necessitated policy initiatives, even though the subsequent reforms may later have come to benefit particular capitalist interests:

The interaction of long-term socio-economic trends, the political strategy of the capitalist state and the ongoing class struggle rule out any simple single-factor explanation of social policies. Above all it is essential to distinguish their concrete historical *origins* from the ongoing *function* they play within that particular social formation. Social policies originally the product of class struggle will, in the absence of further struggle, be absorbed and adapted to benefit the interests of the dominant classes. [Gough 1975, p. 76]

Seen in this way, theories that deny the causal significance of the working class in bringing about state intervention and that assume the functionality of such intervention for dominant economic interests in society are clearly inadequate, for there is no necessary reason for believing that the state always responds to some fraction of capital while excluding popular demands, or for assuming that the effects of its policies will always aid capital accumulation and fragment the non-capitalist classes. It is not true to suggest, as Dickens does, that the working class may win but capital never loses; for questions concerning the causes and long-term consequences of state intervention in housing or other areas of social provision can be addressed only through research on specific cases at specific periods in specific societies. As we shall now see, there are good grounds for arguing that the requirements of capital accumulation take precedence over demands for social provisions in capitalist societies, but this in no way implies that the interests of capital are necessarily reflected in those social provisions that are made. Indeed, there appear good grounds for suggesting that social provisions won through popular political struggles often represent more of a problem than an aid in respect of the long-term profitability and viability of the private sector.

Capital accumulation and social consumption

The characteristic feature of the work of Harvey, Ball and other writers in what may be termed the 'urban political economy' tradition is a common and primary concern with analysing the significance of space and the built environment for capital accumulation. While they certainly differ among themselves over such questions as the problem of over-accumulation or the relevance of differential rent in capitalist urbanization, they share a common focus in so far as they seek to explain the production of the urban environment with reference to the interests of various 'fractions' of capital (for instance in reproducing labour-power, extending markets, countering the falling rate of profit, legitimating capitalist social relations or redistributing surplus value between less powerful and more powerful fractions).

Where such approaches encounter a major problem, however, is in relating this emphasis on accumulation and the interests of capital to an analysis of consumption and the interests of non-capitalist classes. This problem is revealed both in the assumption that urban struggles represent displaced class struggles, and in the assertion that consumption provisions function in the interests of capital, for both of these arguments appear crudely economistic (not to say functionalist) in that they attempt to reduce political struggles and state intervention in the sphere of consumption to the economic categories of capital and wage-labour which are constituted in the sphere of capitalist production. The assumption, in other words, is that processes of consumption mirror those of production and that a mode of analysis adequate to the latter can simply be transferred to an analysis of the former. Thus, if the fundamental antagonism in the workplace is that between capital and labour, then it is assumed that this is reproduced (albeit in distorted forms) in the community: 'The housing struggle analyzed objectively is a struggle between capital and labour over the provision of housing, even if it is a struggle which is diffused both by the fragmentation of capital and by the fragmentation of the working class' (Clarke and Ginsburg 1975, p. 4). Similarly, if the fundamental role of the state lies in maintaining conditions favourable to capital accumulation, then it is assumed that state intervention in the provision of consumption items must in some way reflect the interests of capital.

Such arguments appear problematic for two reasons. First, urban struggles seem not to correspond to the categories of capital and labour. Of course, in conflicts over housing, welfare provisions or whatever, individual members of the working class will often confront individual representatives of capital, but they do so not as a class, but as members of a particular consumer group (in Weber's terms, a status group). Furthermore, as Clarke and Ginsburg recognize, such conflicts often involve different individual members of the same class confronting each other on opposite sides (landlords against industrialists, for example, or owner-occupiers against council tenants). For such struggles to be represented as expressions or mystifications of the underlying class antagonism between capital and labour, resort is made in some cases to an untheorized concept of fractions of capital (in the case of conflicts between different groups of capitalists), and in others to a crudely instrumentalist theory of ideology (for example, the familiar argument that owner-occupation functions to fragment the working class and to incorporate a growing proportion of the work-force into an individualistic and acquisitive ethic which is seen as an aspect of the ideology of capital imposed upon working-class groups to whom it is 'naturally' alien). Thus, in order to maintain the argument that urban struggles are merely phenomenal expressions of the class struggle, total reliance has to be placed upon an untheorized concept of class fractions and an untheorized notion of ideological dominance (the catch-all explanation in terms of capitalist 'hegemony'), and history is systematically reinterpreted in order to show how the spread of owner-occupation, for example, was 'in fact' a deliberate strategy for dividing the working class (cf. Cockburn 1977, p. 45: 'Successive governments have used owner-occupation purposively as an inducement to workers to identify with bourgeois values'; Clarke and Ginsburg 1975, p. 25: 'The capitalist class as a whole has a clear commitment to owner-occupation on ideological grounds, and it was this ideological commitment which was fundamental in determining the emphasis on owner-occupation from the fifties onwards'; and so on). The effect of a given policy is thus taken as indicative of its cause.

As we saw above, such arguments rest not only on an instrumentalist theory of ideology (in which the working class is the passive receptacle of hegemonic values which work against their interests), but also of an instrumentalist theory of the state (since, for example, the interests of industrial capital in ensuring a compliant labour force are directly translated into state policies aimed to foster a growth in home ownership, just as its interests in maintaining an adequate supply of cheap labour-power were directly reflected in rent control legislation during and after the First World War). This, however, is the source of the second problem, for state intervention in the sphere of consumption may, as Castells and others have shown, create severe problems as regards future capital accumulation (since it may represent a deduction from surplus value, either directly, through company taxation, or indirectly, through taxation on workers and consumers which raises the costs of their labour-power). Furthermore, even if such intervention may sometimes have ideological spin-off effects (such as in placating popular unrest), this too is a double-edged sword since any future reduction in the level of provision may presumably be expected on the basis of this argument to provoke what Habermas has termed a 'crisis of legitimation' (Habermas 1976).

As the first step in transcending these problems of economism and in relating the questions of production and reproduction, capital accumulation and consumption, the requirements of capital and the effects of struggle on the part of non-capitalist interests, it is useful to refer to the work of two Marxist writers who have addressed the question of the tension between capitalist profitability and social provisions – James O'Connor (1973) and Ian Gough (1979).

For O'Connor, the capitalist state must attempt to fulfil two distinct and often contradictory functions, for not only must it ensure the profitability of the most significant sectors of the economy (namely 'monopoly capital'), but it must also ensure the continued commitment of strategic sections of the working class by maintaining legitimacy. The state attempts to meet the first of these requirements through what he terms 'social capital' expenditures and the second through 'social expenses' (a category that includes expenditure on both instruments of coercion such as the police force, and instruments of legitimation such as welfare concessions). O'Connor recognizes that these two aspects of expenditure are not mutually exclusive (that is, that the same policy may perform both functions), but they are analytically distinct and any item of expenditure may be classified in terms of the primary function it performs.

In terms of his category of social capital expenditure, he then further distinguishes between 'social investment', which represents state investment in constant capital, and 'social consumption' which represents state investment in variable capital, labour-power. Both aid capital accumulation by socializing necessary costs of production which would otherwise have to be borne by monopoly capital directly (for example, provision of necessary but non-productive physical infrastructure such as roads or rail links, financing of escalating research and development costs, provision of housing for the workforce and so on). Unlike Harvey, therefore, who sees investment in the secondary and tertiary circuits in terms of problems of over-accumulation in the primary circuit, O'Connor emphasizes the role of the state in such investments and explains them not only in terms of their function in sustaining effective demand, but also in terms of the need to maintain capital accumulation in the primary circuit through what may be termed a 'devalorization' of capital. In other words, social investment is a way of maintaining the rate of profit in the monopoly sector rather than of soaking up surplus capacity, since it provides necessary infrastructure without raising the organic composition of capital. As Gamble and Walton explain, 'The state intervenes to take the burden of many costs from private capital. It finances, in a sense, the overhead costs of the whole process of capital accumulation. By doing this . . . it prevents the organic composition of capital rising. Without the huge volume of state spending, capital would make no profits at all' (1976, p. 165).

The crucial point in O'Connor's analysis is that, although the state has progressively socialized the costs of monopoly capital (to the advantage of both capital and labour in this sector, since this has underwritten high profits and high wages), it has not socialized the profits that have accrued as a result. This, together with the fact that social expenses have been rising (particularly in respect of workers in the competitive sector of the economy where wages are lower and unemployment is higher), has generated a 'fiscal crisis' as state expenditures have outstripped revenues. In the short run this becomes manifest in escalating rates of inflation; in the longer term it becomes manifest in attempts by the state to cut back on its spending and hence in the onset of economic slump and mounting political crisis.

O'Connor's analysis is useful in that it distinguishes different aspects of state intervention and points to the tension between them. It is, however, still a strongly functionalist argument in that all three aspects of state expenditure (expenses, investment and consumption) are explained in terms of their contribution to the interests of monopoly capital, even though their effects are contradictory. The basic problem here is that, like those writers discussed in the previous section, O'Connor deduces the causes of state intervention from an analysis of their subsequent effects.

Gough, on the other hand, argues that

> What distinguishes Marxist theory is not the view that a particular class dominates the institution of the state (though this is the normal state of affairs), but that whoever occupies these positions is constrained by the imperatives of the capital accumulation process. But at the same time the separation and relative autonomy of the state permits numerous reforms to be won, and it in no way acts as the passive tool of one class. Within these constraints there is room for manoeuvre, for competing strategies and policies. [Gough 1979, pp. 43–4]

A number of important points arise from this argument.

First, Gough stresses the importance of disentangling an analysis of the causes of state intervention from an analysis of its functions; as we saw earlier (page 240), it is quite possible for the working class to achieve gains that are only later subverted to the interests of capital, in which case state interventions that operate to the benefit of capital should not be explained simply in terms of the prior requirements of capital. A crucial issue here will be whether provisions won by the working class can be adapted to the commodity form.

Second, the necessity that the state maintain capital accumulation in the private sector enters into Gough's analysis as a constraint on, rather than a determinant of, social consumption provisions: 'The structural relationship between the state and the economy ... cannot explain the origin and development of any single act of social policy' (1979, p. 44). This structural relationship is crucial in that the capitalist mode of production sets limits upon such provisions and the requirements of accumulation are necessarily primary, but none of this dictates the character or scale of social provisions. What is required for an adequate causal analysis is therefore thorough comparative and historical research into the origins of particular types of social legislation based upon a theoretical perspective that recognizes the constraints imposed by the requirements of capitalist profitability.

Third, this emphasis on constraints opens up the possibility for analysing the causal significance of the working class in bringing about a wide range of policies and state initiatives. There is no assumption here that the functional requirements of capital are reflected in all aspects of state activity (as is implied by much of the literature discussed in this chapter), for an analysis of the needs of capital 'is only a starting point, and no single instance of social policy can be explained simply in terms of such a requirement' (p. 32). The requirements of capital simply set limits on what other groups may achieve through political mobilization. This is a crucial point, for in effect it enables Gough to break down the problem of the relative autonomy of the capitalist state by recognizing the significance of both the functional needs of capital and the political demands of non-capitalist interests in respect of different aspects of state activity. His argument here is not well developed, but what it essentially amounts to is a dualistic approach in which social investment is explained in terms of the requirements of capital accumulation and social consumption in terms of the relative power of different classes engaged in political struggles. Thus he suggests that this approach

has the merit over pluralist theories of social policy in situating the 'conflict' within an ongoing mode of production, and it has the merit over functionalist theories of social policy in relating the socio-economic 'system' (its structure and its development through time) to the class conflict which is an integral feature of it. Of course, it does not simply sit these two theories side by side: both elements are developed within a completely different theoretical framework. [Gough 1979, p. 56]

We shall attempt to develop this implicit dualistic approach in the next chapter. Here we need only note that it points to the possibility that the distinction between social investment and social consumption becomes manifest at the political level in a tension between the privileged position enjoyed by large capitalist interests *vis-à-vis* the state (for instance through relatively exclusive 'corporate' modes of interest mediation which Gough himself discusses) and the competitive struggles waged by non-capitalist interests through pressure group campaigns, rank and file movements, electoral struggles and so on. In other words, Gough's framework may be developed once we recognize not only that the state responds to capitalist and non-capitalist interests, but that it does so in a different way and in respect of different types of policy.

The problem with Gough's approach as it stands, therefore, is that it does not go far enough. Thus, although it represents a considerable step forward from the crude instrumentalism that characterizes much of the literature discussed above, it finally fails to resolve the two key questions thrown up by that literature regarding the relationship between the state and capital and between urban struggles and class struggles. On the first of these questions, Gough recognizes the constraints imposed by the requirements of capital accumulation, but as in Pahl's later work, he cannot theorize the limits of these constraints. As regards the second question, he, like the other writers already referred to, persists in conceptualizing struggles over social consumption as class struggles. As we shall see in Chapter 8, both of these problems can be overcome only if it is explicitly recognized that the question of capital accumulation and the question of social consumption are theoretically distinct and specific, and that explanations and concepts developed in respect of one cannot unproblematically be carried over into analysis of the other.

We have seen that the weakness of the urban political economy literature is that it elides precisely these two questions, which must be kept distinct. Given its primary focus on capital accumulation, it assumes that state intervention and political struggles in the sphere of consumption simply reproduce the character of state intervention and political struggles in the sphere of production, and in this way its analyses of social provisions such as housing and of the conflicts that surround them collapse into economism and functionalism and fail to recognize the specificity of the social consumption process. From Harvey onwards, the strength of this work has been the way in which it approaches the question of space and the built environment through an analysis of commodity production, but its weakness has been its assumption that processes of social consumption can be explained in much the same way.

8   On the specificity of the urban

We saw in Chapter I that, despite their very different approaches and concerns, Weber, Durkheim and Marx and Engels all came to very similar conclusions as regards the analysis of urban questions. All agreed that the city played an historically specific role in the development of Western capitalism, but they all also argued that, once capitalism had become established, the city ceased to be a theoretically significant category of analysis. This was because it was no longer the expression and form of a new mode of production (Marx), or because it ceased to be the basis of human association and social identity (Weber), or because it no longer corresponded to the geographical boundaries of the division of labour (Durkheim). To the extent that these writers discussed the city in the context of their analyses of advanced capitalist societies, they treated it either as an illustration of the most developed tendencies within such societies (such as class polarization or anomic social organization), or as a secondary condition of the development of certain tendencies (for example of organized working-class struggle or of the erosion of the collective conscience). The city, in other words, was not seen as a significant object of study in its own right, and urban questions were addressed only in so far as they could contribute to an understanding of certain processes associated with the development of modern capitalism.

The development of urban sociology as a distinct sub-discipline with its own professorial chairs, journals, syllabuses and so on changed all this, for urban sociology was premised on the assumption that the city was theoretically important in its own right, that certain social phenomena were characteristic of and peculiar to cities, and that it was therefore possible and necessary to generate specific urban theories in order to explain urban phenomena. These assumptions, which were generally consistent with popular and governmental concerns regarding 'urban problems' (inner-city decay, street crime, black ghetto unrest, mental stress and so on), necessarily led researchers to confront the basic problem of how the city was to be conceptualized, for only by resolving this question was it possible to identify the problems that urban sociology was to address and the range of factors that it might explore in its search for answers.

It is this question of how different theoretical approaches have attempted to conceptualize the urban, with which we have been concerned in previous chapters. What has become evident from our review of the various perspectives is that the basic stumbling block that all have encountered in different guises has been the need to relate certain social processes to particular spatial categories. The history of urban sociology, in other words, has been the history of a search for a sociological phenomenon the source of which may be located in the physical entity of the city. It has been the history of an institutionalized sub-discipline in search of a subject./

Spatial categories and social processes

Within sociology, there have been four main attempts at identifying a set of social phenomena that are specific to cities. These are summarized in Table 1. In addition, as we saw in Chapter 7, it is possible to identify a fifth approach, associated more with geography and political economy than with sociology, in which space is analysed in terms of its significance in the process of capital accumulation rather than as the location of specific social processes. This approach is distinct from the other four in that it does not attempt to locate social processes in a spatial context, but rather to locate spatial processes in a social context, and we must therefore consider it separately. /

The first attempt to develop a conceptual framework for a distinctive urban sociology is represented by Park's theory of human ecology. However, as we saw in Chapter 2, this approach was from its very inception torn between a concern to explain processes of city growth and differentiation on the one hand, and processes of human adaptation to environmental changes within society as a whole on the other. In terms of the former, Chicago-school human ecology was a theory of the city; in terms of the latter, it was a theory of unconscious processes of adaptation in any human aggregate.

We saw that this division reflected the influence of Durkheim's methodology with its concern both to discover hidden forces in human society and to avoid theoretical speculation by grounding

Table 1 *Sociological conceptualizations of urbanism*

Definition of 'urban'	Analytical tension			Resolution of analytical tension
Ecological community		(a) theory of cities (observable processes) versus		(a) community studies (city as microcosm)
		(b) theory of adaptation (non-observable biotic forces)		(b) functionalist sociology
Cultural form	(Simmel)	(a) sociology of number versus		(a) theories of moral density
		(b) sociology of modernity		
	(Wirth)	(a) demographic causality versus		(b) cultural theories of capitalism
		(b) class/life cycle analysis		
Socio-spatial system	(Pahl)	(a) political analysis versus		theory of corporate state
		(b) analysis of spatial logic		
	(Rex)	(a) class analysis versus		theory of black under-class
		(b) theory of city processes		
Spatial unit of collective consumption		(a) collective consumption versus		theory of social reproduction (non-spatial urban sociology)
		(b) spatial articulation of capitalist mode of production		

scientific knowledge in direct experience of the empirical world. This mixture of realism and positivism was carried over into the theory of human ecology by Park with the result that the theory itself was from the outset founded on a logical contradiction. As a theory of the city there was no reason to limit analysis to the biotic level of human organization, yet as a theory of adaptation there was no reason to limit its empirical reference to cities. Increasingly, therefore, a split developed within the ecological approach. One set of researchers held on to the city as an empirical object of analysis but lost any coherent theoretical framework within which their studies could be situated, and the result was a long series of community study monographs and demographic mapping exercises which provided interesting descriptive data but proved essentially non-cumulative and largely a-theoretical. Another group, following Hawley, held on to processes of adaptation as the theoretically specific problem for analysis but severed this from the question of space, and the result of this approach was a growing integration between ecological and functionalist analysis and an abandonment of any attempt to develop a theory of the city. We are thus confronted today with a choice between a-theoretical descriptions of cities and neighbourhoods and theoretical analyses of processes that have no specific relation to cities.

A second attempt to develop a coherent conceptual basis for urban sociology, discussed in Chapter 3, is represented by the work of Simmel and Wirth in which some causal relation is hypothesized between the demographic characteristics of cities and typical cultural patterns. Here too, however, we found the familiar tension between a concern with the city as an empirical object of analysis, and the attempt to theorize a specific social phenomenon (a cultural way of life) that could not be limited to spatial boundaries.

In the case of Simmel, this tension reflected the two distinct concerns of his work with, first, a sociology of number and, second, a sociology of modernity. The first analysed the effects of size on social relationships, while the second was more concerned with the significance of factors such as the development of the division of labour and the growth of a money economy. In his essay on the metropolis, Simmel attempted to put these two areas of analysis together, but the result, inevitably, was a confusion of factors inherent to cities (population size) with factors inherent to specific modes of economic organization of society as a whole (division of labour and monetary exchange).

Wirth's essay can be seen as an attempt to clear up this muddle in Simmel's approach. He was careful to distinguish between an analysis of urbanism and an analysis of capitalism, and he limited his concern with the former to just three variables (size, density and heterogeneity of population). He then constructed an ideal type of the urban way of life (that is, as social relationships characterized by anonymity, superficiality and so on), and hypothesized that, to the extent that cultural patterns came to approximate this ideal type in any given human settlement, this could be explained as the result of the demographic factors he had identified. The problem with Wirth's analysis is not (as is often suggested) that social relationships in cities do not measure up to his ideal type (such a criticism both fails to understand Wirth's project and rests on a misinterpretation of the ideal type method), but is rather that his hypothesis appears implausible in the light of subsequent empirical research. We saw, for example, how the work of Pahl and Gans has suggested that variations in cultural patterns can better be explained in terms of, say, class differences than as the effects of demographic determinants, and the consequence of this is that we are once again forced outside the city in order to explain sociological phenomena found within it.

Both ecological and cultural theories of urbanism thus appear inadequate as the basis for an urban sociology, although both have left some small residue for urban analysis. In the case of human ecology, this residue is the community study tradition in which communities are studied as microcosms of society, while in the case of cultural approaches, this residue is a theoretical concern with the effects of what Durkheim termed 'moral density' on patterns of social relationships. Neither, of course, takes us very far, for the first simply indicates that the city may prove useful in illustrating certain processes which must be explained in terms of some other theory (in other words, it does not itself provide any theoretical rationale for studying the city except as a means for studying processes in society as a whole), while the second suggests that the size and concentration of population may have some effect on the way people live, but this effect is likely to be relatively insignificant when compared with other sociological variables.

In Chapter 4 we considered a third approach, which was based on three main propositions: that space is inherently unequal; that the way in which these inequalities are distributed among the population depends upon social processes (that is, on the actions of strategic urban managers); and that these processes will in turn affect and reflect struggles between different competing groups within the population. From this perspective, urban sociology is defined in terms of its theoretical concern with the distributive consequences of urban managerial decisions and with social conflict between different 'housing classes' over the allocation of scarce and crucial urban resources. Subsequent analysis on these two questions, however, has indicated that neither the urban managerialism nor the housing class concept can adequately specify peculiarly 'urban' processes.

We saw that Pahl's initial definition of urban managers lacked any theoretical criteria of identification and failed to recognize the political and economic constraints on managerial autonomy. This led him to reconceptualize urban managers as local state bureaucrats mediating between the private sector, central government and the local population; but although this resolved the problem of identification, it failed to clarify the question of managerial autonomy and discretion. The result was that Pahl was driven increasingly to address the problem of the national state and the national (and international) economy, and this established a new tension in his work between his continuing concern with the spatial logic of inequality and his growing concern with general issues of political economy. His interest in the latter posed a broad range of questions that had nothing to do with space, while his attempt to hang on to the former led to an artificially narrow scope for analysis in which some state services and provisions were analysed and others were not, according to whether they had an inherently spatial character. Taken as a whole, his approach became incoherent, for if he was interested in, say, the question of housing provision in a given locality, his analysis swiftly led him away into questions of international trade, government fiscal policy and so on, while if he began with the 'big' questions of political economy, his lingering concern with spatial inequalities came to appear virtually redundant. The irony in all this, of course, is that, writing from a mainly Weberian perspective, Pahl failed to make use of Weber's ideal type method which was developed precisely to guard against the problems of incoherence that Weber suggested would necessarily follow from any attempt to explain a given reality in all its aspects.

The housing class concept has fared even worse than that of urban managerialism. The main reason for this is the confusion in Rex's work between empirical and conceptual criteria of identification. Thus we saw in Chapter 4 that Rex identifies housing classes in two different ways: sometimes in terms of current housing situation (owner-occupiers, council tenants, etc.), and at other times in terms of potential power in the housing market (blacks, one-parent families, etc.). Clearly his theoretical concern is with the latter, but this means that social divisions he draws correspond simply to status divisions cross-cutting the class structure. His is not an 'urban' sociology, but a sociology of blacks and other groups whose status characteristics are such as to distinguish their economic, political and social situation from other members of their class. This becomes clear in Rex's latest study with Tomlinson, where the authors argue that the main areas of conflict between blacks and whites in Handsworth concern educational and employment opportunities, not housing. The question that this study addresses is not that of urban struggles and urban inequalities, but rather the issue of racial stratification (hence the concept of a 'black underclass'). Just as the study of urban managers leads us outside and beyond the city to an analysis of political power in society as a whole, so too the question of housing classes takes us away from any specifically urban or spatial reference into an analysis of class structure and its relation to social divisions grounded in race, gender or whatever. Neither concept can provide the basis or justification for an urban sociology.

In the next three chapters, we considered some of the recent Marxist writing on space and the urban question. This fell broadly into two categories: work (such as that by Castells) that remains in the tradition of urban sociology in so far as it attempts to identify a specific social phenomenon which coincides with the spatial object of the city, and alternative approaches (notably those of Lefebvre and Harvey), which begin not with the question of urbanism but with that of capitalism, and which address the problem of space only to the extent that it is seen as significant for an analysis of capital accumulation in the contemporary period. The former is a theory *of* the urban, the latter is a theory *applied to* the urban (in other words, a theory of capital accumulation which takes space into account as an increasingly important factor affecting capitalist profitability).

We saw in Chapter 5 that both approaches are highly critical of earlier non-Marxist perspectives which are attacked as 'ideological', either in functional or in epistemological terms, and that they are equally critical of each other (for example, Castells attacks Lefebvre for his utopianism and humanism, while Lefebvre attacks Castells for his structuralism and functionalism). Much of this mutual criticism is, however, misguided, partly because it is based on epistemological rather than theoretical or empirical grounds (yet we saw in Chapter 5 that no epistemology is self-justifying and that alternative theories have to be evaluated on their own terms), and partly because these two different approaches are basically interested in different questions, and thus in different aspects of the city. For Castells, the city is theoretically significant as the physical context within which the process of reproduction of labour-power is situated; for Harvey and Lefebvre, on the other hand, it is significant as a spatial configuration which facilitates and expresses the process of capital accumulation.

It is this difference in theoretical interests that lies at the heart of the criticism advanced by Lojkine and others to the effect that Castells's conceptualization of the urban system as a spatial unit of collective consumption is inadequate because it fails to take into account the significance of the city in the process of production in capitalist societies. Lojkine, for example, wishes to conceptualize the city in terms of the socialized provision of both social and economic infrastructure, and in this respect his work bears comparison with that of both Harvey (in his analyses of the role of the city in combating crises of under-consumption and its function in the circuit of capital, for example) and Lefebvre (in, say, his emphasis on the commodification of space). For these writers, space itself is the object of analysis, in which case it is illegitimate to separate its functions in consumption and production; whereas for Castells, space is significant only in so far as it is the location of a specific social process (namely the reproduction of labour-power through collective consumption).

The division within the recent Marxist literature therefore corresponds to the tension that has recurred throughout the different non-Marxist approaches to urban sociology between a concern with social processes operating within a spatial context and a concern with spatial units themselves. Castells, of course, attempts (as previous theorists have also attempted) to keep the two together, and he does this by arguing that consumption is the specific process through which space articulates with the social structure as a whole, but as we saw in Chapter 6, this is clearly not the case since many aspects of collective consumption have no spatial reference. A theoretical concern with collective consumption, in other words, does not imply a necessary concern with the question of space.

What emerges out of a consideration of the Marxist literature, therefore, is an appreciation that 'the' urban question is in fact two distinct questions. On the one hand, we derive from Castells a theoretical concern with collective consumption; on the other, we derive from Lefebvre, Harvey and others a theoretical concern with the function of space in the process of capital accumulation. These two questions are both valid, but they must be kept analytically distinct, for a concern with collective consumption cannot be limited to its spatial forms (since collective consumption provisions may be both spatial and non-spatial), while a concern with space cannot be limited to processes of consumption (since the various functions of space also include production and other processes).

Seen in this way, the problem with urban sociology is that, far from keeping these two questions distinct, it confuses them. If our theoretical concern is with a specific social process (say, the process of collective consumption) divorced from the question of space, then we certainly have the basis for a sociology, but to term it 'urban' can be no more than a convenient convention. If, on the other hand, our concern is with the significance of spatial arrangements for the maintenance of capital accumulation, then our problem may indeed be designated as 'urban' (meaning spatial), but our approach to it can hardly be termed 'sociological' (it is, rather, the application of theories of political economy to a geographical object). It seems, to put it somewhat crudely, that we are confronted with a choice between sociological non-urban theories and urban non-sociological theories. /

The conclusion to which all this leads is that the city may constitute a valid object of analysis for the historian (since, as we saw in Chapter 1, the city played a crucial role in the transition from feudalism to capitalism) and for the political economist (since, as we saw in Chapter 7, space may perform a crucial function in sustaining capitalist profitability), but that its significance for the sociologist is limited either to its usefulness as a social microcosm (the 'residue' from the ecological tradition), or its importance in terms of the effects of moral density on social relationships (the 'residue' from the cultural tradition, which is, as Dewey suggested, relatively unimportant). In the former case, the city becomes a research tool (the so-called community study method) rather than an object of analysis in its own right (in other words, we study the city or different areas within it to see what it can tell us about certain phenomena in society as a whole). In the latter case, the city does constitute an object of study in so far as concentration of population can be shown to have a causal effect on patterns of social relationships (for example through studies of the impact of high-rise living on interaction between neighbours, the effects on family life of migration from sparsely to densely populated areas, and so on), but the scope for such analysis appears very limited given the arguments in Chapter 3.

All that is left to an urban sociology that seeks to retain the question of space as a specific aspect of study is therefore a very limited theoretical problem (namely, that of the social significance of variations in moral density) and a particular research technique (the community study) which may prove useful to other researchers. Yet as we have seen, work that has conventionally been defined as 'urban' sociology has attempted to go beyond such restricted concerns and has posed questions that appear crucial to an adequate understanding of contemporary capitalist societies. Both Weberian and Marxist approaches, for example, have directed attention to the need to analyse the causes and consequences of social provisions (housing, education, health care, etc.) in the context of the relationship between the state, the private sector and the working population; yet both traditions failed to establish a framework for such analysis owing to their inability to relate such processes to spatial categories.

Once we reject the problem of space as a defining feature of urban sociology, however, these questions can fruitfully be addressed. As we shall now see, Pahl's concern with the role of urban managers and Castells's concern with the provision of collective consumption may both be retained as elements of a distinctive problem for sociological analysis provided that such an analysis is severed from the very different theoretical question of space. To term such a sociology 'urban' is, of course, merely a matter of convention, the application of a convenient label to designate certain specific theoretical problems that have no necessary relation to the empirical analysis of cities. For the sake of clarity, therefore, we may distinguish between urban political economy (analysis of the significance of space for capital accumulation), spatial sociology (analysis of the significance of spatial concentration for social relationships), and 'urban' sociology (analysis of social provisions in the context of the relationship between the state, the private sector and the population of consumers). The remainder of this chapter is concerned with the development of the third of these distinct areas of analysis, a non-spatial urban sociology.

Social consumption, local government and competitive politics

The starting point for a reformulation of the scope of urban sociology is provided by Castells's concept of collective consumption. There are two reasons for this. First, as Castells himself suggests (see page 169), urban sociology has generally been concerned with analysing resources and facilities that are denoted in one way or another by the term 'collective consumption' (the traditional concern with housing is an obvious example). A reconceptualization of the specific theoretical questions addressed by urban sociology should clearly attempt to encompass the main concerns of earlier work, and the concept of collective consumption, suitably refined and amended, is therefore a useful first step. Second, as we saw in Chapter 6, the concept does point to certain processes that appear crucially important in the analysis of advanced capitalist societies (see page 215, for example). It is therefore not only useful in encompassing existing theoretical and empirical work, but also relevant in indicating a range of questions of central contemporary concern.

At the end of Chapter 6, however, we saw that, as it stands, the concept of collective consumption appears too ambiguous and imprecise for analytical purposes. Two problems in particular need to be addressed: first, by what criteria can collective resources be distinguished from non-collective ones, and, second, how can processes of consumption be distinguished from those of production?

The first of these problems was considered by Dunleavy, who identified twelve different types of consumption, falling into four main categories (individualized, quasi-individualized, quasi-collective and collective), according to the application of four criteria (commodity/service, public/private management, market/non-market access and subsidy/non-subsidy by the state). From this perspective, collective consumption refers specifically to publicly organized facilities characterized by non-market access, or by state subsidy, or both, and Dunleavy argued that the scope of urban sociology could be defined in terms of the analysis of such facilities together with a concern with quasi-collective (privately organized facilities with non-market access, state subsidy or both) and quasi-individualized (state-subsidized) resources.

Dunleavy's exercise in clarification is useful as far as it goes, but it tends to leave unanswered the second question of the definition of consumption processes. It could be argued, for example, that publicly managed and state-subsidized facilities such as public transport services should not be classified as consumption at all since they represent investment in resources that contribute directly to private sector profitability (by transporting labour to and from work, carrying raw materials and finished products between different firms and so on). Of course, as Marx showed, every act of production is itself also an act of consumption (since commodities are produced by consuming other materials), and every act of consumption may similarly be seen as both an act of production (in that it produces fresh labour-power) and as a condition of existence of production (since production is no more possible without consumption as an end-point than is consumption without production as a starting-point). However, this inherent relation between production and consumption need not imply that they cannot be isolated from each other analytically as objects of study in their own right; for ultimately every social process is related to every other social process, and we have therefore to identify specific aspects of social reality for study if we are to avoid the situation where we must know everything before we can know anything. If our primary interest is in processes of consumption, it is therefore necessary to stipulate the criteria by means of which such processes can be identified.

It is in this context that O'Connor's distinction (discussed in Chapter 7) between social investment and social consumption may prove useful. O'Connor recognizes that 'Nearly every state expenditure serves . . . two (or more) purposes simultaneously, so that few state outlays can be classified unambiguously' (1973, p. 7). Nevertheless, he suggests that different areas of expenditure may be distinguished on the basis of the primary function they perform, and on this basis he classifies expenditure in terms of three categories: social expenses (policies designed to maintain social order), social investment (policies that contribute principally to private sector profitability through provision of necessary means of production), and social consumption (policies that contribute mainly to the social and material support of the working population).

There are dangers in adopting this classificatory schema, for O'Connor's argument is that all three types of state expenditure function in the interests of monopoly capital, and as we saw in Chapter 6 in relation to Castells's theory, such an argument must be treated with some caution. Social consumption expenditure (on housing, hospitals, etc.) may in certain circumstances prove beneficial to certain capitalist interests (by ensuring an adequate supply of labour-power, by stimulating demand for certain commodities and so on), but we should avoid any formulation that defines social consumption in such functional terms since the relation between capitalist profitability and the level of social provisions must be established through empirical research in specific societies at specific times rather than asserted as an *a priori* basis for research. The application of O'Connor's typology does not therefore imply any endorsement of his theoretical position, and the usefulness of his work for our present purposes lies simply in the heuristic value of his distinction between policies that primarily represent a direct subsidy to capital (such as provision of economic infrastructure) and those that represent principally a subsidy to the working population (for example social welfare provisions).

My argument is that the first defining element of a (non-spatial) urban sociology is that its field of theoretical interest relates to the provision and role of social consumption resources. The concept of social consumption may then be broken down into the three categories identified by Dunleavy in so far as each of these contains an element of state subsidization. In empirical terms, this means that such an urban sociology will be interested in a rather more specific range of questions than those identified by Dunleavy, in that it will not be concerned with resources that cost the state nothing to provide (it will therefore exclude the examples of the National Trust and independent voluntary welfare agencies which Dunleavy includes), nor with resources that function more in the interests of capital than directly as a support to the working population (it will therefore exclude public provision of transport facilities such as roads, rail links, ports and, perhaps, public passenger transport). It should also be noted that such a perspective is in some ways the reverse of that set out by Pahl (see page 116), for it excludes certain provisions, such as roads, that Pahl includes (on the grounds that they have a spatial character), while including others, such as family allowances, that Pahl rules out (because they are a-spatial). From the point of view developed here, the crucial criterion of an urban resource is public consumption, not spatial location.

This emphasis on social consumption entails two further elements in our conceptualization of the urban question, and these relate to the mode and level of social consumption provisions. The argument is summarized in Table 2.

Whenever the state becomes involved in providing and financing certain resources, irrespective of whether these constitute social investment or social consumption, it faces the problem of how this can be achieved in such a way as to fulfil the requirements to which its

Table 2 *The three elements of the urban question*

Conceptual criterion	Urban aspect	Relational aspect	Principal tension
Primary function	Social consumption	Social investment	Economic management *v.* social provision
Mode of interest mediation	Competitive politics	Corporatist politics	Planning *v.* democratic accountability
Level of administration	Local government	Regional/ national government	Centralization *v.* peripheral autonomy

intervention is addressed. Claus Offe (1975), for example, has suggested that, in its traditional 'allocative' role (in which the state maintains the conditions of capital accumulation in a purely authoritative way – for example, through the enforcement of compulsory minimum levels of education in the nineteenth-century Factory Acts, through the regulation of the money supply, by laying down certain standards of public health and safety and so on), the state has generally been able to fulfil its functions simply by responding to the pressures exerted upon it by the most powerful interests in society. The allocative state of the nineteenth century, for example, was, as Marx suggested, little more than a committee for managing the common affairs of the bourgeoisie, for until the enfranchisement of the working class the only groups that enjoyed formal political power and could directly influence state policies were the landowners and the capitalists, with the result that state regulation generally reflected the demands and requirements of these classes.

As the 'productive' role of the state has increased through the twentieth century (as the state has assumed responsibility for producing various resources in addition to its traditional regulative function), so, according to Offe, its responsiveness to the power of these classes has necessarily altered. This is because the basic requirement of the state in a capitalist society (namely that it maintains the conditions for future capital accumulation) will not necessarily be met by subordinating its interventions to the immediate demands of the most powerful interests. In its productive interventions, therefore, the state must develop its own criteria for action and must determine for itself the best way to achieve its aims. It is at this point, however, that it encounters the problem of rationality.

Offe outlines three possible strategies by means of which the state may attempt to develop its productive policies, but argues that all three eventually prove inadequate for resolving the rationality problem. The first possibility is to locate responsibility in the state bureaucracy, but Offe sees such a strategy as ineffective since bureaucracies may be efficient at administering policies but they are ineffective as the means for initiating them. The second is to increase the scope of state planning, but this option is limited by the inability of the state to plan effectively in an economy in which investment decisions are still mainly the responsibility of private capital operating on the criterion of anticipated rates of return. The third possibility is to sponsor participation in policy-making as the means of determining priorities, but Offe sees this as counter-productive in that it may result in the subordination of policies to the demands of non-capitalist interests and hence to inconsistencies between the requirements of future capital accumulation and the policies followed by the state. For Offe, therefore, the rationality problem of the modern capitalist state is finally irresolvable, and there is a growing tendency towards a 'rationality crisis'.

This analysis, which I have discussed in more detail elsewhere (Saunders 1979, pp. 174–80), is in many respects plausible if not convincing, but it is worth considering the third strategy – which Offe calls the 'participatory mode' – a little more carefully. As Offe (1974) has himself recognized in an earlier paper, the state may sponsor selective participation by including some interests in the policy-making process while excluding others. Of particular significance for such a strategy is the structural organization of the state itself, for as Offe suggests, 'One can only have power over something which according to its own structure allows power to be exercised upon it and responds to it' (1974, p. 35). It is this question of structural organization and selective accessibility that leads us to the two problems of the mode and level of state operations.

The question of the mode of state activity takes us back to the literature on corporatism discussed briefly in Chapter 4. We saw there that the theory of the corporate society developed by Pahl and Winkler may be rejected, both on the grounds of internal inconsistency and on all available evidence. However, Jessop (1978) has suggested that the concept of corporatism may be retained in rather a different form to refer not to a qualitatively new mode of production, but rather to a distinct mode of political interest mediation. According to Jessop, the state in a society like Britain appears to have developed a new way for discharging its traditional function of maintaining the conditions of capital accumulation. He suggests that representatives of large companies and of organized labour have increasingly been drawn directly into the policy-making process, and that a new 'corporate sector' of politics has developed as a result. State intervention in the economy is thus increasingly the product of negotiation and consultation between large capital, organized labour and the state, and this enables the state both to mould its policies more accurately to the needs of the large companies, and (to some extent) to regulate economic class struggles by co-opting trade union leaders into a strategy whose purpose is to ensure the continued profitability of the most significant sections of private capital.

To the extent that Jessop's analysis is correct, it follows that the state now tends to operate in two different ways. On the one hand, the traditional institutions of representative democracy (notably elections, pressure group lobbying, demonstrations, petitions and so on) function primarily as a forum for non-incorporated interests such as small business, welfare state clients, consumers and so on to press their demands; on the other, the newly emergent corporate sector, which is exclusive to the representatives of the functional economic interests of big capital and organized labour, functions primarily as the means for the state to overcome its rationality problem by developing economic policies that are broadly consistent with what is required by the private sector.

The problem, however, is that there exists, according to Jessop, a 'contradictory unity' between these two modes of interest mediation, in that popular pressures exerted through the competitive democratic sector tend to pull in an opposite direction to the economic commitments that emerge from the corporate sector. There is, in other words, a continuing tension between economic planning and democratic accountability, between the economic policies developed within the corporate sector and the demands articulated in the competitive sector. This tension tends to be overlaid by that between social investment and social consumption expenditures (that is, between the commitment of resources to the support of private sector profitability and their allocation to the support of various groups in the population as a whole). Thus the question of how to reconcile the demands of big capital with the demands of various other sections of the population is at one and the same time the question of how to reconcile corporate planning with democratic accountability.

One way in which this dual tension may be mediated is by locating the different functions and different modes at different levels of government. It is, of course, important to remember that local government has different degrees and types of responsibility in different countries, and that there is probably no country in which the local/national division may be said to correspond exactly with that between social consumption and social investment policies, or between competitive and corporate modes of interest mediation. In Britain, for example, although corporate politics are organized mainly on regional levels (such as development boards and agencies) and national levels (the NEDC, the NEB and so on), there is some evidence that corporate strategies may be developing to some extent at the local level also (see for example the case study of the development of a county structure plan discussed in Flynn 1979). Similarly, although local government responsibilities today relate mainly to the provision of social consumption, local authorities do still exercise some control over social investment (such as road building), and there have been some moves in recent years to extend this sphere of action (see the discussion by Minns and Thornley (1978) of various examples of local authority shareholdings in local enterprises).

In general, however, it may be suggested that social consumption policies are the characteristic responsibility of local government, and that in most advanced capitalist countries there has been a long-term tendency for social investment functions to be transferred from local to regional or national levels of administration. What this means is that crucial economic policies not only are increasingly determined outside the competitive democratic sector of politics, but they are also increasingly removed from local control (the growth of regional levels of government is particularly significant in this respect given the total lack of elected bodies at this level in Britain).

Whatever the reasons for this segregation, its effects are further to insulate crucial economic policies from the influence of non-capitalist interests, for as Friedland and his co-authors have noted, it is at the local level that the state appears most susceptible to popular pressures and struggles:

> The electoral-representative arrangements which underpin municipal governments make them vulnerable to popular discontent . . . local governments are often important loci for popular political participation because they are structurally accessible, the point of daily contact between citizen and state. The relative visibility of local government policies and the relative accessibility of local government agencies make them a more susceptible target of political opposition than other levels of the state. [Friedland *et al.* 1977, pp. 449 and 451]

Evidence from Britain (Clay Cross, Lambeth, South Yorkshire, etc.), Italy ('red Bologna'), France (various communist-controlled towns) and elsewhere all tends to suggest that it is possible for the radical Left to gain control of elected agencies at the local level. To the extent that local government powers are limited to the sphere of social consumption, however, such municipal victories will not necessarily undermine or affect key economic policies. Indeed, to the extent that social consumption policies are subordinated to those of social investment (for example through public spending cuts designed to increase the profitability of the private sector), and that local government is subordinated to central agencies, then radical local administrations are likely to find that even their scope for action in the social consumption sphere is extremely limited.

In ideal typical terms, then, we may suggest that different types of economic policies correspond to different types of political arrangements. While social investment tends to be associated with corporate policy-making at national or regional levels of government, social consumption tends to be associated with competitive political struggles waged at the local level. It is this division that provides the conceptual basis for an urban sociology. In other words, I wish to argue that the framework for a potentially very fruitful urban sociology may be given in a complex of three main elements consisting of (a) social consumption, (b) competitive political struggles and (c) local government policy-making.

We saw in Table 2 that each of these three 'urban' elements must be specified in terms of their relation to three other aspects (social investment, corporate strategies and central/regional administration respectively), and that in each case the relationship involves an inherent tension (namely that between support of capital accumulation and provision of social resources; between coherent planning strategies and democratic accountability; and between centralized control and local autonomy and responsibility). If the specific problems for urban sociology to consider relate to social consumption, competitive politics and local government, it is nevertheless obviously the case that such analyses must be situated in the context of these three sets of contradictory relationships. Thus, for example, although such an urban sociology will not be concerned with social investment provisions, it will clearly need to take these into account in so far as they affect social consumption (for example where investment in new economic infrastructure increases the need for social resources such as housing). Similarly, while central government is not itself theoretically significant for the approach outlined here, it is obvious that any analysis of local government policy-making and administration must address itself to the relation between central and local levels.

In arguing that the urban question may usefully be posed in terms of these three interrelated processes of social consumption, competitive politics and local government, it is not therefore suggested that urban sociology should ignore the broader questions regarding the context within which such processes occur, but only that these broader issues do not constitute the focus of theoretical concern. As conceptualized here, urban sociology is addressed to these processes in the context of their contradictory relation to 'non-urban' processes of social investment, corporate policy-making strategies and centralized control. In this sense, urban sociology may be defined in terms of *a specific theoretical and empirical concern with the related processes of social consumption, political competition and local administration within the context of the tensions between private sector profitability and social needs, strategic planning and democratic accountability and centralized direction and local autonomy.*

Such a specification of the urban question leads directly to a reconceptualization of the problem of urban managerialism discussed in Chapter 4, for local state bureaucrats such as housing managers, planning officers, directors of social services and so on can be seen to straddle the divisions between corporate and competitive politics, central and local government and investment and consumption policies. They are, in a sense, the 'personifications' of the contradictory relations which set the context for urban sociological analysis, the link between what is relevant to such analysis and what is not, between those aspects of reality we have termed 'urban' and the 'non-urban' aspects to which they relate. As Pahl suggests, their role is therefore one of mediation.

What this means, however, is that urban managers are not in themselves significant for urban sociology and certainly cannot constitute the defining focus of such a sociology. Urban sociology is specified in terms of its concern with certain processes, not the actions of certain individuals, and analysis of the latter will be significant only in so far as it bears on analysis of the former. The problem of urban managers thus turns out to be a non-problem in that their actions may be taken as an expression of the relation between consumption and investment, corporate and competitive strategies and centralization and local autonomy at any one time, and hence as a 'given' in analysis. Managerial outcomes, in other words, represent the context within which urban analysis takes place.

Seen in this way, managers are neither autonomous actors pursuing their own goals and values within the limits imposed by economic resources and political controls (as Pahl suggests), nor mere agents of capital by means of which the dominant classes ensure their requirements for continued accumulation, legitimation and so on (as some of the Marxist critics of the managerialism literature would have it). They are, rather, the expression of the balance between two sets of processes at any particular time and place, between centralized investment policies developed in the corporate sector on the one hand, and local consumption policies developed through competitive struggle on the other. It follows that our theoretical interest lies not in what urban managers do, but in the processes that are mediated through their actions.

Class struggle, the state and the urban question

For the remainder of this chapter, we must turn from the conceptual problem of how the urban question may be specified to the theoretical problem of how analysis of the urban question may proceed. As we saw in the discussion of Weber's ideal type method in Chapter 1, conceptual clarification is an essential first step if we are to identify distinctive questions for research and thereby avoid the problems that the various approaches to urban sociology have encountered in the past of the disintegration of urban analysis into analysis of society as a whole. Nevertheless, we also saw the construction of ideal types does not itself constitute any claim to knowledge (which is why critics are mistaken when they dismiss Weber's method as idealist), and that such types have a purpose only to the extent that they aid the development of hypotheses and the guidance of empirical research. The argument to be developed here is that the framework set out above may be seen as fruitful in terms of a theoretical understanding of two questions that have not only been at the centre of recent urban sociology, but lie at the heart of any sociological analysis of advanced capitalist societies; namely the question of class analysis and theories of the state.

As we have seen in earlier chapters, these two questions have been addressed in both Weberian and Marxist urban sociology in recent years. The problem of class struggle has variously been approached through the concepts of 'housing classes' and 'urban social movements', while that of the capitalist state has been considered in terms of the questions of 'corporatism', 'relative autonomy' and so on. However, we have also seen that neither Marxist nor Weberian approaches have adequately theorized either of these problems. This, I would suggest, is due to their failure to specify distinctively 'urban' processes, and thus to recognize that such processes cannot simply be explained by subsuming them under existing theories of 'class struggle in general' or 'the capitalist state as a whole'.

The point is that, if urban processes are specific, then we should not necessarily expect theories developed in respect of 'non-urban' questions to apply to them. /This is, however, precisely the assumption that has been made by previous work. Thus various writers have developed or employed theories of *the* state which have then been applied without discrimination to all aspects of state activity. In much of the Marxist literature, for example, 'the' state is first conceptualized in terms of its function in maintaining the conditions for capital accumulation, and this general theory is then applied to what is termed the 'local state' in order to explain state policies and strategies at the local level (see, for example, Cockburn 1977, especially ch. 2). /The very notion of the 'local state' thus rests on the assumption that there is nothing specific about local levels of government and that theories regarding the operation and function of the state at one level can be applied unproblematically to its operation and function at another. Much the same point applies to non-Marxist approaches which have attempted to develop theoretical explanations of the role of the state without recognizing the possibility that a theory that applies at one level in respect of one aspect of state activity may not apply at another (this would appear to be true of both pluralist and corporatist theories, for example).

The same point can be made about different analyses of class struggle. Castells, for example, falls foul of what Pickvance terms the 'urban fallacy' precisely because he assumes that his theory of class struggle in the conditions of monopoly capitalism can be extended to the analysis of urban struggles (in other words, that struggles over collective consumption can eventually be subsumed, both analytically and politically, under the working-class struggle against monopoly capital). Working with a different theory and towards very different conclusions, Rex too makes the assumption that a general theory of class can be applied to urban conflict (since classes may be identified in any situation of competition over scarce resources), and like Castells he ends up confronting the problem of the relation between urban and non-urban class struggles, a problem that he 'resolves' by effectively abandoning the concept of 'housing classes' altogether.

In contrast to these writers, my argument is that the dualism identified in the previous section between social investment/corporate interest mediation/central and regional government on the one hand and social consumption/competitive interest mediation/local government on the other should be reflected in a theoretical dualism as regards both the question of the state and that of class struggle.

This means that the emphasis of urban sociology on the second set of processes should lead to the development of a theoretical perspective on the state and social stratification that is specific to these processes.

We have seen that the basic problem confronted by theories of 'the' capitalist state concerns how the state can both support the interests of capital or fractions of capital and yet at the same time reflect and respond to the demands of non-capitalist interests. Some theories have effectively ignored this problem, either by denying that there is any necessary relation between state policies and the interests of capital (such as pluralist theory), or by denying that non-capitalist interests may significantly affect state activity (for instance crude instrumentalist theories). Such approaches do not resolve the problem but side-step it, and as general theories they appear totally inadequate since it is clear (as Gough, for example, argues) that the state in a capitalist society is ultimately dependent upon the private sector and must therefore accord priority to the maintenance of capital accumulation (a point that pluralist approaches conspicuously fail to recognize), and that, in all capitalist societies, non-capitalist interests have achieved real economic and political gains over the last 100 years (a point that instrumentalist theories find it difficult to explain without resorting to notions of ruling-class cunning in buying off political opposition).

Other approaches have addressed this problem, but have failed to explain it. Notable here is recent Marxist work on the 'relative autonomy' of the state which in many ways offers a fairly accurate description of what 'the' state does overall (by emphasizing that its commitment to ensuring future capital accumulation does not rule out the possibility of policies in support of non-capitalist interests), but which fails to explain how these results come about.

What I wish to suggest is that the recognition of the 'relative autonomy' of the state appears paradoxical only for as long as we hold to a unitary concept of the state itself. It is, in other words, necessary to break down the concept of relative autonomy through the application of a dualistic perspective. Thus it may be suggested that the reason why the state (viewed as a whole) appears both to act in the long-term interests of capital and to respond to the demands of other groups in the population is that social investment policies are typically developed at national level in close consultation with capitalist interests within corporate state agencies, while social consumption policies are relatively responsive to localized popular pressures exerted on and through representative state agencies. The reason why the interests of capital generally prevail in the long run is that social investment must necessarily take precedence over social consumption (owing to the dependence of the state on private sector accumulation), and this is reflected in the subordination of local to central government.

It follows from this that some sort of pluralist hypothesis may be pertinent to the analysis of social consumption policies at the local level where state agencies are relatively open to popular demands (cf. Cawson 1978). Local government, of course, is not entirely open, and some sections of the population may still effectively be excluded from any effective participation in local politics and it follows that any analysis must take account of the possibility of 'non-decision-making' strategies so as to avoid naive pluralist assumptions (see Saunders 1979, ch. 1). Indeed, it is possible that in some areas, one particular section of the population may achieve a virtual stranglehold over the local political process, thereby reducing any effective political competition to a minimum. The important point, however, is that questions regarding the relative openness of different state agencies to different types of groups in different areas must be answered through empirical research, and that the long-running debate within the community power literature between pluralist and elitist interpretations of local politics appears more relevant to such research than do more recent state theories which assume that the determination of policy at the national level is simply reflected in the local political process.

We should not expect pluralist and elitist theories to have much to offer to an analysis of social investment policies at national or regional levels of government, however, for here the state is relatively insulated from popular demands (thereby rendering pluralist approaches untenable) and may, as Offe suggests, distance itself from any one sectional interest in order to pursue policies in the interests of capital as a whole (thereby rendering elitist formulations problematic). A different type of theory is therefore required: one that emphasizes the privileged access of capital to state agencies at this level while also recognizing the priority of maintaining capital accumulation through social investment and fiscal policies. Recent work by Miliband (1977) would seem to go some way in this direction, although we need not consider this in any detail here given that our concerns, as identified in the previous section, are with social consumption at the local level rather than social investment nationally. The important point is that the two spheres of state activity are distinct and should be analysed by means of different theoretical approaches.

If a dualistic theoretical approach to the problem of the state is adopted, then not only does it enable a potential resolution of the problem of relative autonomy, but it also overcomes the difficulties encountered by an approach such as that of Castells with regard to the question of empirical testing. This is because an approach that seeks to explain different types of policies as the effects of different types of factors is in principle falsifiable in a way that the inherently tautological theories discussed in Chapter 4 are not. Thus a dualistic perspective that holds that local consumption policies will reflect competitive political struggles between different groups while national investment policies will reflect the particular demands and general requirements of different sections of capital implicitly contains two crucial counterfactual statements which can be assessed in empirical research; that non-capitalist interests will not generally exert any significant influence over the determination of social investment, and that capitalist interests will not generally exert any significant influence over the determination of social consumption. Three points, however, should be emphasized about these counter-factual statements.

First, given that social investment and social consumption are in a contradictory relationship with one another, it is obvious that factors that determine one must have an effect on the other. Capitalist demands on social investment, for example, will clearly be reflected in levels of social provisions, just as popular demands for increased welfare expenditure will have ramifications for state support of capital accumulation. The two counterfactuals do not, therefore, imply that capitalist interests have no effects on social consumption, nor that popular pressures leave social investment untouched, but rather that the way in which these two areas of state involvement come to be determined will reflect different types of strategies by different types of interests. The influence of capital on social investment thus provides the context within which the influence of other interests on social consumption must be analysed, and vice-versa.

Second, as we saw in Chapter 5 (page 209), the specification of counterfactuals does not imply that there is any metatheoretical criterion of adequacy or validity, but only that the theory itself is capable of indicating how it may be empirically evaluated. To assert empirical testability as a requirement of any approach is not to adopt a naive falsificationist position but merely to reject inherently tautologous 'explanations' in favour of approaches that can in principle support empirical evaluation on their own terms and according to their own criteria (see Appendix). With a dualistic perspective, this becomes possible.

Third, these two counterfactual statements can, of course, be specified more precisely for empirical purposes. Thus the statement that non-capitalist interests will not generally exert any significant influence on social investment may be clarified or modified to take account of variations between investment policies determined nationally and locally, or within the corporate and competitive sectors. It may be, for example, that those few aspects of social investment that remain the responsibility of local government may be determined by non-capitalist interests (for example, road and car park provisions made by socialist local authorities), in contrast to investment policies determined nationally. These are questions for empirical research, organized on a comparative basis, to answer, the point being that it is only because we can specify counterfactuals that such research is made possible.

The framework developed in this chapter may, therefore, prove very fruitful as regards analysis of different aspects of state activity, both in enabling the development of hypotheses and in pointing to new and important areas for research. For example, it indicates the need to consider how far social investment at the local level is becoming organized through corporate strategies (for instance through the development of 'corporate planning'); how far the reorganization of local government in different countries and at different times has reflected a growing need to segregate different aspects of state activity; to what extent different types of interests influence different types of policies in local authorities in different types of areas; and so on. Most crucially of all, however, this approach provides a way of analysing questions of the capitalist state while avoiding both the naive pluralist assumption that capital is no more significant politically than any other section of the population and the naive functionalist assumption that whatever the state does must in some way reflect the interests of the capitalist class. The potential significance of this dualistic perspective is thus by no means limited to analysis of 'urban' questions, for it provides a way of explaining the fundamental question of the relative autonomy of the state while avoiding the tautologous and self-confirming formulations that have tended to characterize debate on this question and

have effectively stifled any significant empirical developments.
The framework developed in the previous section not only contributes to analysis of the question of the capitalist state, but also has
significant implications for theories of class struggle. Political
struggles, like state policy-making, exhibit a dual character. On the
one hand, political struggles take the form of class struggles to the
extent that they directly derive out of or relate to the state's role in
supporting capital accumulation (that is, the social investment
function, including fiscal policy). Examples would include struggles
over prices and incomes legislation, regulation of trade unions, state
support of ailing industries, worker participation and so on. On the
other hand, political struggles take the form of 'sectoral' or 'urban'
struggles to the extent that they derive out of or relate to state
provision of social consumption, and examples here would include
struggles over welfare cuts, the management of council housing,
provision of day nursery facilities, levels of health care, the content of
educational courses and so on. Clearly, the same individuals or
groups may be involved in each of these two types of political struggle
and often are, but the important point is that when they mobilize in
relation to the former, they do so as a class on the basis of definite
class interests, whereas their mobilization in relation to the latter does
not constitute class struggle (even though the groups involved may be
drawn overwhelmingly from one particular class) and is grounded
not in class interests but in specific sectoral interests defined in
relation to the process of consumption. Analytically, there is a
'necessary non-correspondence' between class struggles and sectoral
struggles, although empirically the two may overlap.

The argument that the process of social consumption gives rise to
specific sectoral alignments which cannot be subsumed under class
categories has recently been developed by Dunleavy who suggests
that, 'Consumption locations cannot be assimilated into or explained
in terms of occupational class. Instead the relative independence of
some consumption locations needs to be recognized' (1979, p. 417).
He argues that the primary basis for consumption cleavages between
different sectors of the population is the distinction between
resources provided by the state and/or allocated on non-market
criteria, and resources provided and allocated through the market,
and he cites the divisions between public and private housing and
public and private transport as two important examples. While
recognizing that there is obviously a correlation between class
divisions and sectoral divisions (for example, both owner-

occupation and private car ownership are less widespread among manual than among managerial workers), Dunleavy nevertheless holds that sectoral alignments cross-cut class divisions and give rise to distinct conflicts of interest in relation to questions of social consumption: 'Basically sectors are lines of vertical division in a society, such that certain common interests are shared between social classes in the same sector, while within a social class, sectoral differences reflect a measure of conflict of interests' (p. 419). He then presents evidence to show that, in both housing and (though to a lesser degree) transport, the division between collective and individualized modes of consumption has a significant effect on political alignment (as indicated by voting patterns), independently of class position. He also shows that such sectoral fragmentation is most pronounced among the working class since it is here that variations in consumption locations are most developed.

Dunleavy's argument is important in that it underlines the specificity of consumption-based ('urban') struggles. The assertion made by those such as Clarke and Ginsburg (discussed in Chapter 7) that housing struggles represent simply an extension of class struggle into spheres outside the world of work is thus just as misleading as the argument developed by Rex and Moore (discussed in Chapter 4) to the effect that class alignments may be said to develop in both the urban and industrial contexts. Urban struggles are constituted in the sphere of consumption on the basis of specific sectoral interests which may or may not coincide with class alignments. They are neither one aspect of class struggle, nor a different type of class struggle. They are, rather, a specific type of political struggle distinct from political struggles grounded in class interests and class antagonisms.

All this, of course, poses a direct challenge to those such as Castells and Lojkine who argue that urban protests can provide the basis for an alliance between different non-capitalist classes which can be recruited into the socialist struggle against monopoly capital. On the contrary, we have seen that urban politics have their own specificity with no necessary relation to class politics. Given our earlier conceptualization of 'urban' processes, this specificity may be defined in three ways. First, urban struggles develop around questions of social consumption, and the corollary of this is that they are typically isolated from the labour movement and strategically limited in their objectives. Second, they are generally oriented towards the competitive rather than corporate spheres of politics, and the corollary of this is that they are typically fragmented between themselves. Third, they are mainly locally based, and the corollary of this is that they tend to be both issue-specific and locality-specific. In short, urban struggles are typically fragmented (for instance, different groups in different areas compete against each other for the same resources), localized (different groups with common interests find it very difficult to combine at a national level), strategically limited (the basis for mobilization is highly specific and any attempt to extend the scope of political activity into broader political issues often results in fractional disintegration), and politically isolated (links with more enduring political movements such as the Labour Party or the trade union movement are at best tenuous and more often non-existent). In the light of Dunleavy's arguments, it may also be added that these characteristics are likely to be more pronounced in relation to groups drawing primarily on a working-class member-ship than in relation to middle-class groups where sectoral divisions are likely to be less in evidence.

In Britain at least, empirical evidence strongly supports these hypotheses. I have discussed such evidence elsewhere (Saunders 1979, pp. 127–36), and need note here only that the conclusions drawn by those who have studied and been actively engaged in a variety of different campaigns and movements point time and again to the limited and fragmented character of urban struggles. I do not wish to suggest that such struggles will always and necessarily remain fragmented, isolated, localized and limited, but only that there are no grounds for assuming an inherent relation between them and political class struggles. This means that there is no basis in the often repeated claim that, when groups mobilize around common consumption interests, they are exhibiting a false consciousness of their class position, for consumption interests are real and vital and cannot be dismissed as mere ideological barriers to class solidarity (see, for example, my discussion of the political significance of political divisions between home-owners and tenants – Saunders 1979, ch. 2). It also means that those whose primary concerns lie in furthering the conditions for the development of socialism will derive little return from either analysis of or activity in urban politics (Saunders 1980).

Just as the application of the framework of the three elements of the urban question may prove useful in analysis of the capitalist state, so too it may prove fruitful in regard to the question of the relation between political struggles and class categories. Again the point is that general theories appear grossly misleading, for the pluralist assumption that political conflicts are waged not between classes but between shifting alliances of different interest groups is no more generalizable than the characteristic reductionism of so many Marxist approaches that seek to relate all crucial political conflicts to the wage labour-capital relation. The dualist approach developed here, by contrast, recognizes that political mobilization in some cases may be analysed in class terms while in others it cannot, and it therefore indicates the different types of situations in which different theoretical perspectives may be applicable.

The argument developed in this chapter clearly has implications both for urban sociology and for the sociological analysis of the state and class struggle. This is because the ideal type distinctions that have been drawn between social investment and social consumption, corporate and competitive modes of interest mediation and central and local levels of political activity provide the basis for a theoretical dualism which breaks down the analysis of the state and of political struggle into two related aspects, one of which is specified as the particular concern of a reformulated urban sociology. Seen in this way, urban sociology represents a crucial area of the discipline, for it is addressed to one aspect of the fundamental question of political power and social conflict which arguably lies at the heart of the discipline.

Such a specification of the theoretical concerns of urban sociology rests on three assumptions. First, it suggests that theories that have hitherto often been seen as incommensurable may be taken as complementary. Put in over-simple terms, the suggestion is that pluralist approaches may be most relevant to the analysis of local competitive consumption processes (the 'urban' question, as designated here), Marxist approaches may be most relevant to the analysis of national corporate investment processes, and managerialist approaches may provide the means through which the relation between the two sets of processes may be studied. As it stands, this argument is oversimplified both because the theoretical approaches to which it refers need to be carefully specified and to some extent modified (for example, pluralist theory must take account of the problem of non-decision-making; Marxist theory must take account of social action as well as structural constraint), and because it represents an analytically pure framework through which empirical research may proceed and develop (it may be found that pluralist explanations are less applicable to the analysis of local authorities controlled by one party rather than another, or to particular spheres of local policy as opposed to others, and so on). The argument is, therefore, both rudimentary and hypothetical.

The justification for this position is that it does appear potentially fruitful, both in specifying a particular set of theoretical problems and concerns to which urban sociology may be addressed (that is, it avoids the tendency of urban sociology to collapse into the analysis of capitalist society as a whole), and in providing a framework for analysing the relation between economic and political processes while avoiding the tautologous formulations associated with the concept of relative autonomy. This leads us to recognize the second assumption on which this approach is based; namely that the urban question can only be specified ideal-typically, and that evaluation of any ideal type conceptualization will depend upon its value in aiding and guiding empirical work in areas that appear theoretically relevant from the point of view of particular researchers. Lying behind this assumption, of course, is the argument that any approach should in principle be able to sustain criteria of empirical adequacy – in other words, that it should not only prove useful in guiding empirical research, but should also provide the means whereby it may be evaluated against the results of such research (see the Appendix).

The third assumption is that the problem of space to which urban sociology has traditionally been oriented can and must be severed from the concern with specific social processes. There is a sociological problem associated with the question of spatial forms, and this concerns the effects of moral density on patterns of social relationships, but the scope for such a 'spatial sociology' appears highly restricted in the light of the arguments discussed in Chapter 3. Space may also be theoretically significant as regards an analysis of the political economy of advanced capitalism, but a concern with the role of space in the extended reproduction of capital does not appear to constitute a distinctively sociological problem. As defined here, therefore, urban sociology is not specified in terms of the question of space (although spatial factors may be relevant to particular questions it poses, just as they are to other areas of the discipline, for all social processes occur within a spatial and temporal context), but rather in terms of the question of social consumption, competitive struggles and local politics. Seen in this way, urban sociology has lost the city as a specific object of analysis, for as we saw in Chapter 1, the city is not itself theoretically significant in the conditions of advanced capitalism. What it has gained, however, is a distinctive perspective on questions that are basic to the sociological analysis of advanced capitalist societies.

Appendix   A note on the empirical testing of theories

It has been suggested at various points in this book that empirical testability is one important criterion of theoretical adequacy. We saw in Chapter 4, for example, that one reason for rejecting Castells's theory of the relative autonomy of the state is that it is essentially tautologous and effectively immune from any critical empirical evaluation. The reason for this is that the concept of relative autonomy combines two opposing principles into a single general statement which cannot support counterfactual conditions, for to argue that the state both supports the long-term interests of monopoly capital and responds to the interests of non-capitalist classes without specifying the conditions under which these two contradictory tendencies become operative is simply to provide a self-confirming theory which is descriptively accurate but devoid of explanatory power. It was for this reason that it was suggested in Chapter 8 that a dualistic perspective may prove fruitful, for by distinguishing those situations in which capitalist interests are dominant from those in which the state responds to different interests engaged in competitive struggles with one another, it is possible to develop a range of hypotheses that may be assessed in the light of empirical research.

One possible objection to this whole argument, however, is that it betrays a naive view of the relation between theory and empirical evidence. Thus social scientists have increasingly come to recognize that the traditional assumption behind positivist research that 'facts' can be assembled through direct experience of the social world must be treated with some caution. It is now generally agreed that knowledge cannot be the product of unmediated experience through the senses, but that the way in which we come to 'see' the world is in some way dependent upon the theoretical assumptions and conceptual frameworks that we apply to it. As we saw in Chapter 1 when discussing the problems with Durkheim's sociological method, what we take to be 'facts', and thus 'evidence' and 'proof' for our assertions, will depend upon the way we conceptualize the world. There is no 'pure' observation, no neutral body of evidence, no 'facts' that are independent of prior conceptual assumptions.

If observation is theory-dependent, then resort to empirical evidence to arbitrate between competing theoretical explanations is clearly problematic. As Hindess suggests in relation to Popper's arguments regarding the need for empirical falsification in science, 'If all observation is to some extent theoretical, then how is it possible to maintain that all knowledge is reducible to observation and that theory is to be tested against the "facts" of observation?' (1977, p. 18). The point is not simply that theory determines where we look, but that it to some extent governs what we find.

The theory dependency of empirical research findings does not, however, undermine my earlier argument that empirical testability is an essential condition of theoretical adequacy. Three points need to be considered.

The first is that theory dependency does not imply theory determinacy. There is, in other words, no reason to suggest that different theoretical perspectives cannot agree on common areas of conceptualization and common criteria of empirical evidence. To argue otherwise would be to suggest that different theorists always talk past one another, never engage in meaningful debate and mutual criticism, and never concur over what is actually happening in the world; yet this is clearly not the case. For example, although they certainly disagree over the explanations they offer, and sometimes disagree over criteria of adequate or valid empirical evidence, conflict and consensus theorists nevertheless broadly agree on the sort of evidence that may indicate the perpetuation or break-down of social order. Similarly, while we may doubt, say, Castells's reasons for predicting the growth of urban social movements, and we may criticize the very concept of an urban social movement, none of this precludes the possibility of Castells and his critics agreeing on the existence or non-existence of such movements in a particular place at a particular time on the basis of the criteria which Castells himself puts forward.

The point is, therefore, that any theory employs both relatively high- and relatively low-level concepts, and that there is always likely to be a fairly broad conceptual 'lower common denominator' between different perspectives. As Andrew Sayer notes in his defence of Marxist methodology, ' "Looking at the evidence" need not imply an empiricist notion of observation as theory-neutral, but in relation to concepts like "socialization of consumption", those employed in observation are liable to be of a *"lower order"*. That is, they are unlikely to be exclusive to Marxism' (A. Sayer 1979, p. 48). Thus Sayer distinguishes between the (correct) view that evidence is theory-laden and the (incorrect) view that it is therefore theory-determined. Different theories share a broad (though low-level) area of agreement regarding their conceptualization of the world and their criteria of empirical evidence, and, this being the case, the theory dependency of empirical research need not rule out some degree of empirical evaluation of different theories, nor need it result in a collapse into cognitive relativism.

Before leaving this point, and as a prelude to the second point, it is important to take issue with one aspect of Sayer's argument concerning his critique of Hirst's rejection of epistemology which we discussed briefly in Chapter 5. It will be recalled that, in criticizing Althusser's epistemological imperialism, Hirst came to the conclusion that there are no epistemological principles divorced from particular discourses that can determine the correct mode of scientific analysis. We cannot, that is, criticize any given perspective simply on epistemological grounds, although different perspectives can be attacked on criteria internal to their own discourse. While himself rejecting Althusser's position, Sayer also rejects Hirst's argument as 'fatuous' and 'silly' on the grounds that it assumes that 'all observation is completely theory-determined' (A. Sayer 1979, p. 73). For Sayer, in other words, a rejection of epistemology is tantamount to an endorsement of cognitive relativism (despite the fact that Hirst has stressed that his is not a relativist – or, indeed, any other episte-mological – position).

Given our endorsement of Hirst's argument in Chapter 5, it is clearly necessary to answer this criticism, for we have seen that Sayer is quite justified in arguing against the theory determinacy view of observation. The point is, however, that Hirst's argument does not entail such a view. Hirst and his various co-authors do not necessarily deny that different discourses may agree on epistemological principles; only that any one epistemology can be taken as self-evident and thus as the basis for rejecting alternative approaches grounded in alternative methodologies. His critique of epistemology suggests simply that no approach can be dismissed on the grounds that it is epistemologically invalid because no general epistemology can be self-justifiable. This does not, however, imply that different discourses cannot engage in mutual criticism based on common agreement regarding what is to count as a valid mode of analysis or adequate empirical evidence.

Neither Sayer nor other like-minded critics of Hirst's position have been able to demonstrate the superiority of one epistemological position over others. In his critique, for example, Collier suggests that, for knowledge to be possible, it must be assumed that reality is structured in a certain way:

> If our faculties of knowledge depend for their possibility on the structure of the world outside them in this way, why should we not assume that the world really has that structure and hence makes them possible, rather than that they have the additional magic ability to force the world into a knowable form which it doesn't have in itself? [Collier 1978, p. 16]

The answer, of course, is that there is no reason why we should not *assume* that our concepts develop in such a way as progressively to map and hence reveal the real structure of the world, and that dialectical materialism is the method that is most appropriate to such a voyage of discovery since 'its result depends on the structure of external reality, not on us' (Collier 1978, p. 19), provided we always remember that this is a starting assumption which is not an *a priori* truth (as Althusser seems to believe), and which cannot in itself justify the rejection of other approaches based on other initial assumptions. It is not Hirst and his colleagues who must 'come clean', as Sayer and Collier both suggest at the end of their respective papers, but rather those Marxist theorists who claim to work with a privileged epistemology yet who have failed to demonstrate the source of its superiority. It does seem that the hostility shown by many academic Marxists towards Hirst's arguments is born of a fear of losing the 'scientific' basis of their political analyses, the paradox being (as Hirst himself has shown) that it is precisely this claim to scientific privilege that has so consistently weakened rather than strengthened the political impact of Marxism over the last 100 years.

What is specific to the Marxist method is, as we saw in Chapter 1, the distinction that it draws between essence and phenomenal appearance, and hence its claim to be able to explain the latter through the discovery of the former. This leads us to consider the second point relating to the question of empirical testability; namely, that Marxist laws cannot and should not be tested through any simple notion of empirical falsification. Sayer's paper is again relevant here.

Sayer argues, quite justifiably, that the Marxist method involves the attempt to discover necessary tendencies (such as the tendency within capitalism for the rate of profit to fall), and that the question of whether or not these tendencies are realized is contingent on a variety of empirical conditions (for example the mobilization of counter-acting tendencies to prevent the rate of profit from falling). Drawing an analogy with the natural sciences, he argues that, just as the chemical laws of combustion are not falsified if a particular pile of gunpowder fails to explode when a flame is applied (since, for example, it may be damp), and just as the law of gravity is not falsified whenever aeroplanes fail to drop from the sky, so too Marxist laws cannot be rejected as false simply because they fail to become manifest in particular situations. He then argues on the basis of this that Marxist theories cannot be subjected to the test of empirical falsification (since this ignores the question of counteracting tendencies), or even to the test of their success in guiding political practice (since political intervention changes the situation to which they refer). He concludes that 'In social science there are no "tests", only applications' (A. Sayer 1979, p. 33).

This argument, which is also advanced by Collier, is largely consistent with Derek Sayer's interpretation of Marx's method discussed in Chapter 1. A retroductive method that posits essential relations or tendencies as the means of explaining phenomenal forms should be applicable to empirical situations but cannot be tested against empirical evidence. The explanations that it offers of particular situations may thus be more or less plausible but can never be evaluated as true or false. Yet in the natural sciences, retroductive inference does not exclude empirical testing, and this is because it is intrinsically linked to the development of counterfactuals. In other words, natural science explanations involve *both* the development of theories of essences or necessities (say, that gunpowder is inherently combustible) *and* the stipulation of contingent conditions, in the form of counterfactual statements, regarding the empirical cases in which such inherent tendencies will fail to be realized (as when gunpowder is damp). It is doubtful whether chemists would place their faith in a law of combustion that provided no way of predicting the conditions under which combustible substances such as gunpowder could be expected to explode and which failed to specify the criteria by which such conditions could be recognized empirically. This, however, is precisely the situation in which Marxist 'explanations' find themselves when they fail to develop counterfactual conditions.

Now it is clearly the case, as Andrew Sayer suggests, that the specification of contingencies is likely to be far more difficult in the social than in the natural sciences given the infinite complexity of the social world (that is to say, it is impossible to take all variables into account) and its responsiveness to human intervention. This, however, appears to be a quantitative rather than qualitative difference since natural science predictions may also fail to take all significant variables into account (even experimental conditions frequently fail to hold all contingencies constant), and the question of human intervention in the social world can itself be included as a contingent factor. The development of counterfactuals may be more difficult in the social sciences, but this does not negate the need for them.

The argument that Marxist theories and laws can be applied but not tested necessarily results in tautological reasoning. It is simply not enough to posit the existence of necessary tendencies while at the same time refusing to be drawn on the question of whether and under what sort of conditions these tendencies are likely to become manifest, for this results in the constant and retrospective invocation of the fail-safe assumption that is built into such approaches to the effect that, if necessary tendencies do not develop, then counteracting tendencies must have occurred. Like functionalist theories, Marxist theories that make no attempt to specify counterfactuals amount to little more than the argument that, if things were not as they are, they would be different. To be taken seriously, Marxist approaches must, like any other approach in the social sciences, attempt to develop counterfactual statements and the criteria for recognizing the empirical cases to which such statements refer, for if they do not they are likely to represent little more than assertions of faith.

It follows from our earlier discussion of Hirst's critique of epistemology, of course, that the specification of counterfactuals and of the criteria by which they can be identified empirically will be specific to particular discourses. An insistence on empirical testability as an important condition of theoretical adequacy does not, therefore, rest on a naive falsificationist position. This is because, first, predictions may fail without falsifying the theory on which they are based (since it is never possible to take account of all contingencies), and, second, there are no general criteria of empirical falsification (since there is no general epistemology against which different discourses can be evaluated). This leads us on to the third main point regarding the problem of the empirical testability of theories, which is that any given perspective must be testable, but only on its own terms.

My insistence on the importance of counterfactuality refers only to the necessity of any theory to support the possibility of disconfirming instances and to stipulate the criteria by which such instances may be recognized in empirical research. Theories should not be merely self-confirming tautologies, but should be open to empirical test in accordance with conditions that they themselves lay down. To the extent that different approaches can agree on these conditions, they can be evaluated empirically against each other; to the extent that they cannot so agree, they can be evaluated empirically only on their own terms. But to the extent that they fail to provide such conditions, they cannot be evaluated empirically at all, in which case any claim they make to scientific knowledge can safely be ignored.

It is on this basis that I would justify the dualistic approach developed in Chapter 8, for as we saw there, such an approach can sustain counterfactual testing in terms of the argument that different types of political strategies tend to be associated with different aspects of the state's role performed at different levels of its organization. It was not, of course, suggested that this is universally the case, but only that this may be taken as an ideal-typical framework within which empirical research on a variety of different cases may fruitfully proceed. The significance of this approach, in other words, is that it enables the development of hypotheses that are not true by definition but that can be amended, developed, further specified or even abandoned in the light of empirical evidence from different studies of different aspects of state activity in different countries at different times. It therefore facilitates the development of Castells's call for a 'theorized history of states' in a way that Castells's own use of the concept of relative autonomy does not.

One final point should be made in conclusion, and this concerns the possible criticism that an insistence on counterfactuality and empirical testability is inconsistent with a rejection of general epistemological principles. Such a criticism would appear valid in the sense that my argument does point to a universal principle (internal testability) by means of which all perspectives are to be evaluated, and this reflects my assertion that sociological explanations that are inherently immune from empirical evaluation, even on their own terms, in effect explain nothing. Those who remain content to accept such 'explanations' will obviously reject my emphasis on counterfactuality. However, for those approaches that seek to go beyond tautology and resolute faith, an insistence on counterfactuality does not represent an unwarranted epistemological intrusion since it does not attempt to impose external and general principles regarding correct procedure or universal criteria of empirical adequacy (for such questions are determined within discourses), but merely holds that some such criteria must be specified. This is a minimal epistemological principle, yet it is one that much of the literature discussed in the later chapters of this book fails to address.

Further reading

As we saw in the later chapters of this book, there has been little short of a revolution in urban sociology over the last few years, and there are as yet few general texts that provide a comprehensive coverage of the main perspectives found in the contemporary literature. However, for the reader who wishes to consult some other texts, Reissman (1964) and Mellor (1977) both provide interesting and useful discussions of some of the more established approaches in urban sociology, while more recent work is covered in a number of books to be published in a new series on sociology, politics and cities under the Macmillan imprint (notably in forthcoming titles by Hooper, Dunleavy and Elliott and McCrone). For those who wish to follow up particular themes discussed in this book, I identify below a few key references in respect of each chapter.

Chapter 1: Social theory, capitalism and the urban question

Marx's discussions of the urban question are scattered and fragmented, although an important reference is undoubtedly part 1c of Marx and Engels (1970), in which the town–country division is considered in the context of the development of the division of labour in society. This may usefully be read alongside some of the later chapters of the first volume of *Capital* (1976 – notably chs. 26, 27 and 30–32), which also contains a short discussion of the causes and effects of capitalist urbanization (pp. 811–18 in the 1976 edition), although this latter theme is more fully elaborated in Engels (1969a, b). The best secondary source on all this is Lefebvre (1972), although this is unfortunately not available in English translation. Giddens (1971, ch. 2) is, however, a useful and readily accessible source.

Weber's essay on the city can be found in Weber (1968, ch. 16) or in a separate publication edited and introduced by Martindale (Weber 1958). As was suggested in Chapter 1, this essay has suffered some neglect within sociology – even Martindale's introduction focuses more on work by other writers such as Park and Wirth than it does on Weber – but there are short, useful discussions of it in Mellor (1977, pp. 189–94) and Bendix (1966, pp. 70–9). The latter in particular is useful in showing how this essay relates to other parts of Weber's work, and especially to his concern with the role of puritanism in the development of capitalist rationality.

The principal reference with regard to Durkheim's discussion of urbanization is Durkheim (1933, see especially pp. 1–10, 18–28, 181–90 and 256–301). This work has rarely been discussed in the context of its contribution to urban sociology, although S. Lukes, *Emile Durkheim: His Life and Work* (Allen Lane 1973, ch. 7) provides a thorough and critical review of its main arguments while J. Eldridge, *Sociology and Industrial Life* (Nelson 1973, pp. 73–91) is useful on the concept of anomie and its relation to Durkheim's discussion of a new nationally organized guild system.

Chapter 2: The urban as an ecological community

Probably the most concise statement of Park's theory is his essay on human ecology which was first published in the *Americal Journal of Sociology*, vol. 42, 1936, and which is contained in Park (1952, ch. 12). This collection of Park's essays should also be consulted for ch. 15 (in which he discusses the concept of natural areas in the context of his sociological method) and ch. 19 (a paper originally written in 1939 in which he comes to his final conclusions on the biotic–cultural distinction). His original essay on the city is also included in this collection, and can also be found in Park and Burgess, *The City* (University of Chicago Press 1925; re-issued in 1967), which contains other important contributions by Burgess (his famous paper on concentric rings) and McKenzie.

Of the avalanche of critical discussions of the Chicago school, the most important is probably that by Alihan (1938, especially chs. 2, 3 and 4), part of which is reprinted in G. Theodorson, *Studies in Human Ecology* (New York: Harper Row 1961). The Theodorson collection also contains papers or excerpts by Wirth, Robinson, Firey, Hawley and others, in addition to short summaries of the various papers by the editor. Hawley's reformulation of human ecology is summarized in his 1968 paper, although this should be read in conjunction with his earlier book (Hawley 1950, especially ch. 4). Brief and useful résumés of the ecological tradition can be found in Robson (1969, pp. 8–15 and 35–8) and Berry and Kasarda (1977, ch. 1); and further critical commentaries are provided by Reissman (1964, ch. 5), Mellor (1977, ch. 6) and Castells (1977a, ch. 8).

Chapter 3: The urban as a cultural form

Simmel's essay on the metropolis and mental life first appeared in English translation in Wolff (1950), though it has subsequently been reprinted elsewhere (e.g. in K. Thompson and J. Tunstall, *Sociological Perspectives* (Harmondsworth: Penguin 1971). Wirth's 1938 essay on urbanism as a way of life has also subsequently appeared in a number of edited collections including P. Hatt and A. Reiss, *Cities and Society* 2nd ed. (New York: Free Press 1957) and A. Reiss, *Louis Wirth on Cities and Social Life* (University of

Chicago Press 1964). The Reiss collection also contains Wirth's essays on the ghetto (1927) and human ecology (1945), as well as his unfinished but important article on rural–urban differences. Useful supplementary reading on Simmel includes his essay 'On the significance of numbers for social life' (in Wolff 1950, Part II, ch. 1) and the piece on 'Group expansion and the development of individuality' included in Levine (1971). Levine's introduction to this latter collection is also useful on Simmel's formalism, his sociological emphasis on number, and his relation to Park's later work.

The history of urban–rural dichotomies in sociology is discussed and summarized in Pahl (1968), which is also an important article in its own right for the critique that it develops of any attempt to relate cultural patterns to spatial locations. The other major contribution to this debate is by Gans (1968) who shows that, at most, Wirth's theory of urbanism applies only to deprived groups in inner-city areas of high population turnover. See also Dewey (1960) for an evaluation of the effects of location on cultural patterns, and the final chapter in Lewis (1951) for a critique on Redfield's work on folk culture. Mellor (1977, ch. 5) provides a critical overview of this whole tradition, while Williams (1973) develops a fascinating argument regarding the ideological significance of rural and urban imagery in Western capitalism (see especially chs. 1 and 25; also his article on 'Literature and the city' in the *Listener*, vol. 78, 1967, pp. 653–6).

Chapter 4: The urban as a socio-spatial system

The original concept of a socio-spatial system is set out in Pahl (1970, ch. 4) and in ch. 7 of the second edition of *Whose City?* (Pahl 1975). The latter is a collection of Pahl's essays which clearly documents the shift in his thinking on urban managerialism from the earlier conception of managers as independent variables (as in ch. 10) to the later recognition of their mediating role in a context of economic and political constraint (ch. 13). This shift is clarified and discussed in Williams (1978) and Norman (1975). Its relation to Pahl's later writings on corporatism is never made entirely clear in Pahl's own work, although his 1979 article perhaps comes closest to spelling out the common methodological and theoretical position that lies behind his approach to both urban managerialism and corporate state strategies (cf. his argument on p. 34 that 'The process of resource allocation has certain common elements no matter what the scale of organization. . . .'). His discussions of corporatism can be found in Pahl (1977b, c), and these should be read alongside the two articles by Winkler (1976, 1977).

On the concept of housing classes, see Rex and Moore (1967, chs. 1 and 12), Rex (1968), and, for the various amendments made in the light of later criticisms, Rex (1971), on the problem of multiple value systems, Rex (1977) where the emphasis shifts from current tenure to potential access, and Rex and Tomlinson (1979, pp. 20–4 and chs. 5 and 8). This last reference also contains a methodological appendix in which recent Marxist work is attacked for its metaphysical assumptions and a Weberian emphasis on meaningful action and the use of ideal types is asserted and defended. The most important critique of the housing class model remains Haddon (1970), but see also Davies (1972, chs. 3 and 4), Couper and Brindley (1975) and C. Bell, 'On Housing Classes', *Australian and New Zealand Journal of Sociology*, vol. 13, pp. 36–40. Recent Marxist work on housing tenure, referred to in Chapter 7, is also clearly relevant to this debate, while Lambert *et al.* (1978) provides a useful evaluation of both the managerialism and housing class concepts (see especially chs. 1 and 7). My own work on urban politics (Saunders 1979) also provides a fairly comprehensive review of the arguments in chs. 2 and 3.

Chapter 5:   The urban as ideology

Most of the relevant work by Lefebvre is still unavailable in English, although the flavour of his arguments can be sampled in Lefebvre (1976), especially ch. 1 (on the relation between space, capitalist accumulation and the state) and ch. 2, section 7 (which contains an attack on Althusserian Marxism). Lefebvre's ideas are discussed in the final chapter of Harvey (1973) and in Castells (1977a, ch. 6).

Castells's critique of urban sociology (including the work of Lefebvre) is contained in two early papers (1976a, b) and in *The Urban Question* (1977a, chs. 5–8). These should be read in the light of Althusser's papers on Marxist methodology, especially chs. 3, 6 and 7 in Althusser (1969), and his discussion of ideology in his 1971 paper. A useful guide to Althusser's arguments can be found in A. Callinicos, *Althusser's Marxism* (Pluto Press 1976), especially chs. 2 and 3, while his approach has been subjected to a merciless critique from a humanist position by E. Thompson in his essay on 'The poverty of theory', which is contained in a book of the same title published in 1978 by the Merlin Press.

The key chapter in *The Urban Question* as regards Castells's formal conceptualization of his object of analysis is ch. 10, and much of his later work represents a gradual retreat from the position set out there. Significant milestones in this retreat include the 1975 Afterword to the English edition (which is important both for the auto-critique of his earlier formalism and for its clarification of the conceptualization of urbanism in terms of collective consumption) and ch. 1 in Castells (1978).

Chapter 6:   The urban as a spatial unit of collective consumption

Castells has published a number of papers that provide a concise summary of his arguments regarding the causes and political implications of crises of collective consumption. See, for example, ch. 2 in Castells (1978), his article on 'The class struggle and urban contradictions' in J. Cowley *et al.*, *Community or Class Struggle?* (Stage 1 1977), and his paper on 'The wild city' (*Kapitalistate*, no. 4/5, 1976, pp. 2–30). None of these, however, was written later than 1975/6, and for Castells's more recent work it is important to refer to chs. 1, 8 and 9 in his 1978 collection.

Various Marxist approaches to the analysis of the capitalist state are discussed and reviewed in Gold *et al.* (1975) and in Saunders (1979, ch. 4). These debates provide the context for the divergence between Castells and Lojkine which is discussed in some depth by Pickvance (1977b) and Harloe (1979). Castells's own position draws heavily on that outlined by Poulantzas (1973), particularly as regards the analysis of the relation between structures and practices (see pp. 85–92 and 142–5) and the theory of the relative autonomy of the state (see, for example, pp. 187–94 and 275–89). The problems entailed in this approach have been ably diagnosed by Clarke (1977) and Hirst (1977); and the change of emphasis from structures to practices, which is characteristic of the later writings of both Castells and Poulantzas, has done little to overcome the basic problems they identify.

The specific problems associated with the concept of urban social movements are discussed in Pickvance (1976b, 1977a), while the usefulness of the concept of collective consumption is considered by Pahl (1977a), who points to the inconsistencies in the work of both Castells and Lojkine, and by Dunleavy (1979b). Finally, the relation between recent Marxist work and the traditional concerns of urban sociology is traced in simple terms by M. Harloe, 'The new urban sociology' (*New Society*, 5 October 1978), and this article may provide a useful starting point for those coming to this literature for the first time.

Chapter 7: Political economy and the urban question

The work of David Harvey is scattered throughout a number of journals and edited collections, although a new book encompassing the recent ideas is promised. In the meantime, Harvey (1973) remains his single most important statement, although the 1978a paper is perhaps somewhat clearer and provides an indication of the way in which his work is now developing. This should ideally be read against the background of Baran and Sweezy (1966), which is in turn discussed by Gamble and Walton (1976, pp. 88–110; see also ch. 4 for a clear discussion of the theory of the falling rate of profit).

Harvey's work on rent ('Class monopoly rent, finance capital and the urban revolution', *Regional Studies*, vol. 8, 1974), although much criticized, remains an important contribution to Marxist discussions of urban rent and provides an interesting contrast to much sociology of the inner city. The rent question is also addressed in both volumes of the CSE housing workshop papers, although Ball's 1978 paper is arguably the most fundamental of recent Marxist contributions, concentrating as it does on the sphere of capitalist production. Berry's work provides a useful elaboration and critique of the political economy of housing literature (Berry 1979).

O'Connor's analysis of fiscal crisis is presented in his 1973 book and is criticized (along with work by Yaffe and others) in Gough (1975) and by E. Mingione ('The crisis, the corporations and the state', *International Journal of Urban and Regional Research*, vol. 1, 1977, pp. 370–8). The applicability of theories of fiscal crisis to the British situation is considered by C. Pickvance, *Urban Fiscal Crisis, Theories of Crisis and Theories of the State* (Urban and Regional Studies Unit, University of Kent 1978), who also takes up the problem of the functionality of state intervention discussed by Gough (1979). Although not specifically discussed in this chapter, it should also be noted that the various publications from the Community Development Project groups provide useful and interesting material informed by the overall perspective outlined here.

Chapter 8:   On the specificity of the urban

The dualistic approach developed in this chapter is an elaboration of an argument first set out in an article entitled 'Community power, urban managerialism and the "local state" ', which is to appear in a collection of papers from the 1979 CES conference edited by M. Harloe and published by Heinemann. In addition to O'Connor's work (1973), it draws heavily on various writings by Offe (notably his 1975 article) and on the paper on governmental structures by Friedland *et al.* (1977). Recent discussions of corporatism by Cawson (1978) and Jessop (1978) are also significant for the argument. Empirical evidence on the fragmented character of local consumption-based political struggles can be found in Bell and Newby (1976) and in a variety of case studies, some of which are discussed in ch. 3 of Saunders (1979).

Since completing this book I have tried to develop the arguments in this final chapter a little further in 'Towards a non-spatial urban sociology' (University of Sussex: *Urban and Regional Studies Working Papers*, no. 21, 1980). This paper adds a fourth dimension to the conceptualization of the urban question and clarifies the use of ideal type constructs. It also contains an interesting critique by Andrew Sayer.

It should also be noted that Dunleavy's book, *Urban Political Analysis*, has been published since the completion of this book; it contains an extremely interesting attempt to develop a framework for urban research based on a rejection of the spatial factor. Dunleavy's book may fruitfully be read in the context of the arguments developed here.

References

Abu-Lughod, J. (1961), 'Migrant adjustment to city life: the Egyptian case', *American Journal of Sociology*, vol. 67, pp. 22–32

Alihan, M. (1938), *Social Ecology: A Critical Analysis*, New York: Columbia University Press

Althusser, L. (1969), *For Marx*, London: Allen Lane

Althusser, L. (1971), 'Ideology and ideological state apparatuses', in L. Althusser, *Lenin and Philosophy and Other Essays*, London: New Left Books

Anderson, J. (1975), *The Political Economy of Urbanism: An Introduction and Bibliography*, London: Architectural Association

Ball, M. (1977), 'Differential rent and the role of landed property', *International Journal of Urban and Regional Research*, vol. 1, pp. 380–403

Ball, M. (1978), 'British housing policy and the house-building industry', *Capital and Class*, vol. 4, pp. 78–99

Baran, P., and Sweezy, P. (1966), *Monopoly Capital*, New York: Monthly Review Press

Becker, H. (1959), 'On Simmel's "Philosophy of Money" ', in K. Wolff (ed.), *Georg Simmel 1858–1918*, Columbus: Ohio State University Press

Bell, C., and Newby, H. (1971), *Community Studies*, London: Allen & Unwin

Bell, C., and Newby, H. (1976), 'Community, communion, class and community action', in D. Herbert and R. Johnson, *Social Areas in Cities*, London: John Wiley

Bendix, R. (1966), *Max Weber: An Intellectual Portrait*, London: Methuen

Benton, T. (1977), *Philosophical Foundations of the Three Sociologies*, London: Routledge & Kegan Paul

Berry, B., and Kasarda, J. (1977), *Contemporary Urban Ecology*, London: Collier Macmillan

Berry, M. (1979), *Marxist Approaches to the Housing Question*, University of Birmingham, Centre for Urban and Regional Studies, research memorandum no. 69

Beshers, J. (1962), *Urban Social Structure*, New York: Free Press

Boddy, M. (1976), 'Building societies and owner-occupation', in Conference of Socialist Economists Political Economy of Housing Workshop, *Housing and Class in Britain*, London: Conference of Socialist Economists

Bruun, H. (1972), *Science, Values and Politics in Max Weber's Methodology*, Copenhagen: Munksgaard

Burger, T. (1976), *Max Weber's Theory of Concept Formation*, Chapel Hill, North Carolina: Duke University Press

Burgess, E. (1967), 'The growth of the city: an introduction to a research project', in R. Park and E. Burgess, *The City*, London: University of Chicago Press

Byrne, D. (1977), 'Allocation, the council ghetto and the political economy of housing', *Antipode*, vol. 8, pp. 24–9

Castells, M. (1976a), 'Is there an urban sociology?', in C. Pickvance (ed.), *Urban Sociology: Critical Essays*, London: Tavistock

Castells, M. (1976b), 'Theory and ideology in urban sociology,' in Pickvance, *Urban Sociology*

Castells, M. (1976c). 'Theoretical propositions for an experimental study of urban social movements', in Pickvance, *Urban Sociology*

Castells, M. (1977a), *The Urban Question*, London: Edward Arnold

Castells, M. (1977b), 'Towards a political urban sociology', in M. Harloe (ed.), *Captive Cities*, London: John Wiley

Castells, M. (1978), *City, Class and Power*, London: Macmillan

Castells, M., and Godard, F. (1974), *Monopolville: l'entreprise, l'état, l'urbain*, Paris: Mouton

Castells, M., and Ipola, E. (1976), 'Epistemological practice and the social sciences', *Economy and Society*, vol. 5, pp. 111–44

Cawson, A. (1978), 'Pluralism, corporatism and the role of the state', *Government and Opposition*, vol. 13, pp. 178–98

Clarke, S. (1977), 'Marxism, sociology and Poulantzas' theory of the state', *Capital and Class*, vol. 2, pp. 1–31

Clarke, S., and Ginsburg, N. (1975), 'The political economy of housing', in Conference of Socialist Economists Political Economy of Housing Workshop, *Political Economy and the Housing Question*, London: Conference of Socialist Economists

Cockburn, C. (1977), *The Local State*, London: Pluto Press

Collier, A. (1978), 'In defence of epistemology', *Radical Philosophy*, vol. 20, pp. 8–21

Community Development Project (1976), *Profits against Houses*, London: CDP Information and Intelligence Unit

Coser, L. (1965), *Georg Simmel*, Englewood Cliffs, New Jersey: Prentice-Hall

Couper, M., and Brindley, T. (1975), 'Housing classes and housing values', *Sociological Review*, vol. 23, pp. 563–76

Damer, S. (1974), 'Wine alley: the sociology of a dreadful enclosure', *Sociological Review*, vol. 22, pp. 221–48

Davie, M. (1937), 'The pattern of urban growth', in G. Murdock (ed.), *Studies in the Science of Society*, New Haven, Conn.: Yale University Press

Davies, J. (1972), *The Evangelistic Bureaucrat*, London: Tavistock

Davies, J., and Taylor, J. (1970), 'Race, community and no conflict', *New Society*, vol. 9, pp. 67–9

Dawe, A. (1970), 'The two sociologies', *British Journal of Sociology*, vol. 21, pp. 207–18

Dawe, A. (1971), 'The relevance of values', in A. Sahay, *Max Weber and Modern Sociology*, London: Routledge & Kegan Paul

Dennis, N. (1968), 'The popularity of the neighbourhood community idea', in R. Pahl, *Readings in Urban Sociology*, London: Pergamon Press

Dewey, R. (1960), 'The rural-urban continuum: real but relatively unimportant', *American Journal of Sociology*, vol. 66, pp. 60–6

Dickens, P. (1977), 'Social change, housing and the state: some aspects of class fragmentation and incorporation', in M. Harloe (ed.), *Proceedings of the Conference on Urban Change and Conflict*, London: Centre for Environmental Studies

Duncan, O. (1957), 'Community size and the rural–urban continuum', in P. Hatt and A. Reiss, (eds.), *Cities and Society* (2nd edn), New York: Free Press

Duncan, O. (1959), 'Human ecology and population studies', in P. Hauser and O. Duncan (eds.), *The Study of Population*, Chicago: University Press

Duncan, O. (1964), 'Social organization and the ecosystem', in R. Faris (ed.), *Handbook of Modern Sociology*, Chicago: Rand McNally

Duncan, O., and Schnore, L. (1959), 'Cultural, behavioral and ecological perspectives in the study of social organization', *American Journal of Sociology*, vol. 65, pp. 132–46

Duncan, S. (1978), 'Housing reform, the capitalist state and social democracy', *Urban and Regional Studies Working Papers*, no. 9, University of Sussex

Dunleavy, P. (1979a), 'The urban bases of political alignment', *British Journal of Political Science*, vol. 9, pp. 409–43

Dunleavy, P. (1979b), 'Rehabilitating collective consumption', Unpublished paper, Department of Politics, London School of Economics

Durkheim, É. (1933), *The Division of Labour in Society*, Toronto: Macmillan

Durkheim, É. (1938), *The Rules of Sociological Method*, New York: Free Press

Durkheim, É. (1952), *Suicide: A Study in Sociology*, London: Routledge & Kegan Paul

Elliott, B., and McCrone, D. (1975), 'Landlords as urban managers: a dissenting opinion', in M. Harloe (ed.), *Proceedings of the Conference on Urban Change and Conflict*, London: Centre for Environmental Studies

Engels, F. (1969a), *The Condition of the Working Class in England*, St Albans: Panther Books

Engels, F. (1969b), 'The housing question', in K. Marx and F. Engels, *Selected Works*, vol. 2, Moscow: Progress Publishers

Firey, W. (1945), 'Sentiment and symbolism as ecological variables', *American Sociological Review*, vol. 10, pp. 140–8

Flynn, R. (1979), *Managing Consensus: The Infrastructure of Policy-making in Planning*, paper given at the Centre for Environmental Studies conference on urban change and conflict, University of Nottingham

Ford, J. (1975), 'The role of the building society manager in the urban stratification system', *Urban Studies*, vol. 12, pp. 295–302

Forrest, R., and Lloyd, J. (1978), 'Theories of the capitalist state: the implications for policy research', in *Papers in Urban and Regional Studies*, no. 2, University of Birmingham, Centre for Urban and Regional Studies

Freund, J. (1968), *The Sociology of Max Weber*, London: Allen Lane

Freund, J. (1978), 'Emile Durkheim', in T. Bottomore and R. Nisbet (eds.), *A History of Sociological Analysis*, London: Heinemann

Friedland, R., Fox Piven, F., and Alford, R. (1977), 'Political conflict, urban structure and the fiscal crisis', *International Journal of Urban and Regional Research*, vol. 1, pp. 447–71

Gamble, A., and Walton, P. (1976), *Capitalism in Crisis*, London: Macmillan

Gans, H. (1962), *The Urban Villagers*, New York: Free Press

Gans, H. (1968), 'Urbanism and suburbanism as ways of life', in R. Pahl, *Readings in Urban Sociology*, London: Pergamon

Gettys, W. (1940), 'Human ecology and social theory', *Social Forces*, vol. 17, pp. 469–76

Giddens, A. (1971), *Capitalism and Modern Social Theory*, London: Cambridge University Press

Giddens, A. (1974), 'Introduction' to A. Giddens (ed.), *Positivism and Sociology*, London: Heinemann

Giddens, A. (1979), *Central Problems in Social Theory*, London: Macmillan

Glass, R. (1968), 'Urban sociology in Great Britain', in R. Pahl (ed.), *Readings in Urban Sociology*, London: Pergamon Press

Gold, D., Lo, C., and Wright, E. (1975), 'Recent developments in Marxist theories of the capitalist state', *Monthly Review*, vol. 27, pp. 37–51

Gough, I. (1975), 'State expenditure in advanced capitalism', *New Left Review*, no. 92, pp. 53–92

Gough, I. (1979), *The Political Economy of the Welfare State*, London: Macmillan

Gray, F. (1976), 'The management of local authority housing', in Conference of Socialist Economists Political Economy of Housing Workshop,

Housing and Class in Britain, London: Conference of Socialist Economists

Habermas, J. (1976), *Legitimation Crisis*, London: Heinemann

Haddon, R. (1970), 'A minority in a welfare state society', *New Atlantis*, vol. 2, pp. 80–133

Hall, P., Gracey, H., Drewitt, R., and Thomas, R. (1973), *The Containment of Urban England*, vol. 1, London: Allen & Unwin

Harloe, M. (1975), 'Introduction' to M. Harloe (ed.), *Proceedings of the Conference on Urban Change and Conflict*, London: Centre for Environmental Studies

Harloe, M. (1977), 'Introduction' to M. Harloe (ed.), *Captive Cities*, London: John Wiley

Harloe, M. (1979), 'Marxism, the state and the urban question: critical notes on two recent French theories', in C. Crouch (ed.), *State and Economy in Contemporary Capitalism*, London: Croom Helm

Harloe, M., Issacharoff, R., and Minns, R. (1974), *The Organization of Housing*, London: Heinemann

Harvey, D. (1973), *Social Justice and the City*, London: Edward Arnold

Harvey, D. (1974), 'Population, resources and the ideology of science', *Economic Geography*, vol. 50, pp. 256–77

Harvey, D. (1977), 'Government policies, financial institutions and neighbourhood change in United States cities', in M. Harloe (ed.), *Captive Cities*, London: John Wiley

Harvey, D. (1978a), 'The urban process under capitalism: a framework for analysis', *International Journal of Urban and Regional Research*, vol. 2, pp. 101–31

Harvey, D. (1978b), 'Labour, capital and class struggle around the built environment in advanced capitalist societies', in K. Cox (ed.), *Urbanization and Conflict in Market Societies*, London: Methuen

Hawley, A. (1944), 'Ecology and human ecology', *Social Forces*, vol. 22, pp. 144–51

Hawley, A. (1950), *Human Ecology: A Theory of Community Structure*, New York: Ronald Press

Hawley, A. (1963), 'Community power and urban renewal success', *American Journal of Sociology*, vol. 68, pp. 422–31

Hawley, A. (1968), 'Human ecology', *International Encyclopedia of Social Science*, vol. 4, Macmillan and Free Press

Heraud, B. (1975), 'The new towns: a philosophy of community', in O. Leonard (ed.), *The Sociology of Community Action*, Sociological Review Monograph, no. 21

Hill, R. (1977), 'Two divergent theories of the state', *International Journal of Urban and Regional Research*, vol. 1, pp. 37–44

Hindess, B. (1977), *Philosophy and Methodology in the Social Sciences*, Hassocks: Harvester Press

Hindess, B. (1978), 'Class and politics in Marxist theory', in G. Littlejohn, B. Smart, J. Wakeford and N. Yuval-Davis (eds.), *Power and the State*, London: Croom Helm

Hirst, P. (1975), *Durkheim, Bernard and Epistemology*, London: Routledge & Kegan Paul

Hirst, P. (1976), *Social Evolution and Sociological Categories*, London: Allen & Unwin

Hirst, P. (1977), 'Economic classes and politics', in A. Hunt (ed.) *Class and Class Structure*, London: Lawrence & Wishart

Hirst, P. (1979), *On Law and Ideology*, London: Macmillan

Jessop, B. (1978), 'Capitalism and democracy: the best possible political shell?' in G. Littlejohn, B. Smart, J. Wakeford and N. Yuval-Davis (eds.), *Power and the State*, London: Croom Helm

Jones, G. (1973), *Rural Life*, London: Longman

Keat, R., and Urry, J. (1975), *Social Theory as Science*, London: Routledge & Kegan Paul

Lambert, J., Paris, C., and Blackaby, B. (1978), *Housing Policy and the State*, London: Macmillan

Lebas, E. (1979), 'The evolution of the state monopoly capital thesis in French urban research', unpublished paper, Centre for Environmental Studies, London

Lefebvre, H. (1968a), *The Sociology of Marx*, London: Allen Lane

Lefebvre, H. (1968b), *Le droit à la ville*, Paris: Anthropos

Lefebvre, H. (1970), *La révolution urbaine*, Paris: Gallimard

Lefebvre, H. (1972), *La pensée marxiste et la ville*, Paris: Castermann

Lefebvre, H. (1976), *The Survival of Capitalism*, London: Allison & Busby

Lefebvre, H. (1977), 'Reflections on the politics of space', in R. Peet (ed.), *Radical Geography*, Chicago: Maaroufa Press

Levine, D. (1971), *Georg Simmel on Individuality and Social Forms*, London: University of Chicago Press

Lewis, O. (1951), *Life in a Mexican Village: Tepoztlán Restudied*, Urbana: University of Illinois Press

Lipton, M. (1977), *Why Poor People Stay Poor*, London: Maurice Temple-Smith

Lojkine, J. (1976), 'Contribution to a Marxist theory of capitalist urbanization', in C. Pickvance (ed.), *Urban Sociology: Critical Essays*, London: Tavistock

Lojkine, J. (1977a), *Le Marxisme, l'état et la question urbaine*, Paris: PUF

Lojkine, J. (1977b), 'Big firms' strategies, urban policy and urban social movements', in M. Harloe (ed.), *Captive Cities*, London: John Wiley

McBride, W. (1977), *The Philosophy of Marx*, London: Hutchinson

McKenzie, R. (1967), 'The ecological approach to the study of the human community', in R. Park and E. Burgess, *The City*, London: University of Chicago Press

Mann, P. (1965), *An Approach to Urban Sociology*, London: Routledge & Kegan Paul

Marx, K. (1964), *Pre-capitalist Economic Formations*, New York: International Publishers

Marx, K. (1969), 'Preface to "A contribution to the critique of political economy" ', in K. Marx and F. Engels, *Selected Works*, vol. 1, Moscow: Progress Publishers

Marx, K. (1973), *Grundrisse*, Harmondsworth: Penguin

Marx, K. (1976), *Capital*, vol. 1, Harmondsworth: Penguin

Marx, K., and Engels, F. (1969), 'Manifesto of the Communist Party', in K. Marx and F. Engels, *Selected Works*, vol. 1, Moscow: Progress Publishers

Marx, K., and Engels, F. (1970), *The German Ideology*, London: Lawrence & Wishart

Massey, D., and Catalano, A. (1978), *Capital and Land*, London: Edward Arnold

Mellor, J. (1977), *Urban Sociology in an Urbanized Society*, London: Routledge & Kegan Paul

Menzel, H. (1950), 'Comment on Robinson's "Ecological correlations and the behaviour of individuals" ', *American Sociological Review*, vol. 15, p. 674

Miliband, R. (1977), *Marxism and Politics*, London: Oxford University Press

Mills, C. (1959), *The Sociological Imagination*, London: Oxford University Press

Miner, H. (1952), 'The folk–urban continuum', *American Sociological Review*, vol. 17, pp. 529–37

Minns, R., and Thornley, J. (1978), *State Shareholding*, London: Macmillan

Moore, R. (1977), 'Becoming a sociologist in Sparkbrook', in C. Bell and H. Newby, *Doing Sociological Research*, London: Allen & Unwin

Morris, R. (1968), *Urban Sociology*, London: Allen & Unwin

Newby, H. (1977), *The Deferential Worker*, London: Allen Lane

Nisbet, R. (1966), *The Sociological Tradition*, New York: Basic Books

Norman, P. (1975), 'Managerialism: a review of recent work', in M. Harloe (ed.), *Proceedings of the Conference on Urban Change and Conflict*, London: Centre for Environmental Studies

O'Connor, J. (1973), *The Fiscal Crisis of the State*, New York: St Martin's Press

Offe, C. (1974), 'Structural problems of the capitalist state', in K. Beyme (ed.), *German Political Studies*, vol. 1, London: Sage

Offe, C. (1975), 'The theory of the capitalist state and the problem of policy-formation', in L. Lindberg, R. Alford, C. Crouch and C. Offe (eds.), *Stress and Contradiction in Modern Capitalism*, London: Lexington Books

Pahl, R. (1968), 'The rural–urban continuum', in R. Pahl (ed.), *Readings in Urban Sociology*, London: Pergamon

Pahl, R. (1970), *Patterns of Urban Life*, London: Longman

Pahl, R. (1975), *Whose City?* (2nd edn), Harmondsworth: Penguin

Pahl, R. (1977a), 'Collective consumption and the state in capitalist and state socialist societies', in R. Scase (ed.), *Industrial Society: Class, Cleavage and Control*, London: Tavistock

Pahl, R. (1977b), 'Stratification, the relation between states and urban and regional development', *International Journal of Urban and Regional Research*, vol. 1, pp. 6–17

Pahl, R. (1977c), 'Managers, technical experts and the state', in M. Harloe (ed.), *Captive Cities*, London: John Wiley

Pahl, R. (1977d), 'A rejoinder to Mingione and Hill', *International Journal of Urban and Regional Research*, vol. 1, pp. 340–3

Pahl, R. (1978), 'Castells and collective consumption', *Sociology*, vol. 12, pp. 309–15

Pahl, R. (1979), 'Socio-political factors in resource allocation', in D. Herbert and D. Smith (eds), *Social Problems and the City*, London: Oxford University Press

Panitch, L. (1978), 'Recent theorizations of corporatism: reflections on a growth industry', paper given at the Ninth World Congress of Sociology, Uppsala, Sweden

Paris, C., Blackaby, B., and Lambert, J. (1977), 'State urban policy and the housing problem', *Antipode*, vol. 8, pp. 51–7

Park, R. (1952), *Human Communities*, New York: Free Press

Parsons, T. (1951), *The Social System*, New York: Free Press

Parsons, T., Bales, R., and Shils, E. (1953), *Working Papers in the Theory of Action*, New York: Free Press

Pickvance, C. (1976a), 'Introduction: historical materialist approaches to urban sociology', in C. Pickvance (ed.), *Urban Sociology: Critical Essays*, London: Tavistock

Pickvance, C. (1976b), 'On the study of urban social movements', in Pickvance, *Urban Sociology*

Pickvance, C. (1977a), 'From social base to social force; some analytical issues in the study of urban protest', in M. Harloe (ed.), *Captive Cities*, London: John Wiley

Pickvance, C. (1977b), 'Marxist approaches to the study of urban politics', *International Journal of Urban and Regional Research*, vol. 1, pp. 218–55

Poulantzas, N. (1973), *Political Power and Social Classes*, London: New Left Books

Redfield, E. (1941), *The Folk Culture of Yucatan*, University of Chicago Press

Redfield, R. (1947), 'The folk society', *American Journal of Sociology*, vol. 52, pp. 293–308

Reissman, L. (1964), *The Urban Process*, London: Collier Macmillan

Rex, J. (1968), 'The sociology of a zone of transition', in R. Pahl (ed.), *Readings in Urban Sociology*, London: Pergamon

Rex, J. (1971), 'The concept of housing class and the sociology of race relations', *Race*, vol. 12, pp. 293–301

Rex, J. (1977), 'Sociological theory and the city', *Australian and New Zealand Journal of Sociology*, vol. 13, pp. 218–23

Rex, J., and Moore, R. (1967), *Race, Community and Conflict*, London: Oxford University Press

Rex, J., and Tomlinson, S. (1979), *Colonial Immigrants in a British City*, London: Routledge & Kegan Paul

Robinson, W. (1950), 'Ecological correlations and the behaviour of individuals', *American Sociological Review*, vol. 15, pp. 351–7

Robson, B. (1969), *Urban Analysis*, Cambridge University Press

Runciman, W. (1966), *Relative Deprivation and Social Justice*, London: Routledge & Kegan Paul

Saunders, P. (1978), 'Domestic property and social class', *International Journal of Urban and Regional Research*, vol. 2, pp. 233–51

Saunders, P. (1979), *Urban Politics: A Sociological Interpretation*, London: Hutchinson

Saunders, P. (1980), 'Local government and the state', *New Society*, vol. 51, pp. 550–1

Saunders, P., Newby, H., Bell, C., and Rose, D. (1977), 'Rural community and rural community power', in H. Newby (ed.), *International Perspectives in Rural Sociology*, London: John Wiley

Sayer, A. (1979), 'Theory and empirical research in urban and regional political economy: a sympathetic critique', *Urban and Regional Studies Working Papers*, no. 14, University of Sussex

Sayer, D. (1979), *Marx's Method*, Hassocks: Harvester Press

Sjoberg, G. (1964), 'The rural–urban dimensions in pre-industrial transitional and industrial societies', in R. Faris (ed.), *Handbook of Modern Sociology*, Chicago: Rand McNally

Stacey, M. (1969), 'The myth of community studies', *British Journal of Sociology*, vol. 20, pp. 134–45

Swingewood, A. (1975), *Marx and Modern Social Theory*, London: Macmillan

Szelenyi, I. (1979), 'Autonomie relative de l'état ou mode de production etatique?', Paris: *URBI*, pp. 107–22

Tonnies, F. (1963), *Community and Society*, New York, Harper & Row

Torrance, J. (1974), 'Max Weber: methods and the man', *European Journal of Sociology*, vol. 15, pp. 127–65

Walther, U. (1978), 'Politics and sociology on "The Urban Question": the case of Manuel Castells', in *Papers in Urban and Regional Studies*, no. 2, University of Birmingham, Centre for Urban and Regional Studies

Walton, P. and Gamble, A. (1972), *From Alienation to Surplus Value*, London: Sheed & Ward

Weber, M. (1948a), 'Science as a vocation', in H. Gerth and C. Mills (eds.), *From Max Weber: Essays in Sociology*, London: Routledge & Kegan Paul

Weber, M. (1948b), 'Politics as a vocation', in Gerth and Mills, *From Max Weber*

Weber, M. (1949), *The Methodology of the Social Sciences*, New York: Free Press

Weber, M. (1958), *The City*, Chicago: Free Press

Weber, M. (1968), *Economy and Society*, New York: Bedminster Press

Westergaard, J. (1977), 'Class inequality and corporatism', in A. Hunt, (ed.), *Class and Class Structure*, London: Lawrence & Wishart

Williams, P. (1978), 'Urban managerialism: a concept of relevance?', *Area*, vol. 10, pp. 236–40

Williams, R. (1973), *The Country and the City*, London: Chatto & Windus

Winkler, J. (1975), 'Corporatism', *European Journal of Sociology*, vol. 17, pp. 100–36

Winkler, J. (1977), 'The corporate economy: theory and administration', in R. Scase (ed.), *Industrial Society: Class, Cleavage and Control*, London: Allen & Unwin

Wirth, L. (1927), 'The ghetto', *American Journal of Sociology*, vol. 33, pp. 57–71

Wirth, L. (1938), 'Urbanism as a way of life', *American Journal of Sociology*, vol. 44, pp. 1–24

Wirth, L. (1945), 'Human ecology', *American Journal of Sociology*, vol. 50, pp. 483–8

Wirth, L. (1964), 'Rural–urban differences', in A. Reiss (ed.), *Louis Wirth on Cities and Social Life*, London: University of Chicago Press

Wirth, L. (1967), 'A bibliography of the urban community', in R. Park and E. Burgess, *The City*, London: University of Chicago Press

Wolff, K. (1950), *The Sociology of Georg Simmel*, Glencoe, Ill.: Free Press

Young, K., and Kramer, J. (1978), 'Local exclusionary policies in Britain: the case of suburban defence in a metropolitan system', in K. Cox (ed.), *Urbanization and Conflict in Market Societies*, London: Methuen

Young, M., and Willmott, P. (1957), *Family and Kinship in East London*, London: Routledge & Kegan Paul

Index